NOTORIOUS MURDERS, BLACK LANTERNS, & MOVEABLE GOODS

SERIES ON INTERNATIONAL, POLITICAL, AND ECONOMIC HISTORY

Jack Gieck, *Lichfield: The U.S. Army on Trial*

John M. Knapp, *Behind the Diplomatic Curtain: Adolphe de Bourqueney and French Foreign Policy, 1816–1869*

Martha McLaren, *British India and British Scotland, 1780–1830: Career Building, Empire Building, and a Scottish School of Thought on Indian Governance*

Charles John Fedorak, *Henry Addington, Prime Minister, 1801–1804: Peace, War, and Parliamentary Politics*

Chip Bok, *Bok!: The 9.11 Crisis in Political Cartoons*

Peter K. Gifford and Robert D. Ilisevich, editors, *European Capital, British Iron, and an American Dream: The Story of the Atlantic & Great Western Railroad*

David R. C. Hudson, *The Ireland That We Made: Arthur & Gerald Balfour's Contribution to the Origins of Modern Ireland*

Peter John Brobst, *The Future of the Great Game: Sir Olaf Caroe, India's Independence, and the Defense of Asia*

Deborah A. Symonds, *Notorious Murders, Black Lanterns, & Moveable Goods: The Transformation of Edinburgh's Underworld in the Early Nineteenth Century*

NOTORIOUS MURDERS, BLACK LANTERNS, & MOVEABLE GOODS

The Transformation of Edinburgh's Underworld in the Early Nineteenth Century

DEBORAH A. SYMONDS

THE UNIVERSITY OF AKRON PRESS

Copyright © 2006 by Deborah A. Symonds
All rights reserved
First Edition 2006
Manufactured in the United States of America.
10   09   08   07   06   5   4   3   2   1

All inquiries and permission requests should be addressed to the Publisher,
The University of Akron Press, 374B Bierce Library, Akron, Ohio 44325-1703.

LIBRARY OF CONGRESS CATALOGING-IN-PUBLICATION DATA

Symonds, Deborah A., 1951–
Notorious murders, black lanterns, and moveable goods : transformation of Edinburgh's underworld in the early nineteenth century / Deborah A. Symonds.— 1st ed.
  p. cm. — (Series on international, political, and economic history)
  Includes bibliographical references.
  ISBN 1-931968-27-6 (cloth : alk. paper)
  1. Crime—Economic aspects—Scotland—Edinburgh—History—19th century.
  2. Murder—Scotland—Edinburgh—History—19th century.   3. Theft—Scotland—Edinburgh—History—19th century.   4. Informal sector (Economics)—Scotland—Edinburgh—History—19th century.   5. Edinburgh (Scotland)—Social conditions—19th century. 6. Edinburgh (Scotland)—Economic conditions—19th century.
  I. Title: Murder, theft, and the transformation of Edinburgh's shadow economy.
  II. Title.   III. Series.
HV6950.E3S95 2005
364.1'09413'409034—dc22
                        2005004167

The paper used in this publication meets the minimum requirements of American National Standard for Information Sciences—Permanence of Paper for Printed Library Materials, ANSI z39.48–1984. ∞

Cover image: *Head of the West Bow,* by William Geikie. Illustration courtesy of West Port Books, 145-7 West Port, Edinburgh, Scotland.

All illustrations appear courtesy of West Port Books, 145-7 West Port, Edinburgh, Scotland.

For my Uncle Mike, Michael Pukish,
Who has taught me a thing or two.

Contents

Preface	ix
Prologue	xi
Introduction	1
1. The Notorious Murders in the West Port in 1828	21
2. Common Thievery in the Old Town in 1828	52
3. The Spectacular "Burke mania" Trial	74
4. The Criminal Household	101
5. The Transformation of the Shadow Economy	126
Notes	142
Bibliography	166
Index	175

Preface

This book began when I read William Roughead's *The Murderer's Companion*, because I wanted to read about nineteenth-century Edinburgh after working in earlier Scottish records for many years. I knew the streets where his Scots murderers had lived; I had lived in the neighborhood in the 1970s, before the coal soot on the buildings was sandblasted off for the tourists and the greater glory of the Enlightenment. I finished Roughead in a few hours, and began making notes. I was not ready to leave the old alleys near the Grassmarket, nor the peddlers, street sweepers, or doctors at Surgeons' Hall. This book is the result of various felonies committed in Edinburgh in 1828, William Roughead's elaboration of several of them, a great deal of work, scholarly and less so, done on the history of crime, the efforts of archivists at the National Archives of Scotland, and my own attachment to Edinburgh's Old Town.

In research that goes on for years, there is as much forgetting as there is discovery, and this preface will be a short, sharp attempt to remember all those people and institutions who contributed to this book, and to my ability to think, and to travel. I can begin by mentioning the old reliables. First, the Drake University Center for the Humanities, and the Arts and Sciences Dean's Faculty Travel Budget, which together have paid for much of my research and travel. Second, my partner Melissa Cano, who has repeatedly saved me from becoming an antiquarian rather than a historian. Third, my dear friends Marney Queen and Julia Johnson, who have never failed to supply a front door key, room, and much board for all my visits to Edinburgh, and have not yet found a way to declare my fairly regular visits a charitable contribution. Fourth, my friend and mentor Elizabeth Fox-Genovese, who always makes me see more than I had the day before; and Eugene D. Genovese, who may be the only person who truly knows what NSRV means. To paraphrase Virginia Woolf from *A Room of One's Own*, money, a room, good food, and good company are the foundation of all good work. For *all* those included in the "good company," you know, I hope, who you are.

I have the pleasure of thanking the readers of this manuscript for their adroit and professional comments, which have made this a much more sturdy, pointed, and accessible book. And Michael J. Carley, the former director at the University of Akron Press, has been timely, congenial, and forthright in getting this book out of my hands, as has Amy Freels, the production coordinator. I must also thank a number of Drake students who have been excellent research assistants on this project, most recently Kandis Meinders and Michaela Waszgis, who worked on anatomists, and over several years Monica Black, Michal Piszczuk, Jessica Tarbox, Hanssen Wendlandt, and Jeri Krutsinger, who worked on Edinburgh newspaper reports of crime.

But I am most indebted to the staff of the National Archives of Scotland, both at Register House and West Register House, as well as the staff of the National Library of Scotland, and the Edinburgh City Library. I have found the staffs of all these institutions to be unfailingly adept and professional. I have particularly relied on the help and advice of Robert Gibb, Register House, who has helped with aspects of this project and with several others that have not yet seen the light of day. I am also in debt to Ruth Jones and Ian Sommerville at West Register House for finding an elusive single-page document. We conventionally mention the record keepers, the archivists, and the librarians who make our work possible, but I think we do not do them justice. Without their work over the centuries there would be no sources, and no history.

Of course, errors and misjudgments are my responsibility; indebtedness is no excuse for inattention to one's craft.

Prologue

After dark on a spring evening in 1828, three people equipped with a "dark lantern" and some skeleton keys broke into a storage cellar in Whiskey Row, in an old street called the Cowgate in Edinburgh's Old Town. The thieves were looking for tea but had to content themselves with hams, double Gloucestershire cheeses, raisins, orange peel, figs, and candles. They carried these away one box at a time, in a bed tick, to the nearby house of Elizabeth Allan and James Wood in Blackfriar's Wynd. Suddenly the three were interrupted. When one Bertram the Cowfeeder came down the street, the last of the thieves coming out of the cellar, Alexander Reid, fled, leaving two double Gloucestershire cheeses and two hams under Bertram's cart in the street. As he burst back into Allan and Wood's house at five o'clock that morning he cursed, complaining of his colleagues' "damned carelessness in not keeping a look out for the watching."[1]

It was very much a neighborhood crime, possibly overly ambitious, for not only were they caught, they seemed to have little idea of how to dispose of their goods. They ate one of the hams, some of the raisins, and a little orange peel. James Wood, landlord to one of the thieves, sold their candles and a cheese to Christian McKay, a widow who kept a small grocery shop in the ground floor of the same building. She later admitted to police that she, too, had one of the hams, but said she providently "laid it aside" when she heard about the cellar. The three thieves, David Adams, Alexander Reid, and Margaret Robertson, had been meeting for more than a week at Elizabeth Allan and James Wood's upper-story house, where Robertson lived. On the night in question, Allan testified, the thieves met there, Adams

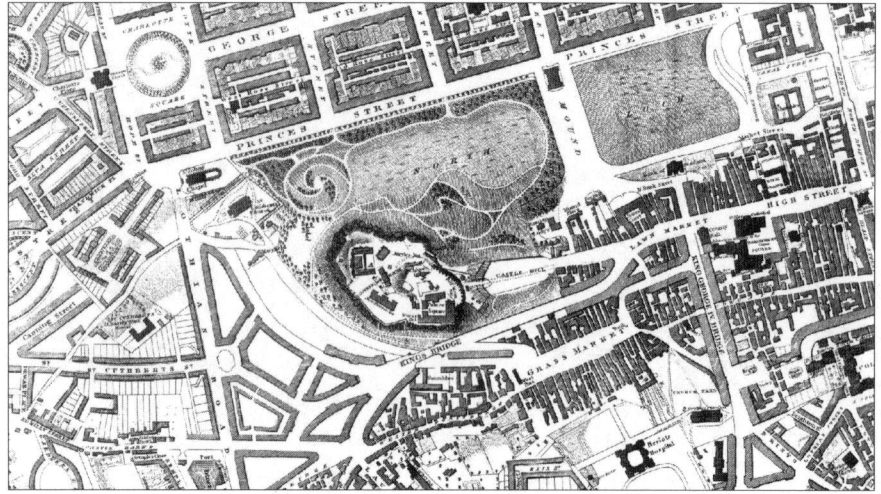

A map of Edinburgh's Old Town.

showed Maggie Robertson some keys, Reid asked her to file them, and then they went out. Allan testified that Reid and Adams were "for 8 days before that time talking about a Cellar in the Whiskey Row which they said would be Easily done." The cellar, probably beneath a post office building, was rented by a grocer named Mr. Rymer, possibly the same grocer who figures in chapter 3.

It was not as easily done as they thought. The police record refers to the three as "bad characters," but not as practiced, habitual thieves. It listed David Adams's occupation as watchmaker and Alexander Reid's as laborer. Maggie Robertson may well have been at Allan and Wood's house not as a boarder, but as a servant. If they were bad characters, they nonetheless seem to have found congenial neighbors willing to profit from stolen goods. Neither Allan nor Wood turned them in, and Wood helped dispose of some of the food in Christian McKay's shop at the bottom of the stair. The police found the neighborhood couple who hid their dark lantern—probably one with a dark glass, or some cover for the flame—for them afterwards. They were young. Maggie Robertson was sixteen, Adams twenty-nine, and Reid twenty-one, and inexpert, but well-connected enough on that street to be far from innocent or starving thieves in 1828.

This story is not remarkable, and that is why I have chosen it. This book examines an exceptional series of brutal and by now fairly well known murders. But the questions about crime that arise have only a little to do with horror or exception, and everything to do with the typical structures of the criminal underworld of Edinburgh in 1828. The first question is, what does the criminal underworld look like in 1828; the second, does it change in or around 1828? It does, and the change tells us how the criminal underworld was a kind of shadow economy that was necessarily transformed by the continuing capitalist transformation of the much larger public economy.

We begin with Margaret Robertson, and her relation to Reid and Adams. In 1828 she was sixteen, had been in jail once, and had lived with Elizabeth Allan and James Wood in Blackfriar's Wynd, off the High Street, since January. She hardly could have been the leader of the gang, nor is it likely that they could not have filed the keys without her—although it is possible that she alone had that skill. Nonetheless, the question of why she was there at all would seem to loom large. Unlike other women, she was not skilled in the resetting of goods—the sale of stolen bits and pieces, usually to a pawnshop owner—nor did she have the interpersonal skills of a "girl of the town," stealing watches from drunken gentlemen who were expecting something quite different to happen.[2] And she was apparently not married to either Adams or Reid. Given her role in the theft, she could as easily have been male.

Margaret Robertson exists for us as a question that unfortunately cannot be answered. But she is also one of a number of women from Edinburgh's Old Town and its westward outgrowth, the West Port, who were jailed and tried in 1828 for theft, reset, or murder. From their lives we can begin to reconstruct Edinburgh's underworld, and speculate on how it was changing in the 1820s. Of particular use will be the fairly well documented lives of the infamous murderers, Lucky Log, Helen M'Dougal, William Hare, and William Burke. Log and M'Dougal worked alongside their husbands, Hare and Burke, and shared in their notoriety when their string of sixteen murders was discovered. Neither woman would hang, but both, along with their husbands, so enraged the public that an eager press gleaned scraps of biographical information before, during, and after the trial. It is this trial and the surviving documentation that make 1828 an important year, and it is with this year and this trial, and all that it can tell us about this neighborhood, that we will begin.

NOTORIOUS MURDERS, BLACK LANTERNS, & MOVEABLE GOODS

The Cowgate ran east from the Grassmarket and lay at the heart of the network of wynds and closes that housed the poorer residents.

Introduction

1828 might seem an inauspicious year to choose as the basis of a discussion of anything so grand as a transformation, which certainly implies that something very old has been markedly superseded. There were no great acts of Parliament, no treaties, no great riots or famines in 1828. No European wars began or ended. Yet the larger world outside the closes and wynds (alleys) of Edinburgh's Old Town was changing rapidly in the wake of Waterloo, the great battle of 1815 that stopped Napoleon, but could not stop liberal democracy or economic revolution on the Continent or in Great Britain. The Scottish and English Reform Acts came in 1832, and the long-argued reform of the Scots burghs in 1833. These pillars of the modern British state extended the vote to urban, male, upper-middle-class householders, created new parliamentary districts reflecting the growing importance of industrial cities, and ended the self-perpetuating paternal powers of burgesses in Scottish towns. The mere possibility of such political reform had so provoked the popular author, lawyer, and public figure Sir Walter Scott that he made his conservative loyalties excessively clear, and was hissed at the Jedburgh election of 1831 by critics who yelled "Burke Sir Walter!" This was a direct reference to the notorious murderer William Burke, caught three years before, whose name became a synonym for death by suffocation. Of course, old Sir Walter's world of Scots lords, clan chiefs, and gentlemen who knew their place and gloried in it was not dead yet. Scott had spent his life trying to prove that through his novels, and, rather ironically, in the carefully staged parade of a kilted King George IV through Edinburgh in 1822.[1] But Scott died in 1832, and the transformation that was eroding nobility and elevating the factory manager and the Royal Exchange—in a word, property—did not. Those alive in the year 1828 and living in Edinburgh would, without riot, Parliament, famine, treaty, or war, feel that transformation's effect.

In 1830, as E. J. Hobsbawm said, nothing was clearer than the inability of the great conservative Metternich to stop the clamoring for democratic institutions. Equally clear was the development of an industrial and capitalist economy, for which growth, not merely production, was now a goal. As the British historian Harold Perkin put it in 1969,

> The Industrial Revolution, however, was more than an expansion of commerce, more than a series of changes in the technology of certain industries, more even than an acceleration of general economic growth. It was a revolution in men's access to the means of life, in control over their ecological environment, in their capacity to escape from the tyranny and niggardliness of nature.[2]

If that suggests the magnitude of the social and economic changes afoot, the timing of this economic and political transformation is simply illustrated. Adam Smith died in 1790, the year that the Forth & Clyde Canal began the linkage of Glasgow and Edinburgh; Karl Marx was born in 1818, and in 1822 the Union Canal continued the Forth & Clyde into Edinburgh. The canals were ultimately a curiosity of development, outweighed by good roads, railroads, harbor improvements, and big ships. But they are telling, nonetheless, if one recalls the urgency with which good engineers in many countries worked on the design of routes, locks, and aqueducts for fifty years.[3] In the years between Smith's death and Marx's birth came more than canals; these were the years of Revolution and warfare in France, and ultimately across the Continent. Along with the wars came demand for the materials of war, and the means of transporting them.

If ever there was a period when the smell of something new was in the air, it must have been in 1828, after half a century of Enlightenment in Edinburgh. More important, this timing was international, rather than regional. The Enlightenment, which was both a material and a philosophical undertaking, produced increasing supplies of zeal, Bills of Rights, the bridges of James Telford, and violent upheaval in France. It sent Mary Wortley Montagu to Turkey, James Bruce to East Africa, and finally, George IV marching through Edinburgh in a kilt and bloomers. Its proponents made better clocks, factories, hogs, schools, prisons, governments, carriage fringe, armies, and books. The old order, agricultural and hierarchical, could not stand the shock. Wary peasants took to the roads; hereditary conservatives like Sir Walter Scott railed with horror at the loss, the change, and the license. Others called it liberty.[4]

Between 1815 and 1833 Scotland and much of the Western world, its empires and its ex-empires, were to reconstruct themselves. Those British hallmarks of the new era, the Reform Acts, the abolition of slavery, and the repeal of the English Corn Laws, reflect not only internal changes in the British political economy, but a re-creation of Britain's place in the nineteenth-century world economy. Slavery in the remaining British colonies, and in Britain, ended between 1833 and 1838. This mattered most in the Atlantic world, where there were more than a few Scots. Further east, the old and rarely honorable East India Company would slowly be reshaped between 1766 and 1857, as Britain replaced its literate freebooters with government bureaucrats. And all this mattered to Scots, and to Scotland, for Scots figured prominently in this wider world, finding careers and money that had never been available to them at home in virtually every nook and cranny of the British imperial world.[5]

In 1828 Scotland was no provincial corner of the world. It was still distinct from England, had generated the Scottish Enlightenment, bred Adam Smith, profited greatly from New World sugar and tobacco, generated a movement for the abolition of slavery, and repealed the servile status of its miners. Throughout the nineteenth century, Scots would do much of the sometimes dubious work of empire, fighting, planting, converting, ruling, and bribing, then returning home with fortunes. Many less fortunate Scots would be shipped to the New World wholesale during the notorious clearances of highland estates, or as indentured servants, or fighting for no more pay than the king's shilling. Consider again the cellar that was robbed in 1828 by Adams, Reid, and Robertson. The teas they were looking for came from India, Sri Lanka, or China, the hams probably from Virginia, and the oranges perhaps only from Spain. The Old Town of Edinburgh may at first appear to have been a decaying corner of an antique, northern British city, but that would be a great misapprehension.

In 1828 Edinburgh was still the capital, albeit no longer a political one, of a country much engaged in a world economy that was both glamorous and vile. Thus, what we are seeing in poor neighborhoods of Edinburgh, chiefly the older, early modern part of town, known literally as the Old Town in 1828, was the wandering, fighting, drinking, thieving, and disorder that accompanied the migrations of enormous numbers of smallholders, peasants, cottagers, and landless laborers toward wages. The resultant jumble of demobilized soldiers after 1815, Irish migrants, Gaelic-speaking highlanders, and lowland Scots continued to move, following seasonal work and demand for domestic servants, or shuffling back and forth between the different economies of Edinburgh and Glasgow. If some were miserable, others were probably hopeful, and kept an entrepreneurial eye out for any small opportunity. Migration, and the need for labor, including Irish Catholic labor, were sufficient to provoke the passage of a very unpopular Catholic Emancipation act in London in 1829. By 1844, Scotland was trying out its new Poor Law, designed to deal with the wandering poor, as they moved out of the villages where they were born, and toward a future that was not yet clear to anyone.[6]

Edinburgh in the 1820s could be seen as a city still balancing at the very end of the early modern era, when the great social and economic changes of that era were about to be abetted by changes in government, and in those who controlled the structures of government. And here, with the word government, we come up against a great dilemma in Scots history: whether Scotland constitutes a nation or merely a region within the politically united Great Britain of 1828. The usual answer to this might be to recite the chronology of the political union, beginning with Elizabeth I leaving her crown to her Scottish relative, making him James VI and I, in 1603. This would be followed by the Act of Union in 1707, creating a single Parliament in London, and the defeat of persistent Jacobite rebels who attempted, in 1715 and in 1745, to bring back a Stuart monarch and undo the Union. But this answer begs the question by relying on the obvious.

What is perhaps less obvious is an old Scottish problem, that of weak central authority, which strengthened the nobility in their regional kingdoms. Whether one absorbs one's history from *Braveheart*, *Rob Roy*, or standard texts, it becomes clear that, to steal a line from Arthurian as well as Jacobite mythology, the king was often over the water. Because of that absence, Scotland developed other strengths—a national church that rivaled government at times as a source of order, a banking system separate from the Bank of England, and a widespread, popular interest in Scottish law and the Scottish courts. But for our purposes it is enough to point out that between the 1640s and the 1740s, some Scots used the English to subdue the Stuarts, the Kirk, and certain Scots noble houses. Scotland was not taken or colonized. It was the Scots Parliament, with some bribery and coercion, that wrote and ratified the Act of Union.

If they found it more efficient to have their governing done for them in London, they did not put it in those words. But by waving goodbye to a resident king in the seventeenth century, and by sending away the Parliament in the eighteenth, an act that was seen as a national tragedy by many in 1707, Scots got some peace in the later eighteenth century. Edinburgh became a center of Enlightenment learning, wealthy tobacco merchants rebuilt Glasgow, the Kirk moderated its principles, and Scots made great fortunes throughout the British Empire. It seems doubtful that the Stuart pretenders to the throne could have done more.[7]

But someone had to represent central authority in Scotland, and London first entrusted direct local power and the privilege of patronage to the hands of a noble family, the Campbells of Argyll. But when they failed to forestall or contain the Jacobite uprising of 1745, they were replaced by a family of Edinburgh lawyers named Dundas. A precedent was established by which the lawyer raised to the office of lord advocate (attorney general for Scotland) would act unofficially as a sort of secretary of state for Scotland, assuming many of the powers of the old Scots Privy Council which had been abolished in 1707. From the ascendancy of the Dundas family through 1828, when one William Rae held the office, the lord advocates who acted as the agents of the London government in Scotland all were, at least while in office, resolute Tories. Nonetheless, despite their conservative allegiances, these men were lawyers, bourgeois gentlemen whose very access to power was new in Scotland, and they showed the flexibility of conservatives soon to make their peace with a rapidly changing society in the Reform Act of 1832.[8]

The lord advocate came to represent Crown authority in Scotland, and that meant that any criminal case might suddenly, especially during the explosive years of the French Revolution, become a political affair. Scots Whigs who could not openly criticize the government could always hope to embarrass its chief representative in court, especially if his ineptitude threatened to set loose a dangerous miscreant or hang a harmless citizen. There were always talented Whig lawyers ready to take on the lord advocate in these years, men who would take a case without payment, merely for the joy of beating the government's man in the courtroom. These men were interested both in moderate political reform, and in their own advancement, and saw both blocked by Tory placeholders with talents far inferior to their own. With Enlightenment figures like Henry Erskine, Francis Jeffrey, and Henry Cockburn snapping at various lord advocates' heels, it is little wonder that Edinburgh courtrooms sometimes attracted great audiences. The law had always been a popular diversion in Scotland, and by the late eighteenth and early nineteenth centuries, it was a political forum as well. In Edinburgh, crowds attended two kinds of learned and discreetly political gatherings: the Sunday sermon and the High Court of Justiciary.

Crime

Much has been written about crime already, especially in the tradition of the great criminal narratives. Much of that was contemporary and some marginally fictional, offering little more than dramatized horrors, recalling muck-raking reports on the evils of the slums, Engels's *Conditions of the Working Class in England*, the careers of notorious English highwaymen, the fictional Moll Flanders, or the real Moll Cutpurse. Crime—outside the older sociological discussion, which goes back to Beccaria, and then the Enlightenment and the Panopticon, not to mention the Book of Genesis—is merely a pastime, until it is studied as an integral part of a complex society. It makes no sense apart from the development of the rule of law, which in turn depends upon those who make the law, who in turn have themselves been elevated to their position by some political system, social order, and economy.

Some of the best work on crime has taken shape as studies of particular problems, or cases, as they played out in courtrooms. For example, E. P. Thompson's *Whigs and Hunters*, Christina Larner's *Enemies of God*, or Natalie Zemon Davis's *Return of Martin Guerre* have been particularly effective. These books are not about crime as a topic, but about instances of change and conflict, as they happened to be recorded in court cases. Other studies of topics largely salvageable through trial or police records, secular or religious, such as prostitution, witchcraft, illegitimacy, infanticide, militia riots, and grain riots, have also proven valuable insofar as they address complex behavior, with ties to economic, cultural, and social change. What this recent work has shown is that records of crime, once the territory of retired lawyers and other gentlemen antiquarians with an eye for the ghastly or bizarre, can be a rich and usable source for historians.[9]

But the growth of the history of crime, like other forms of social history over the last few decades of the twentieth century, has produced an overwhelming amount of information, and historians' abilities to theorize about what it means have not caught up with the influx of information. This is partly due to the appearance of the personal computer, with its ability to sort vast amounts of quantifiable data, like that provided by indictments, convictions, and cases heard over the years, stretching on for a century or more. As the records have been coded and tabulated, we know more, but with less certainty than the men who wrote happily about their favorite criminals.[10]

What we have gotten from the union of the old criminal narratives with social history has been various. While hardly predominant, English Marxists, following from Marx's insight into the uses of the law to defend and create new forms of property, have investigated the creation of laws enforced to the disadvantage of ordinary people. But this indictment of English law, giving us the term social crime—theft, poaching, or riot committed by decent people, in the face of famine or the loss of traditional perquisites—accounts for only a small portion of the work done on crime.[11]

Much of the work done has been that of unearthing and presenting to the public what evidence we have of the incidence and nature of crime in the past. It is hardly surprising that societies much concerned with their own crime rates would produce historians who demonstrate to us that past societies were also plagued by theft, arson, rape, murder, and so forth. But, to paraphrase G. R. Elton, who raised this question many years ago, what are we talking about when we describe crime? Crime, in the abstract, understood as the breaking of laws, is as old as law, religious or secular, and thus potentially ever-present, and more a matter for moralists than historians. There are no societies, past or present, without crime, and there may be pickpockets in heaven. If crime is continuous, and history is about change, how are historians to make use of criminal court records? The English Marxists who gave us "social crime" hit upon an aspect of crime that changes—the letter of the law—and thus were studying local responses to change, albeit a change imposed from above, by Parliament. Other historians of crime, working quantitatively, have looked to changes in the incidence of various crimes and taken those changes as the problems they must explain. Implicitly, statistics of crime have come to be seen as part of a misery index, as variables dependent on their connection to some quantifiable source of misery, such as famine, unemployment, or new markets that pull goods away and drive up prices.[12]

The problem with all this is that it still leaves criminals outside history, continuing old practices, poaching, thieving, burning down a barn, and gleaning while their social superiors and their economies change around them, goading them to steal more, or punishing them for it more often. This timeless aspect of the criminal is also due to the nature of court records, which reduce the complex squabbles collected there to formulaic instances of those categories of crime that the law of one period or another recognized. And it is precisely that tendency to the formulaic, which suggests the timeless, that historians must dismantle by reconstructing from the anecdotal evidence, not how many thefts, but what was stolen from whom, by whom, and how it was stolen, and how it reentered the economy. The point should be to discover how crime and criminals change over time.

With criminals caught in the headlights of the law, frozen and looking much alike, it is no surprise that several historians remarked in a coauthored piece that "In all societies before the present century, in short, criminals were probably very much more tradition-bound in their practices than many historians suggest. Most stole for one ancient and enduring reason: to survive."[13] This tendency to find change only among the ranks of the rulers, or the state of the economy, while the ruled flail away, stealing to keep body and soul together, rests on an over-simple assumption. This assumption stipulates that social criminals for English Marxists, and that criminals in general for the somewhat quantitative social historian, are linked to the economy through short-term economic failures and other troubling changes, but do not control or innovate within that economy. They are hangers-on, living from hand to mouth: men collect firewood, urban children steal a few pieces of coal, women trade sex for a loaf of bread, all of them driven to commit crimes by persons, forces, or innate characteristics beyond their control. It seems to be true, at least in the British literature, that when times get hard, more people steal. But even more steal anyway, and the suggestion that they do so simply to survive begs the real question, which is why so many chose to survive in that way.

Engels may well deserve more credit for coining the phrase "social crime" than he has gotten, for although he did not use it directly, he certainly had written down something of the concept by 1844 in *The Condition of the Working Class in England:*

> The clearest indication of the unbounded contempt of the workers for the existing social order is the wholesale manner in which they break its laws. If the demoralisation [*sic*] of the worker passes beyond a certain point then it is just as natural that he will turn into a criminal—as inevitably as water turns into steam at boiling point.[14]

This is not quite as sophisticated a definition as has been offered by twentieth-century historians, but it does suggest that the point in time, as well as the site at which people become ungovernable marks something more than a sudden lapse into criminal behavior. Engels went on to call it "social war," while later historians called it "social crime," or "socio-political crime" and described the typical examples, like grain rioters or Wilksite radicals, as people who were not breaking the law, but attempting to negotiate what the law said, and ultimately, how they should be governed. When these arguments work, the erstwhile lawbreakers cease to be criminals, and become protocitizens, participants in the governing process who do not have suffrage.[15]

If some laws may usefully be broken as part of the process of creating a more just—at least from the particular perspective of the rioter, protestor, or poacher—system of laws, we begin to see, as Marx believed that he saw, that the law, and consequently justice, are relative to the particular societies in which they exist, and change as society changes. But this skepticism about the law—"the Marxian critique of justice," in fancier words—was older than Marx. The Scots lawyer Sir George Mackenzie, the right-hand man of Charles II in Scotland, had remarked in the late seventeenth century that there was the law, and then there was justice, and any man who thought they were the same thing was a fool. Mackenzie was, of course, skeptical, or pragmatic, only about the law, reserving to justice its existence, if only as an ideal.[16]

But what does this skepticism about the law, as a means of administering justice, do to our ability to understand crime? It forces us to reconsider what the law is—and recognize that the law in Scotland, as in virtually every other Western country, consisted of many layers of law, from common, old, and traditional understandings to recent statutes. The law, never so unified and rational as the word suggests, was also very variably enforced, as many historians of crime have found. Over centuries, neighbors, elders of the Kirk, landlords, magistrates, sheriffs, police officers, prosecutors, judges, juries, and lawyers had a great deal of personal freedom in the often lengthy process of investigation and trial, and the law was often trampled on, bent, and disregarded. In other words, what Marx attempted to describe systematically, Charles II's lawyer knew intuitively: the law is a tool in the hands of human beings, sometimes in one hand, and sometimes representing a group interest.

This altogether healthy skepticism about law, at least for Mackenzie in the seventeenth century, as a sure means of securing justice, has developed in the late twentieth century into a horror at the thought that any institution should exercise power over anyone. What this influential argument, expressed by Foucault and others, and perhaps ultimately rooted in Rousseau's *Émile* and nineteenth-century anarchism, implies about criminal history is that criminal law is a purely pragmatic tool in the hands of lawmakers and law enforcers, who use law not to defend the rights of citizens, but to selectively punish the dangerous, the disaffected, and the rebellious. Thus, what perhaps began as a little worldly skepticism about the law has extended into a scathing critique of law, and implicitly, a defense of all criminals as social criminals. Whether this was what Engels had in mind seems doubtful, and it has not been historians of crime who have pushed the debate in this direction.[17]

But if the law is more than a pragmatic tool, then the Enlightenment scholars who wrote about universal law must have been right to argue that certain principles were beyond party interest, and were indeed universal. And it does seem that the practice of criminal history implicitly rests on recognizing that those two kinds of law, the pragmatic tool and the universal principle, coexist, generating two kinds of crime, the social and, for lack of a better term, the antisocial. It would seem that since Engels wrote in 1844 about the lawbreakers in revolt, the business of criminal history has been to sort out these two kinds of crime, and force us to confront the larger philosophical questions of whether or not we find the laws broken to have been just, or not, and whether those breaking the laws saw themselves as moral, or not.

Habite [sic] *and Repute*

To quote another historian, the concept of social crime does "not explain why the poor murdered each other, raped each other, or stole from each other." Most criminals, at least as the literature on early modern England has developed, were of this latter sort, breaking laws that protected the lives and property of other people like themselves. And there is still a good deal of work to be done on these people—the petty thieves, various rogues, and sometimes murderers who, at their most dangerous, caught the eye of eighteenth- and nineteenth-century popular writers. This book is an attempt to follow the trail laid for us many years ago when William Roughead wrote "that Sir Walter Scott had a passion for reading murder trials" and "that Tennyson and Jowett once sat up a whole night discussing—murder." If we can resurrect the old antiquarians' untrained insight, that the lives of the ordinary, antisocial majority of criminals were important objects of study, and combine it with the insights of modern historians who place crime in a political and economic framework, we can reconstruct something of the lives of those who were called criminals "habite [*sic*] and repute" in Scots courtrooms in 1828. More importantly those ordinary criminals, both the occasional murderer and the more common thief, allow us to see both crime and the economy in a new light.[18]

The Shadow Economy

Men and women lived by theft, assault, murder, and the disposal of stolen goods, and they had the help of neighbors who were no more honest than they had to be. These people are the object of this study, not because they possessed any special culture or curious vocabulary, but because it is among the habitual thieves of a city that change in the criminal economy—not in the laws—will be found. If re-creating a criminal underworld, like that of Charles Dickens's Fagin was our only goal, this would be shallow antiquarian social history. But the ultimate goal is to describe a shadow economy, replete with criminals who are active, calculating, economically aware agents of something the older writers would have called evil, and possibly of change. To view them in that way is a compliment that has not been paid to them—especially to the women—in many years. And it is something very different from the more common suppositions that the law changes, the enforcement of the law changes, and the economy changes, but that the poor and the ordinary people who break the law muddle along pathetically and violently from century to century.[19]

Women as Criminals

Much has been written, at least for England, about the static nature of women's roles in crime, and the reluctance of juries, and even neighbors, to see them formally tried or severely punished. And there is some truth to those findings. In the late Middle Ages 10 percent of all criminals were women, as they were some years later in Elizabethan Essex. For 140 years before 1800, broken down by kinds of property crime, women constituted from 8.5 percent to 34.3 percent of the recorded criminals in Surrey and Sussex; and finally, in Scotland in 1828, they made up 20 percent of those investigated for all sorts of serious crime by the Lord Advocate's Department.[20]

Those figures of 10 to 20 percent seem generally confirmed, but it is important to understand that crime is a difficult topic, affected by modern notions of what constitutes crime. None of the figures given above, by reason of their dates or the authors' choices, touch on the great witch hunts of the early modern period. And infanticide, which was a subject of the second study quoted, was given as a crime separate from the number of general homicides. These two crimes—witchcraft and infanticide—must have accounted for many of the women brought to trial between the late Middle Ages and the early nineteenth century. And if we look at the numbers of violent crimes committed by women in Surrey between 1660 and 1802—to quote from that noted and thorough study—we find ninety-five homicide indictments, about a tenth of which were charged to women. But if we add to that the number of infanticide indictments, which is again ninety-five, and consider violent crimes as a whole, we see that over 50 percent of all violent crimes were attributed to women through the indictment process. Even without reviewing the literature on witch hunts for England and Scotland, the point is simple. Overviews of female criminality, as that criminality was perceived by past society, must take into account not only the usual offenses that we now recognize as criminal, but also the very old crimes of witchcraft and child murder. Women did not rob travelers or brawl with the frequency of men in England, but they were, all the more ironically, seen as exceptionally dangerous at times, and prosecuted quite viciously. That truism of standard criminal history, that women were consistently treated mildly, rarely convicted, and even more rarely hanged, is not always true, and a criminal history of women from 1500, or earlier, to 1900, will fluctuate wildly in what it shows us about women.[21]

To reconstruct a brief outline of women's criminal acts in Scotland—some morally justifiable to us, others simply felonious—one would begin by identifying who had authority to define crimes of various sorts. In the early modern world, that would have included the state, local landed magnates of varying degrees, and the church. Leaving aside all the civil cases heard by the central civil court, and various city magistrates, which are interesting but essentially different from criminal law, we are left with serious crimes prosecuted by the state in 1690: homicide, infanticide, witchcraft, arson, kidnapping, false coining, bestiality, notorious adultery, incest, rape, deforcement (interfering with government officials), riot, and many kinds of theft. As the eighteenth century began, witchcraft ceased to be a believable crime; infanticide was increasingly difficult to prosecute; and bestiality, incest, and adultery disappeared as capital crimes by the later decades of the century. Church courts continued to shame and fine adulterers, fornicators, parents of illegitimate children, and those who attempted to marry outside its control, notably Episcopalians. Landowners' courts, sometimes known as baron courts, settled disputes among tenant farmers on estates and tried to enforce the landlords' rights to labor and to control the distribution and use of land by their tenants. As cities grew, urban courts and some means of policing the streets grew with them. The godly discipline that John Knox might have enforced in Edinburgh in the sixteenth century was long gone, swamped by population growth and religious controversy. By 1828, citizens of Edinburgh taken up by the police for petty crimes might be sentenced by the city magistrates, or by a police court, and sent to either a house of correction or a prison. More serious crimes —those that are the subject of this study—were tried before the High Court of Justiciary, and those convicted might be imprisoned, transported, or hanged.

Women as well as men living in Scotland in 1828 would have known some of this, even if memory of the old crimes, such as witchcraft, which in Scotland was preponderantly a woman's crime, had faded. Infanticide was re-created by a new statute in 1809 as concealment of pregnancy and was no longer a capital crime. But women also figured as social criminals, protesting publicly and with some force against grain exports and the enclosure of common land during the Napoleonic wars. Of course, they also figured as what would have been called common criminals, but because no systematic studies of crime in medieval, early modern, or modern Scotland exist at this time, we have primarily English studies to use as a guide to women's participation in most kinds of crime. Those suggest that most women, like men, were principally indicted for theft of various kinds, especially housebreaking. They were apt to be young, between fifteen and thirty-four in the early modern period, and stealing in urban rather than rural areas. Women were less likely to rob persons, a particularly male career, and more likely to break into houses. They stole food and textiles. They were sometimes prominent as receivers of stolen goods, and as counterfeiters; in the early modern period, the ratio of women to men in these crimes in Surrey and Sussex was higher than in any other crime, excepting, presumably, witchcraft and infanticide.[22]

Where does this information, much of it drawn from English studies, leave us with regard to Scots in 1828? The witch hunts were long over, and infanticide, unless it could be proven with direct evidence as a murder, was a minor offense. Prostitution, the next specifically woman's crime to be defined by the courts, was an even more minor offense, handled by the recently instituted Edinburgh Police Establishment. Presumably "girls of the town" were not rare on the city streets, but some, at least, preferred to steal, and exchanged sex for a payment only as a last resort. Other women, for the most part younger, stole, while a few, who were older and married, handled the resale of stolen goods. Few of these women worked alone, so we are really examining, not numbers of women engaged in various branches of crime, but the common methods of organization—household, group, gang—used by the men and women who supplied the shadow economy.[23]

The Household Organization of Crime

Women were no more absent from the shadow economy than they were from the larger economy, and in 1828 men and women carried on thieving in concert, often through a rough kind of household organization. Just as the larger society had relied on household production for centuries, so did the inhabitants of the shadow economy, who lived in both worlds. The following brief summary of the particularly nasty case that draws our attention to the year 1828 also illustrates the workings of a criminal household. In that year, in Edinburgh's West

Port, seventeen lodgers, visitors, and traveling peddlers died while in the company of Willie Hare, Lucky Log, William Burke, and Nelly M'Dougal. Sixteen of these people were murdered, and the bodies packed up and sold, generally by both couples working together. The last murder was committed on Halloween, and discovered the day after; the trial took place on Christmas Eve, and scandalized and terrified the city. These exploits, eventually ascribed chiefly to the two men and the anatomist who bought the bodies, provoked a great deal of writing, as people tried to come to terms with what had happened. Early rumors and transcripts of the trial were soon, and continually, replaced by fiction, ranging in quality from Robert Louis Stevenson's *Body-Snatchers* to popular plays and verse.

> Burke's the butcher, Hare's the thief,
> And Knox the boy who buys the beef.[24]

On Christmas Eve in 1828, the High Court of Justiciary in Edinburgh convened before a full house to try William Burke for three murders, and Helen M'Dougal for one. Mary Paterson, James Wilson, and Mary Docherty, the three mentioned in Burke's indictment, had been killed by Burke and his friend William Hare, with much help from their wives, Helen M'Dougal and Lucky Log, for the purpose of selling the bodies to the popular anatomy lecturer Dr. Robert Knox. Knox, like other anatomists, had almost no legal access to corpses for research or teaching, and bought "resurrected" bodies from gangs who dug in churchyards. Burke and M'Dougal were tried alone, because the only witnesses who could give direct evidence against them were their colleagues, William Hare and his wife, Lucky Log. They gave that evidence in return for immunity from prosecution, and the subsequent trial horrified and mesmerized the city, not least because it was apparent that Log and Hare were also guilty. Burke, Hare, and Dr. Knox have since become notorious, representing for many terrified citizens the logical outcome of the grave-robbing that provided Edinburgh medical schools with corpses for dissection. Their notoriety obscured Log's complicity in a business that began in her lodging house, and continued to thrive under M'Dougal and Burke's roof, with considerable help from M'Dougal. Lucky Log and Helen M'Dougal were just as guilty as their husbands, as members of the mobs demanding blood knew in 1828 and early 1829. And their contribution to what began as a household enterprise frames much of the following examination of the men and women in the shadow economy, or underworld, of Edinburgh.[25]

The extraordinary series of sixteen murders that the four carried out in 1828 forces us to examine the peculiar economic, cultural, and scientific development that turned the human body into a commodity, thus making those murders profitable. That development was the rise of anatomy, in the course of the Enlightenment, from the despised, messy, material business of barber-surgeons to a field literally at the cutting edge of medical knowledge. With status came increased demand: students wanted to attend lectures, lecturers wanted bodies, and the best courses provided students with sufficient bodies on which to practice, as well as those required in the lecture hall. The business of resurrecting the very recently deceased, wherever medical schools existed, could not keep up with demand. The prices anatomists paid the resurrection gangs for bodies rapidly inflated in the course of the late eighteenth century, until they fluctuated from eight pounds to as much as twenty guineas in the 1820s.[26]

Certainly none of the other goods stolen by Edinburgh thieves would bring as much as the bodies that were "stolen" from their owners by Log, Hare, Burke, and M'Dougal in 1828. That makes the four murderers entrepreneurs of a very dangerous sort, people both extraordinarily vicious, and quick to understand supply and demand in a very basic way. But if they—none of whom had a record with the police—could grasp this so quickly, surely the habitual criminals of the Old Town, though shy of committing murder, were equally aware of prices and dealers. Of course, the other goods in the shadow economy, such as watches, clothes, food, and household goods, would not bring nearly as much. And their prices were no doubt somewhat controlled by the resetters (resellers of stolen goods), secondhand dealers, and pawnshop keepers of the city, who would not have had many wealthy customers. Then again, Maggie Robertson's nocturnal search for tea suggests that those three thieves had a particular buyer in mind, and perhaps an attractive price. They did not find the tea, but in the West Port, Rymer's grocery supplied Hare, Log, Burke, and M'Dougal with empty tea chests, which they used to transport their victims' bodies to Dr. Knox's rooms.

The West Port, the city's old west gate, grew into a neighborhood known as Wester Portsburgh by 1828. The murderers Burke, M'Dougal, Log, and Hare lived near these buildings.

CHAPTER I

The Notorious Murders in the West Port in 1828

Edinburgh's West Port, a neighborhood outside the old west gate of the city, was the home of the murderers. It extended west from a part of the old city known as the Grassmarket, which in 1828 was a warren of tenements and closes (alleys) surrounding a large central square. The Grassmarket and the neighboring closes running off the High Street, part of Edinburgh's Old Town, had been abandoned by most fashionable people in the last decades of the eighteenth century, when many families migrated north to the recently built, and still building, New Town. With its neoclassical squares, circles, gardens, gates, and sunlit rooms, it was a monument not only to the Enlightenment, but also to a new domesticity. In sharp contrast, the West Port and much of the Old Town came to house the laboring poor. A few indigent gentry in old family property and those stubbornly attached to St. Giles Kirk, the courts, or the Royal Exchange also stayed behind. Most of those who survived and even prospered in the Old Town made shoes, kept lodgings, washed clothes, carted goods, sold matches, collected bones and rags, worked as night watchmen, butchered cows, traded in old clothes, and did what they could. Some regularly left town to work the local harvests; others worked the wrong side of the law.

The West Port, sometimes called Wester Portsburgh as it expanded outside the old city limits, was in 1828 something of a new suburb, really an accretion of tenements, that marked the city's growth toward the west. It was a laborer's neighborhood, particularly marked by a tannery and cobblers. Some of the housing was respectable enough; some was squalid. People kept pigs penned in sties between one tenement and another and grew potatoes in the fields just outside the city. There were grocers, public houses, pawnshops, and lodging houses that catered to the very poor, renting space on a wreck of a bed or a pile of straw for a few pennies a night. The public houses seem to have been open continuously. Religious meetings were held on Sundays, for the poor, especially the Irish Catholic poor, were very much an object of salvation. Thieves and prostitutes mingled with cinder gatherers, night watchmen, washerwomen, shopkeepers, bargemen, saltwives, and clerks. And then, because it was 1828, there were police officers and watch houses, a relatively new institution in old cities.

This was the neighborhood where, late in 1827, "at Hallow-fair," in early November, Margaret Laird, known in the neighborhood as Lucky Log, met up with William Burke and his companion of nine years, Nelly (or Helen) M'Dougal, and "had a dram." Burke, who knew Log, told her that he was thinking of heading west, toward Glasgow, to work as a cobbler, repairing old shoes for resale. Log convinced him that he and his wife should move into the small inner room in her lodging house in Tanner's Close, and he worked there as a cobbler, off and on, over the next year. They seem not to have paid rent, which raises the question of why Log wanted them there, especially as her second husband, Willie (or William) Hare, was as vicious in money matters as Log. Without speculating on the answer to that question at this point, we can begin by considering the house, which was to become infamous, and has since been torn down.[1]

It consisted of three rooms, the entire first floor of a building that sat at the back of Tanner's Close, a narrow alley running north off the West Port, which was itself a proper street running east out of the Grassmarket. Known as Log's Lodgings, after Lucky Log's first husband, the three rooms were quite public, especially the front room, the door of which stood open to the street. Behind that lay a second room, almost as public, again with an open door or doorway, and in a corner, the third inner room. It had a lock on its door, and a window that faced a pigsty and a dead wall. This was the room offered to William Burke and Nelly M'Dougal, creating a household within a household. Burke cobbled, M'Dougal peddled the old shoes, Log watched over her lodgers and her toddler, and Hare seems at this time to have worked unloading barges on the Union Canal.

This continued for a few weeks, when one of the lodgers, an old pensioner named Donald, died owing Log and Hare quite a bit of money. Hare claimed it was four pounds, which seems unlikely, as it would have meant that he had stayed there for nearly a year, all on the promise of his quarter's pension coming due. His debt notwithstanding, a coffin was ordered for him, and possibly even a wake, since the body was not coffined for a day or two. Burke would later say that it was Hare's idea to pry the coffin open, and sell the body to the anatomists, and that it was Hare who pried up the coffin lid "with a chisel." But both of them then filled the coffin with tanner's bark, from the nearby tannery, and nailed down the coffin lid. Neither knew what to do next, and that evening they stood around in the yard of the medical college, eventually speaking at random to a student who directed them to the rooms of Dr. Knox. It is enough to say about Knox at this point that he paid well—the legal acquisition of bodies was difficult, and many anatomists bought bodies illegally resurrected from graves at this time—and that his men accepted bodies in sacks without asking questions. The two men got seven pounds and ten shillings for their work, Hare taking four pounds and five shillings, and Burke three pounds and five shillings. It appears that the extra pound in Hare's pocket may have gone to Log, as Burke later claimed that she got one pound of his share for every "subject" who came from the lodging house. Whether this was her idea, as Burke thought, or a scheme of Hare's to keep more of the money is not clear.[2]

Seven pounds and ten shillings was an enormous sum of money for working people, equivalent to the average wages of a handloom weaver for six months. There are two households here, not one; but the seven pounds and ten shillings had an enormous impact on their fragile household economies. Not long after Donald's timely death, which came somewhere between mid-November and Christmas, there was another death in the lodging house. On February 11, an old woman who was a pensioner of a wealthy family, and now supported herself by selling salt and camstone[3] in the streets, was "decoyed" into the lodging house by Log and Hare. Her name was Abigail Simpson, from the outlying parish of Gilmerton, and she had come into town to collect her "pension": a few pennies and a can of kitchen scraps; and also to sell a bit of salt. Log offered her one shilling and sixpence for the scraps, which was spent on sufficient whiskey to put Simpson to sleep. Hare made merry with her, offering to marry her daughter, and have them all live together. She became too drunk to leave, and was ill and vomiting when she awoke the next morning. As a remedy, Burke said that "they then gave her some porter and whiskey," after which she fell asleep on her bed. Again, according to Burke, "Hare then laid hold of her mouth and nose, and prevented her from breathing. Burke held her hands and feet till she was dead. She made very little resistance; and when it was convenient, they carried her to Dr. Knox's dissecting rooms in Surgeon's Square, and got ten pounds for her." They packed her in a tea chest, and the obliging young men from Knox's sent a porter to carry the body part of the way for them.[4]

The next "subject" was English, a forty-year-old man who sold spunks in the streets, and who "was ill with the jaundice." All Burke would say was that "they murdered him in the same manner as the other," and that they got ten pounds for him as well. The third victim was an old woman, brought into the house by Lucky Log in the forenoon, and given sufficient whiskey that she was put to bed. Log must have been busy with her all the forenoon, because Burke, who was mending shoes in the inner room all the time, reported that the old woman kept getting up to leave, and had to be put back into a bed three times before she fell asleep. Hare, who was at work unloading canal barges, came home for his dinner and found a ready subject. Even so, he was careful, and would only put some of the bed tick over

Old Surgeon's Hall sat on Surgeon's Square near Knox's rooms and just south of the Cowgate Port.

her face, and in her mouth. By evening she had died, apparently without any further help from Log, Burke, or Hare. All three put her in a "tea-box," and she too brought ten pounds from Dr. Knox.[5]

And then in April, the pattern varied, and the scene shifted to another house, that of Burke's brother Constantine. Constantine Burke, his wife Elizabeth, and several children lived in what seems to have been an attic room at the east end of the Old Town, in Gibb's Close in the Canongate. C. K. Sharpe, in his preface to John Macnee's transcript of the Burke and M'Dougal trial, described it carefully:

Ascending a narrow wooden trap-stair, and going along a passage, you find a door, only fastened by a latch, opening into an apartment, in which were a truckle bed, and another with tattered patch-work curtains; the walls adorned with many tawdry prints, carefully nailed on.[6]

Burke and M'Dougal had apparently spent the night there, and Hare and Log joined them in the morning. Perhaps they had been drinking at that end of town, and were unwilling to walk the mile or so that would have brought them back to the West Port, by simply walking along the Cowgate and into the Grassmarket. We know more about this murder than any of the preceding ones because there was a witness, Janet Brown, the companion of the victim Mary Paterson. Both were "girls of the town," and both were making their way home from the Canongate Police Office that Wednesday at 5 A.M., April 9.[7]

They first called at Mrs. Lawrie's lodging house, or perhaps brothel, but they both chose to go out again; they ran into Burke drinking in the house of a spirit dealer named Swanston, and he asked them to join him. According to Brown, they first shared a gill of whiskey, and watched Burke and Swanston drink rum and bitters together. Burke bought them some three gills of rum and bitters, and persuaded both of them to return to his lodgings, saying to Brown "that he had a pension, and could keep her handsomely, and make her comfortable for life." He bought each a bottle of whiskey, and promised them breakfast, which he subsequently ordered his brother's wife, Elizabeth Burke, to cook, after swearing at her for not yet having lit the morning fire.[8]

The breakfast was well beyond what might have been ordinary for any of the Burkes: tea, bread, eggs, Finnan haddocks, and whiskey. Burke, his brother, his sister-in-law, and the two young women ate, with Constantine leaving in the middle to go to his work as a scavenger. M'Dougal was asleep in one of the beds during all of this, only appearing later. Paterson seems to have been falling asleep by this point, for Burke began to concentrate on Brown, insisting that she go to a nearby public house and drink even more, after which they returned to Constantine's. It was then that M'Dougal awoke, rising suddenly from one of the beds, and "whispered" that she was Burke's wife. Brown "apologised for being in his company, mentioning that they did not know him to be a married man." M'Dougal responded by encouraging them to stay, but meanwhile began an argument with her husband, in which she threw eggs into the fire, and he broke a dram glass against her forehead, then locked her out of the room.[9]

With M'Dougal pounding on the door to get back in, Burke apparently commenced attempting to seduce Brown. In her words, "he affected great kindness toward her, and pressed her to go along with him into the bed which M'Dougal had so recently left." At this point they were virtually alone, since M'Dougal was locked out, Constantine's wife had run out during the fight, Constantine himself had left for work, and the unlucky Paterson was stretched unconscious or asleep on one of the beds. Brown, however, was just as sober as Burke, after quite a bit of drinking, and with M'Dougal pounding on the door, she "peremptorily refused." Burke let her leave, although she first had to promise to return in fifteen minutes, and he had to escort her past a still enraged M'Dougal, out on the stairs.

But she was not out of danger yet, nor did she suspect that Paterson was in any, which tells us that life in the Old Town could be fairly disorderly. But when she returned to Mrs. Lawrie, the older woman was suspicious, and immediately sent her out with a servant to get Paterson. She must have been somewhat drunk, however, since she could not remember where the house was, and had to go back to Swanston's to ask about Burke. There, remarkably, she was told that Burke was a respectable married man, and "did not keep company with such as they." But she found the house, and found Hare and Log and M'Dougal there; as she entered, Log rushed forward to hit her. That she then joined them in a glass of whiskey is ludicrous, but perhaps she felt obliged to wait, as they told her that Paterson had gone out with Burke, and would be back shortly. The servant returned to Mrs. Lawrie to report, and M'Dougal began to regale Brown with "a narration of her grievances from Burke's bad conduct."

Had Brown stayed much longer, she too would have been killed. Only because Mrs. Lawrie remained concerned, and sent her servant back to get Brown out of the house did she live, and remain concerned for some time about her friend Paterson. In fact, Paterson had been suffocated by Burke and Hare as soon as Hare arrived, and her body must have been in the room when Brown returned, and had her last convivial glass of whiskey. It was probably in anticipation of Hare's arrival that Burke agreed to let Brown go, since neither he nor Hare seem to have been willing to take on decidedly conscious, if not totally sober victims. And so Brown left, to return to the room that afternoon, when she was told by Elizabeth Burke that Paterson and Burke had still not returned. She continued to ask, for she often saw Constantine Burke at work in the streets in the morning. She was able to report two of his replies: "How the h——ll can I tell about you sort of people; you are here to-day and away tomorrow"; and "I am often out upon my lawful business, and how can I answer for all that takes place in my house in my absence."[10]

There are two points to be made about this episode at Constantine Burke's house. One is that there was not much privacy to be had, not merely in Log's Lodgings, but in any of the houses we shall see in these narratives. Not only is household a complex term; the houses themselves were porous. People came and went, slept here and there; a household might well include several houses. Burke and M'Dougal lived with Log and Hare, but they then drew Constantine and Elizabeth Burke into the circle of overlapping households. Both of these other Burkes probably knew what had become of Paterson; Burke had sent Elizabeth Burke out to fetch Willie Hare, and Elizabeth, Nelly M'Dougal, and Lucky Log must all have been standing by while the killing was done. Two, if Constantine Burke could struggle to disassociate himself from "you sort of people," undoubtedly the others could too. Presumably Log, Hare, Burke, and M'Dougal saw themselves as petty bourgeois entrepreneurs, lesser associates, but associates nonetheless of Dr. Knox; and they probably saw their victims as unlike themselves, as lower, lost, friendless commodities. The ease with which these people literally accommodated murder is stunning, and that ease allows us to see their "natural" pretension to see themselves as better people in a rather garish light.[11]

Burke especially seems to have been able to play on his reputation as a decent, respectable man. Because someone at Swanston's was willing to tell Janet Brown that a man like Burke did not keep company with women like herself, we can assume that Burke could get away with much. One of Knox's students recognized Paterson, a beautiful and well-known prostitute, but asked only a few questions, even though Burke admitted that "Paterson was only four hours dead till she was in Knox's dissecting-room." The student asked where he got the body, to which he replied that "he had purchased it from an old woman at the back of the Canongate." The body was still warm, and the students may have feared something, for they asked him to cut off her hair, and handed Burke a pair of scissors. And Knox may have feared, as well, for he had Paterson kept in spirits for several months. He also had a painter look at her, and possibly paint her, which suggests that he was fearless or a fool. There is more to be said about Burke's manner and reputation, and Knox's, but it can wait.[12]

In June, an old woman and a boy, probably her grandson, came to lodge at Log's. They gave the old woman a dram, and then, as with the other old woman, put "the bed-tick and bed-clothes on the top of her" in the middle of the night. Then they carried the boy, who was not likely to drink, into the little inner room, and suffocated him forcibly. Burke described him variously as "dumb," meaning speechless, and as "weak in his mind," so they probably did not fear much resistance. They stuffed the two into a herring barrel, and carried it to Hare's stable. They then tried a new means of transportation, Hare having bought a horse and cart, apparently for the body trade. But it did not work; the horse was too old or ill to work, and would not haul the barrel very far. Stranded, they had to hire a porter with a cart, deliver the bodies, collect their sixteen pounds, and then take the horse to the tanyard to be shot. What became of the cart we do not know, but presumably Hare sold it. He had probably hoped to avoid the cost of this hired labor, as well as the curiosity or gossip of porters. But he must have known nothing about horses, for he bought one with a great hole in its shoulder, covered over with a bit of horse skin from some other poor beast.[13]

Next came a fellow known only as Joseph the miller, a lodger whose face they covered with a pillow, undoubtedly after getting him drunk. As Burke put it, he and "Hare generally tried if lodgers would drink, and, if they would drink, they were disposed of in that manner." He was worth ten pounds. After Joseph came a curious episode, triggered by a visit Burke and M'Dougal made to friends in the country near Falkirk. While they were gone, Hare "fell in with a woman drunk in the street at the West Port." Hare killed her, and sold her, as usual, but denied that he "had been doing any business" when Burke and M'Dougal returned. Burke went to Knox's and found out that he had, after which Hare "confessed." This is interesting, because neither man seems to have been sure about whether his partner was the other man, or his own wife. After this anonymous woman came Effie the cinder gatherer, whom Burke lured in, as she was used to selling him scraps of leather that she found. She was killed by Burke and Hare in the stable, rather than the lodging house, and sold for ten pounds. And then Burke outdid himself. Seeing the police dragging a drunken woman to the watch house, he stopped them and said, "Let the woman go to her lodgings." He persuaded the police, who were having some trouble getting her to go with them, that he would see her home. He took her to Log's Lodgings, where he and Hare suffocated her that night, and then sold her for ten pounds.[14]

A Lamb to the Slaughter

About their next victim we know a good deal more. He was a local character, the subsequent trial brought his murder before the public, and Burke was willing to confess much more about James Wilson, known in the streets as Daft Jamie. Repeating her performance with old woman number three, Log brought Wilson back to the lodging house, promised him strong drink, and left him in Hare's company while she went to Rymer's, the neighborhood shop. James Wilson was a tall young man with respectable relations, a beggar only because he was "daft." That Log led him into their house was ambitious, for she probably recognized the difficulty of making him a subject. She immediately went to Rymer's, not only to buy a pennyworth of butter, but to collect Burke, who was drinking there. Too smart to order Burke back to her house publicly, she asked to share a dram with him, and stomped purposefully on his foot while drinking it. Burke must have known what was up, because he saw her "take Jamie off the street." Since this comes from Burke's account, he probably exaggerated the degree to which he followed while she led, but her part in the proceedings was obvious.[15]

Considering Jamie Wilson's size and youth, they sent someone for half a mutchkin (one-fourth of a liter) of drink.[16] With it, all three invited Jamie "ben" into the small back room of the lodging house, where Burke repaired shoes. Log "then went out, and locked the outer door, and put the key below the door." In other words, she left Burke and Hare locked in a tiny back room with Jamie, and perhaps Burke, if not Hare, felt like the poor young woman in *Rumpelstiltskin* who had to spin straw into gold. At that moment Log appeared to be in control, at least through Burke's telling of it, after the trial. Burke "declares that Mrs. Hare led poor Jamie in as a dumb lamb to the slaughter, and as a sheep to the shearers; and he was always very anxious making enquiries for his mother, and was told that she would be there immediately."[17]

Juxtaposing Log with Jamie's mother is all the more naively telling as it exaggerates images of good and evil women, through the Christian image of the lamb. And it is hard not to hear Burke's identification with Jamie ring through, as though he wished to claim for himself Jamie's anxiety and his victimization. Burke may have worked with Log, as well as Hare, but he preferred to think that the woman he slept beside, M'Dougal, had nothing to do with the murders. Perhaps he glimpsed himself wanting M'Dougal, much as poor Jamie had wanted his mother. Burke's paradox was that he worked with Log, and eventually, if not immediately, with M'Dougal in the murder business, but he wanted M'Dougal to be different, a shelter perhaps, no matter how rough and tawdry a figure of domesticity she might have been. While he ostensibly left M'Dougal out of his later confessions to protect her, he no doubt also did so to salvage for himself some comfort in the memory of her company.[18]

This murder was something of a turning point for both men, for they could not distance themselves from Wilson, quickly and easily doing away with him as if he were an old pensioner besotted with drink. Wilson drank little, and was strong. When Hare "threw his body on top of Jamie," Wilson fought back, and they rolled off the bed. Burke had to pitch in, holding his feet and hands, probably for some time. When it was over, Burke refused to hand over the extra pound for Log, insisting on half the takings for himself, and shortly after he and M'Dougal moved a few streets over, into a room rented by a cousin of Burke's and her husband John Brogan.[19]

Burke and M'Dougal's House

This move signaled Burke's rise to full partnership in the business, or perhaps his intention to go into business on his own or with M'Dougal. It also further complicates our understanding of household, and household enterprise, since the Brogans also came to know about, if not the murders, the getting and selling of bodies. The first subject to be murdered in their house was a relative, a distant cousin of M'Dougal's first husband. Why this young married woman would have come to see them, on a visit, is a mystery, but probably the offer was extended to her while Burke and M'Dougal were in Falkirk. Perhaps the offer was made with subjects in mind, raising the question of how they determined who was a friend, and who was prey. Because John Brogan knew about the cousin's body, which they had in a trunk in his house, Burke and Hare each paid him one pound and ten shillings, ostensibly to cover his unpaid back rent. The Brogans then left town, eventually, with the money, leaving Burke and M'Dougal to live in the house, without ever seeing the landlord, or paying any rent.[20]

This house, which some subsequent commentators thought was admirably chosen as a place to murder, was simply one of three tidy and inauspicious basement flats, each having one room. Burke and M'Dougal's room was reached by going down the passage, turning right, and opening a door into a shorter passage, which led to their door. The room itself was later viewed by the public, drawn, and described in all the papers. Varying descriptions emerged, suggesting that the room was respectable enough when clean, but often filthy while Burke and M'Dougal occupied it.

The room is so small, that the women who pretended to feel some alarm while Burke was stifling his prey, must have stepped over them to escape. The day after the trial, every thing seemed in the position as when the culprits were first arrested. A crazy chair stood by the fire place, near two broken wooden stools—old shoes, and implements for shoe-making lay scattered on the floor—a pot full of boiled potatoes, and broken glass, with old rags and straw, were near a cupboard, on which were some plates and spoons—the bed, if such it may be called, exhibited a disgusting spectacle; it is a coarse wooden frame, without posts or curtains, and was filled with old straw and rags, among which a man's shirt, stained with blood in front, and something like a child's shift, also bloody, were plainly discernible.[21]

Yet from another source, also published in 1829, came a very different view:

Burk's [sic] room was one of the neatest and snuggest little places I ever saw—walls well plastered and washed—a good wood floor—respectable fire-place—and light well-paned window, without a single spider's web.[22]

Clearly Burke and M'Dougal had improved their condition by the move, even if they had no nice furniture, and Burke could continue to present himself as a respectable person. But the second report of the clean and snug room did not take into account its state when occupied, for scraps of M'Dougal's statements, taken before the trial, reveal a somewhat less cheery version of domesticity.

That the pillow-case was used for containing dirty clothes, and lay at the head of the bed as a pillow... that the marks [of blood] on the pillow-slip were from her nose bleeding [Burke hit her]... and the blood upon the sheet proceeded from the declarant, in consequence of her state at the time, as was known to Mrs. Gray.[23]

The Last Victim at Log's Lodgings

The next victim, old Mrs. Haldane, was lodging with Log and Hare when she happened to get drunk on her own, and fall asleep in the stable on some straw. The two men got rid of her quickly, and Burke remembered no more than that she had only "one tooth in her mouth, and that a very large one in front." It was just luck that this old woman, who had one daughter married, another transported as a habitual criminal, and yet another who was "of idle habits, and much given to drinking," fell victim in Hare's stable. The next three, which were to be the last, all died in Burke and M'Dougal's house, the house the murderers persisted in calling Brogan's.[24]

In Brogan's House

All three were women, and all three seem to have been happy to get whiskey, and not afraid to sleep in Brogan's house, with strangers. The first was Peggy Haldane, who came looking for her mother, and never left. Burke killed her by himself, perhaps because she drank readily, and was unconscious. A washerwoman named Mrs. Hostler was washing clothes in the house, apparently for the Brogans, who were still there, or had suddenly returned, for Burke and Hare waited until Mrs. Brogan was out. In her case Burke also remembered little, save that she had ninepence halfpenny in her hand when she died, and they had a hard time getting it out of her fingers. Burke's confessions were never exact about the order of the victims, as Burke himself said that they—meaning himself, M'Dougal, Log, and Hare—were always quite drunk when they killed, and had only blurry recollections. But concerning the last of these three women we have much better information, and can see all four members of the original household at work, because this murder was discovered, went to trial, and elicited testimony from many people in the neighborhood, the police, and several medical experts.

The Death of Docherty

The four committed their last murder in Burke and M'Dougal's room on Halloween, which fell on a Friday in 1828; they still referred to it as Brogan's house, although the Brogans, with the exception of one son, seem to have finally moved out the week before. The house was a secure ground-floor flat, but neighborhood custom and their own willingness to take in lodgers in their single room made the potentially private room porous and at times virtually public. Consequently, the killing of Madge Docherty, an Irish woman in her forties, and the transportation and sale of her body provided the state with nineteen witnesses at the trial. Because we now have evidence from someone besides Burke, we can begin to see all four working together, in a neighborhood where they were recognized, helped, and suspected.[25]

That Mary or Madge Campbell, M'Gonegal, Duffie, or Docherty came to be drunk, and murdered in Burke and M'Dougal's sunken flat, as Hugh Alston, a neighbor, called it, on October 31, 1828, was pure chance. Docherty, the name she used in talking to Burke, had come from Glasgow in search of her son, Michael Campbell. She arrived at his lodgings, the house of Mary Stewart, just in time to hear that he had moved on. As he left money to pay for a night's lodging for her, it would seem that he either wanted to avoid her, or had work and would join her later. She stayed at Stewart's for one night, perhaps without eating anything, and left the house in the Pleasance on the morning of the thirty-first. She stopped at the shop of the shoemaker Charles McLaughlan, another of Stewart's lodgers, apparently hoping that he could tell her where her son had gone; but what she told McLaughlan was that "she did not know where her son was, and she was leaving town."[26]

Leaving McLaughlan's shop at the foot of St. Mary's Wynd, she walked west, across the Old Town, into Rymer's grocery shop in Portsburgh, "asking charity," as a shop boy put it. Burke was there, heard her Irish accent, could not help seeing her small frame, and asked her name. When she responded with Docherty, he insisted that she must be a relation of his mother's, and offered her breakfast. She left with him, and no witnesses place her outside Burke and M'Dougal's house, and hallway, until the police discovered her body in Dr. Knox's rooms in Surgeon's Square on Sunday.[27]

Docherty, who had been calling herself Margery M'Gonegal at Stewart's, no doubt thought that finding Burke, whom she was now calling Docherty, was a stroke of good luck. She went home with him between nine and eleven, to a tolerable room, and breakfasted with Burke, M'Dougal, and their lodgers, Mr. and Mrs. Gray. She seems to have taken advantage of their meager resources, washing her gown, smoking her pipe by the fire, and eating porridge with milk at three in the afternoon. Two neighbors, Mrs. Law and Mrs. Connoway, saw Burke coming back in at one with Docherty. Since the shop boy at Rymer's remembered only Burke coming in that afternoon, she had probably followed him, but only down the passageway. She would later be reluctant to stay in his house without him, and M'Dougal would complain to the neighbors that Docherty became too familiar with Burke, so she seems to have attached herself to him as best she could.[28]

As night fell, around four or five o'clock in Edinburgh in October, Burke sent away their lodgers, packing Mr. and Mrs. Gray and their child off to Log's boardinghouse for the night. Mrs. Gray recalled that he "put me out," giving as a reason that she and her husband were fighting too much, and "he would not have his house made a boxing-house." Her husband, rather more discreetly, remembered only that "he told us we must go out that night." Burke walked over with Gray, a pensioned soldier, himself; Log had apparently taken Mrs. Gray through the alleys earlier, so it seems that neither had any chance of straying. Once they left, and Lucky Log returned, the whiskey came out, and Docherty, Hare, and Log appeared to make merry. They were observed for twenty minutes or so by one of the downstairs neighbors, Mrs. Law, who stopped in, so she thought, around six or seven that night, and confirmed that the three were "merry[,] dancing and drinking." This party seemed to have continued until about nine, when Mrs. Gray returned for some bit of her child's clothing, and found Docherty singing, M'Dougal and Log dancing, and Hare and Burke drinking. Docherty might have been killed after Mrs. Gray left, and boxed up and put in a cellar at the end of that downstairs passageway, for they had all had a bit to drink by then, but that was not what happened.[29]

Inexplicably, the group broke up. Hare and Log went to their own house for supper; Mrs. Gray was there to see them return. Shortly after they appeared, M'Dougal joined them, probably for a meal of boiled potatoes. Burke also left, but we have no record of where he went. M'Dougal, the last of the group to leave her own house, left Docherty there alone, and stopped in at the Connoways' as she left.

According to Ann Connoway, "sometime after the darkening, Burke's wife came to me, and asked me to pay particular attention to her door, lest anybody should go in, until she came back." Docherty, now alone, must have made some noise, for Connoway's husband sent her to check M'Dougal's door, and she took a "light" and went to investigate. She found no one there but Docherty, whom she referred to as "the stranger," and who was asking her "for the name of the land of [these] houses," because she wanted to go looking for her son, but also to come back. Docherty had been trying to leave all day, but had been kept in the room with various offers and complaints. At this point, Connoway told her not to leave, because she was too drunk to walk, and that "the police would take her up." She ended up following Connoway back to her house, and talking to her husband about Ireland for a while. It seems far more likely that M'Dougal had actually asked her to keep the woman in, rather than keep strangers out, and that she was unwilling to admit that in the trial, because she clearly went to great lengths to keep Docherty there, when she hardly knew the woman. She succeeded in keeping Docherty until Hare and Log returned, Log with a bottle of whiskey in her apron. So this very odd Halloween party started up again, this time in the neighboring flat of John and Ann Connoway, with Madge Docherty, Willie Hare, Lucky Log, and finally Nelly M'Dougal in attendance.[30]

Docherty seemed fairly aware of her best interests that evening, as she followed Connoway down the hall. If she was drunk, she was quite conscious, and she told Connoway that Burke had promised her a bed and her supper. She also said "she intended to stop with them for a fortnight" which sounds as if she was both fairly calculating, and easily bought with offers of room and board. She may have been able to discuss Ireland with Connoway's husband, and when, in about an hour, Log and Hare appeared, she was able to drink and dance and sing with them. Log brought the whiskey, but did not dance with Hare and Docherty, and the lately arrived M'Dougal. Despite the dance, Docherty refused to return to Burke and M'Dougal's room until Burke appeared, so Log and Hare and M'Dougal went down the hall to wait in the familiar small room themselves. Meanwhile,

Docherty sat with the ostensibly annoyed Connoway until at least ten, or perhaps eleven o'clock. Given that none of these people had clocks or watches, it seems likely that the memories are roughly accurate, but the times jumbled, especially for those drinking. The four overt conspirators seem to have roamed from house to house, getting another drink, or relighting a fire. Burke, for example, was reported by Mrs. Gray to have turned up at Log's Lodgings at around seven that night, carrying a "copper measure, with some liquor in it," while Log and Hare were carousing at his house. Log and Hare spent as much time in the Burke and M'Dougal household as in their own, drinking with Docherty in shifts to keep an eye on their property, and to keep her quite drunk.[31]

The exact timing of all this will never be known, and certainly the participants never intended to remember it. Given that they were drinking, and even drunk, the chronological experience of all five that evening must have been quite distorted, all the more so by any attempt to reconstruct it accurately by sober members of the court later. Nonetheless, things happened; while Docherty ate, dozed, washed her bed gown, and drank, Log and Hare were informed. There was a great deal of coming and going, as the Grays were roughly ordered to the other lodging house, and money borrowed to buy whiskey. Much of the work of keeping Docherty in the house fell to M'Dougal, although Connoway knowingly or unknowingly did her share. Mrs. Gray recalled that when Docherty had wanted to leave that afternoon, M'Dougal had insisted that she take a nap.[32]

Burke and Hare Fight

Given the preceding fifteen murders, this was familiar work for all four, but, even allowing for the porous houses in which they lived, work that they repeatedly botched. Burke seems to have vanished for most of the day, after bringing the woman into his house. When he finally returned, somewhere around eleven, or perhaps ten that night, all hell broke loose in the seven and one-half by sixteen foot room, not in the course of Docherty's murder, but because he and Hare attacked each other, apparently as soon as Burke walked into the room.

Something had gone wrong here. Men who had previously killed at all hours of the day and night, as opportunity struck, now hesitated, and fought each other. In the end the two men, now probably thoroughly drunk, and angry, resolved their difference by falling on Docherty and suffocating her in ten or fifteen minutes. Hare's testimony is so garbled and inept that it is hard to make anything of it; he gave away so little that there is no motive for the fighting to be found there. Nor did Burke say much about the fight in his confessions. He did insist that "he was nearly strangled by Hare" but there is no explanation given for the fighting. All that Burke was willing to say, after his conviction, was

> That while he and Hare were struggling, which was a real scuffle, M'Dougal [sic] opened the door of the apartment, and went into the inner passage and knocked at the door, and called out police and murder, but soon came back; and at the same time Hare's wife called out, never to mind, because the declarant and Hare would not hurt one another. That whenever he and Hare rose and went towards the straw where Docherty was lying, M'Dougal and Hare's wife who, he thinks, were lying in bed at the time, or, perhaps, were at the fire, immediately rose and left the house, but did not make any noise, so far as he heard, and he was surprised at their going out at that time, because he did not see how they could have any suspicion of what they (the declarant and Hare) intended doing.[33]

Burke went on to say that after the fight, they drank, and then advanced on the woman, who was asleep in the straw. He claimed that Hare took her by the mouth and nose, and he merely "lay across her." But he was reported to have told guards in the lock-up house on Christmas morning, immediately after the trial, that "after the sham fight was over, she was thrown down on her back; that Hare seized her by the legs; and that he forced the mouth of a bottle into her throat, and poured down whiskey till she was choked or nearly so, and that he himself then sat down upon her, stopping up her nose and mouth so completely that she died in a few minutes." This talk of a "sham fight" may be an interpolation of the editor providing this story, for the idea that Burke and Hare had used sham fights to somehow beguile their prey was taken up by the press after the trial, along with rumors that they laced the alcohol they served with opium. All of these vastly exaggerated the efficiency and cunning of the four, who seem more likely to have been randomly vicious, and aggressive even toward each other. If Burke was using the phrase "sham fight," then he was probably playing to that image of ruthless efficiency in the aftermath of the dramatic trial. Or he was unwilling to admit to how miserable and disorganized the killers' lives were.[34]

The only disinterested, and hence presumably reliable account comes from someone who was not there, and consists only of what he heard. Hugh Alston, on his way home to one of the more respectable upstairs rooms at half past eleven, heard shouting and the sounds of struggle, and strangling. He reported hearing "two men quarrelling" and he ran down the street, called for police, found none, and ran partway into the hall, where he heard a woman with a very strong voice cry out "for god sake get the police, there is murder here." Along with the cry, he heard pounding on what he believed to have been the door to the room, and "then something gave a cry, as if proceeding from a person or animal that had been strangled." After that, he heard two men's voices, but could not hear what they said. Mrs. Law, whose house, or room, did not share a wall with that of Burke and M'Dougal, testified that she heard a quarrel late that night, and recognized Burke's voice, but did not know what he was saying. Mrs. Connoway, whose house did share a wall, reported only that "they were fighting like." The explanation for all this noise has to be that Burke and Hare fought with each other, violently, before killing Docherty, and perhaps over her murder. The testimony of those present, namely Alston, Law, Connoway, Log, and Hare, as well as Burke's confessions all point to a fight between Burke and Hare, with their wives attempting to separate them. Burke claimed in his first confession that "he was nearly strangled by Hare," and that M'Dougal "called out police and murder," and that Log told her "never to mind, because [Burke] and Hare would not hurt one another."[35]

The Wives in the Passageway

The two men had a history of fighting with their wives, and with others; Hare in particular was known for picking fights. But surely the fight was not a part of any plan, especially yelling murder loud enough to be heard by people in the street. They were both inept, and overconfident. No one ever saw them kill, and wives and husbands could not testify against each other. And they served an arrogant doctor, whose arrogance had begun to extend to Burke and Hare, and perhaps to Log and M'Dougal. According to Burke, the two men stopped fighting, drank more whiskey, and moved toward Docherty, who had crawled toward the wall, on a pile of straw. Both women then hid themselves in the passage, between the inner and outer doors, signaling that they understood what would happen, even though Burke took pains to protect them in his first confession. Log testified that while they stood in the hall, they talked about whether they might be murdered as well: "We were just talking about [Docherty], saying, perhaps it would be the same case with her and I." Maybe they said that, but Log was a calculating woman, no doubt capable of foreseeing evil, but also of playing to the audience as a fearful and respectable woman. She also told the court that she and M'Dougal "were both alarmed, and we both flew out of the house." When asked if she had cried out, she replied, "No, sir, I was quite powerless." To confirm her position as wife, mother, and helpless woman, she brought her infant into court with her, and testified that she had three times left her husband, because of the terrible life they led. It would doubtless be more accurate to remember Log as Burke described her, pragmatically telling M'Dougal "never to mind, the declarant and Hare would not hurt one another." And perhaps she and M'Dougal stood in the passageway to keep any unwanted visitors out, although it seems unlikely that they heard Alston calling for the police in the West Port.[36]

On Halloween the two men dominated that room, and even if Log and M'Dougal had participated, working as partners during the day, that night they became vulnerable. Tough and loud-voiced as they were, they both left the room. Killing was work for men, and as Burke later confessed, those men were always careful to have no witnesses, not even their own wives. When Log and M'Dougal left the room, the four acknowledged a complex set of distinctions, about which more will be said in a later chapter. But when they came back into the room, work continued. The men may have stripped Docherty's body and hidden it beneath the straw kept at the foot of the bed before Log and M'Dougal came back into the room. They found seven shillings in her pocket, and split the sum between themselves. Burke then hurried out to find David Paterson, an agent of Dr. Knox who lived just across the West Port; he called at ten, or so Paterson's sister Elizabeth recalled, and did not find him at home. He called again at midnight, and brought Paterson back to the house.[37]

Why he brought Paterson back at that hour is not at all clear, and Paterson, who was in a very difficult position as Dr. Knox's agent or procurer, was not very forthcoming in his testimony. He admitted that he went in, saw Log, M'Dougal, and Hare there, along with Burke. Burke, he said, gestured toward the straw, and said he had gotten something for the doctor. M'Dougal was standing nearby, and probably heard what they said. But Paterson claimed that nothing more was said, except for his own farewell. But that farewell seems a bit premature, and if more was said, it must have incriminated him. Possibly Burke was anxious to ask him about the marks on Docherty's throat, since he or Hare had, uncharacteristically, grabbed her by the throat during the murder. If not that, then perhaps he wanted an opinion on how well the body would keep in late October weather, for they got £10 in the winter, and £8 in the summer. If they really had neither of these conversations, nor any other of substance, then Burke must have been horribly anxious, despite being drunk that night. And he must have hoped that the presence of an official representative of Dr. Knox would help him to convert, in his imagination, the old woman at the foot of his bed from a grisly corpse to a piece of merchandise, a subject. After all the shouting, this denouement seems rather cold-blooded and orderly.[38]

After Paterson left, the four settled in for the night, with the body under a pile of old straw next to the rough box bed. Although Log would later tell the court that she had struggled to get her husband to go home, as a respectable wife might have done, they probably slept at

Burke and M'Dougal's house to protect their share in the newly acquired subject. But they did not get to sleep until after two in the morning, when John Brogan came by to spend the night. Brogan was the son of the former tenants; he had been in the house much of Friday afternoon, seeing the Grays leave for Log's Lodgings, and the old woman entertained. Because of some relation between his mother and M'Dougal, he called her his aunt. Brogan reported finding Hare and Log lying in the bed, and Burke and M'Dougal standing at the window, talking. When all five finally settled down to sleep, Burke and Hare were in the bed, and Brogan slept by the fire, on the floor, with Log and M'Dougal. That Burke and Hare claimed the bed suggests that they also claimed to dominate those in the room: their wives, the young Brogan, and the corpse at their feet. That only an hour earlier they had arranged themselves differently, in couples, suggests that the partnership was tenuous and conflicted with other loyalties.[39]

Saturday Morning

Despite the late, not to mention bizarre night, no one slept in on Saturday morning. Hare and Log were back in their own house before nine. Sometime between eight and nine, Elizabeth Paterson had come through the hallway, looking for Burke and "John," the name Hare used with the medical men. She found Burke, and he then called on her brother David, who "told him if he had anything to say or to do with Dr Knox, to go to himself and settle with him." At about that time, Burke also went to see a porter named M'Culloch, asking him to be at the house at six that evening to carry something. And while he was out, he also stopped at Log's Lodgings where he woke up the Grays, asked Hare to give them "a dram of spirits," and urged them to come back for breakfast. Hare, we might note, would later testify that he saw Burke in Rymer's shop that morning, and that Burke called him into the shop as he was on his way "to feed [his] swine." While Burke was about his errands, M'Dougal was up, and busy fetching Mrs. Law and Mrs. Connoway. Around eight o'clock, she went to Mrs. Law's house to borrow her bellows, and at nine, probably the time that Burke returned, went back down the hall to tell Connoway that "William was wanting [her]." By what seems to have been a few minutes past nine, a group had assembled in Burke and M'Dougal's house. Young Brogan, Mrs. Law, Mrs. Connoway, and the Grays joined Burke and M'Dougal and left a record of the curious performance they witnessed. Had Docherty's body been visible, we would probably call it a wake.[40]

The Ceremony

Mrs. Connoway reported that Burke was sitting with his back to the bed, drinking. He "filled a glass to me," she said, "and I drank it." Perhaps as she was drinking the Grays came in, for they too saw what happened next. Burke continued to drink, but then he began to fling whiskey up toward the ceiling, over the bed, and then under the bed. Mrs. Gray particularly remembered that he "went three times under the bed, and put some [whiskey] on his breast." Brogan, Mrs. Law, the Grays, and Mrs. Connoway all saw this, and the three women all remarked that Burke's explanation at the time for his behavior was that he wished, in Mrs. Gray's words, "the bottle *toom* [empty] to get more." While her husband was flinging whiskey about the room, M'Dougal was singing. Unfortunately no one mentioned what she sang in their testimony. Then Burke left to get his bottle filled, and the odd party broke up. Whether Burke hoped to clear the air in a scientific way, relying on the alcohol to keep down smells, or whether he had something a little more religious, or superstitious, in mind is impossible to know. The first he might have learned from his visits to Knox's dissecting rooms, but the second comes straight from the wake, the old custom of sitting with the dead to keep them company.[41]

Perhaps M'Dougal and Burke, if not Log and Hare, already knew that it was going to be a hard day. When M'Dougal had called on Law at eight that morning, she was already thinking of ways to explain the noise they had made the night before. M'Dougal raised the subject, immediately asking Law if she had heard Burke and Hare

The Cowgate Port, where the Cowgate joined St. Mary's Wynd, would have marked where a porter carrying a body from the West Port would probably have turned south to reach Surgeon's Square, unless he chose to follow the back alleys and closes.

fighting the night before. Law, virtually as a response, "asked her what she had done with the little woman." This must have struck M'Dougal as a rather pointed question, for she was in Law's house, and Law could not see that the woman was gone. Law must have had some suspicion; in any case, she recalled that M'Dougal told her that "she had kicked the d——d b——h's backside out the door," because Docherty "had been using too much freedom with William." And when Connoway had gone to Burke and M'Dougal's house at nine, she too had asked M'Dougal about Docherty, and gotten much the same answer. When Mrs. Gray asked, probably not long after Connoway, she was told that Docherty "was too impudent," and had been "turned... out." Both Gray and Connoway may have been altering M'Dougal's words to sound polite in court, since Mrs. Law had replicated, with some urging ("give us the words she used") M'Dougal's coarse phrase, "damned bitch." And John Brogan, not confined by any sense of female propriety, reported that one of the neighbors who asked about Docherty that morning had referred to her by the odd title of "*spaewife*," meaning fortuneteller. M'Dougal's response as Brogan heard it, and it was always M'Dougal who responded, was that Docherty was so "*fashous*," a Scots word for troublesome, that "she gave her a kick in the ——, and set her to the door... [and] thrust her out of the house, for an old Irish *limmer*," or rascal.[42]

A good many people had seen the old woman, and perhaps Burke, Hare, Log, and M'Dougal thought it wise to keep the body in the straw until six, when it would be quite dark out. It was to be a fatal mistake. Mrs. Gray, her curiosity aroused by all the spilled and thrown whiskey, perhaps saw herself mirrored in the older Docherty, should her husband die. Maybe she saw Docherty not as an abject victim of poverty and dependence, but as playing on the customary ties that made life easier for the working poor. Even if Docherty was drunken and dissolute, she was doing well to keep seven shillings in her purse, while being treated to meals and whiskey. The purse argues for some self-control and calculation on her part, even if her death does not. And Hare and Burke were very imperfectly in control of the business, and were not the masters of her fate that the prosecution would make them out to be. Nor were all four in control, even though they struggled to re-create the simple pattern of the previous murders, suffocation followed by transportation to the doctors' district.[43]

Finding Docherty

Docherty's body remained hidden in the straw all day, while something like normal life went on in the house. The Grays returned after nine on Saturday morning, to the gathering reported above. After the bottle was emptied, Burke left, pointedly asking young Brogan to sit on a chair near where the body was hidden, and not to get up until he returned. But Brogan got up and left a moment later, leaving M'Dougal and the Grays in the house. Mrs. Gray remembered not only the drinking and sprinkling of whiskey, but also that she had moved toward the pile of straw, looking for her child's stockings, and was told by Burke to stay away from there. Then she moved to look under the bed, where potatoes were stored, and Burke asked what she "was doing there with a lighted pipe." What happened after that is not clear, but then no one expected that morning and afternoon to become subject to scrutiny. Burke and Brogan left within minutes of each other; Burke would appear at Dr. Knox's rooms on Surgeon's Square between twelve and two that afternoon, alone, again asking about the subject. Meanwhile, Mrs. Gray washed and sanded the floor, while M'Dougal "was stretched on the bed." Burke seems to have been out walking and drinking, for at one point Mrs. Gray went looking for him, and found him coming up the West Port. He "went into one M'Kenzie's to get a dram," telling Gray to go home, and he would be there shortly. Brogan came and went again, M'Dougal went out, and Mrs. Law's servant girl came in. By then it was getting dark, perhaps at around five in October. Mrs. Gray, her husband, and the servant, apparently all curious, and led by Mrs. Gray, looked in the straw at the foot of the bed. Mrs. Gray later said in court that she "thought there was something that was not right; because he was throwing about the whisky." And what she found was Mary Docherty's right arm. She and her husband uncovered the body, which was naked, and looked at her face, which was bloody. The body had been laid up against the wall, with its feet under the bed. What became of the servant we will never know, but Mr. Gray gathered their belongings and left the room immediately. His wife tarried behind, perhaps still looking for the child's stockings she had been searching for since Friday.[44]

In the hall Mr. Gray met M'Dougal, and confronted her, asking "what was that she had got in the house." She tried to play dumb, but he replied "I suppose you know very well what it is." At that, she fell to her knees, in what the lord justice clerk pressed Gray to call a "supplicating attitude," and she promised him five or six shillings on the spot, and then ten pounds a week, if he would not inform the police. He replied that his "conscience would not allow [him] to do it." At that, M'Dougal left him and went into her house, where she found Mrs. Gray, whom she offered only the five or six shillings. But Mrs. Gray was more direct with her, pointing out that Docherty had been quite well the night before, "singing and dancing on the floor." M'Dougal kept reiterating her offer of money, raising it to ten pounds if both of the Grays would "hold their tongue[s]." Gray replied "God forbid that my husband should be worth that for dead bodies." And then she pushed M'Dougal further, demanding "what did she mean by bringing her family into disgrace by it," to which M'Dougal replied, "my God, I cannot help it." Gray responded by telling M'Dougal that "you surely can help it, or you would not stay in the house."[45]

M'Dougal made no answer to that, but followed the Grays as they made their way down the hall, up the stairs, and into the street. There must have been some yelling, though, for when they quickly ran into Log in the street, Mr. Gray would later remember that "Mrs Hare" asked them "what we were making a noise about." Log, ever quick to take control of a situation, asked them to come into "the house," probably meaning her house, to "decide our matters there." Unfortunately, we have no record of what Log said to them then, for no one on the court asked either of the Grays about it, probably because as king's evidence, Log and Hare were immune from prosecution, and there was no point. Neither of the Grays could have had any illusions about the innocence of the two women; perhaps Mrs. Gray suspected that had she, or her pensioned husband been alone with them, indoors, they might not have survived to tell the police. But Log and M'Dougal could do nothing else, and that evening the Grays reported what they had seen to the police.[46]

The Procession to Knox's Rooms

Ironically, at five in the evening as the Grays were making their way to the police office, Burke was in Rymer's shop, buying an empty tea chest for which he could not yet pay, which suggests that they killed as they ran out of money. Burke told Rymer's shop boy that "he would send Mrs Hare" to get the box. By six o'clock Log had collected the box, and the porter, George M'Culloch, had arrived at Burke's, and he helped to pack the body into the tea chest, pushing in the head. He would later be so afraid to admit to carrying the chest that he had to be warned by the senior judge, the lord justice clerk, to speak plainly. But at the time the five of them made quite a procession as they left the house. An unidentified servant girl, perhaps Mrs. Law's girl, reported to the police that "she had seen Burke and his wife, Hare and his wife, and the porter M'Culloch, going up the stair, the porter carrying a tea-box." Just before they left, M'Dougal had asked Mrs. Connoway to watch the door, and let no one into their house, because Mrs. Gray had been stealing things "out of her house." It was never a very private neighborhood, and from the time the Grays left, and then Hare and Log arrived to follow the body, neighbors and police would swarm around the Brogans' old house. While rumors began to spread in the West Port, the four accompanied their box to Dr. Knox's rooms, where they were met at about seven by Paterson, a sort of caretaker, and Mr. Jones, a student and one of Knox's assistants. Having delivered the body, Paterson and Jones, followed at a few yards' distance by the four, and M'Culloch, walked all the way out to Knox's house in Newington. Apparently they made their way out to Knox's in three groups, with Paterson and Jones walking together, Burke, Hare, and M'Culloch making another group, and Log and M'Dougal following behind. They were rushing out to Knox's because Burke and Hare wanted their money, but the best that Knox would do on a Saturday, without seeing the body, was to give Paterson £5, to be divided between Hare and Burke, plus the small sum owing to M'Culloch. On Monday, Paterson said, when Knox had seen the body, he would pay more, making a total of either £8 or £10.[47]

That Monday reckoning was never to come. Around eight o'clock on Saturday Mrs. Gray found Mrs. Connoway, told her about the body, and dragged her into Burke and M'Dougal's. Mrs. Connoway, however, who may well have known that there had been a body there and that it was gone, claimed to be so afraid that she ran back out without looking at the straw. When Burke and M'Dougal returned from Knox's house shortly after that, Connoway was able to greet them with news of the "noise" in the neighborhood, the rumor that he had killed the old woman. Mr. Connoway asked him about the report, and Burke laughed, and "said that he defied all Scotland to say any thing against him." M'Dougal said "all the world could not say any thing against him." This was just before the police officers, John Fisher and John Finlay or Findlay, accompanied by Mr. Gray, "gripped him on the stair," and Fisher, the senior man, took him into his house.[48]

With almost comic irony, they met Burke and M'Dougal coming out of the building, and very quickly separated Burke and M'Dougal, interviewing each. Burke replied insolently, as Fisher put it, saying that the woman had left on her own, and that many people had seen her go. But he said that Docherty had left at seven in the morning, and M'Dougal said she had left at seven in the evening. This, coupled with the blood that Fisher saw all over the bed, was enough to make him take them into custody. At the police office, they were examined by the superintendent; and then Fisher with the superintendent and the police surgeon Dr. Black went back to the house, where they found more blood under the straw, and Docherty's striped bed gown in the bed. By Sunday morning, Log and Hare also had been taken into custody, roused out of bed while Log laughed, jeered, and insisted that "the police had surely very little to do now to look into a drunken spree like this." At the same time, the police had located the body in Knox's rooms, left a man to guard it, called the Grays to identify her, and within hours carried the body to the police office. Later on Sunday, Burke, M'Dougal, Log, and Hare, shown the body, denied all knowledge of it.[49]

CHAPTER 2

Common Thievery in the Old Town in 1828

Lucky Log stopped the Grays on their way to the police, and consequently knew just as much as M'Dougal about the trouble ahead. It is inconceivable that she would not have urged Hare to see where their self-interest lay, and urged him to join her in turning king's evidence once all four had been jailed. Log lived in a neighborhood, or neighborhoods, where women often played a part, and an aggressive one, in the most common businesses of crime in Edinburgh, theft and reset. Resetting stolen goods meant, to be literal, to set them before the public again: in practical terms, to sell them to pawnshops, or private persons, for cash. Log lived in an extended neighborhood that stretched from the West Port to the High Street, on to the North Back of the Canongate, south along the Pleasance, back into the Cowgate, which led to the Grassmarket, which in turn led to the West Port. She must have known more than a few women and men who could deliver or dispose of shirts, a pair of blankets, salt cellars, watches, or almost anything else.

If Log did not know them, the prosecuting lawyers in the Lord Advocate's Department certainly did. In 1828, 109 women and 532 men were "precognosed" or interviewed by prosecutors as persons potentially guilty of felonies. One out of six suspects was a woman, which tells us that women were neither an overwhelming presence, nor were they absent. In Edinburgh neighborhoods, chiefly the Old Town, in 1828, nineteen women including Log and M'Dougal were taken into custody and interviewed. If one includes the ports north of Edinburgh, Leith and Newhaven, now part of Edinburgh, the number rises to twenty-one. That is not a large number for a city of 136,000 in 1831, and it suggests that we are not seeing social crime—some large-scale shift that leaves many destitute, stealing to keep from starving or to protest the sudden loss of their livelihoods. Rather, it looks like most of the twenty-one, some of whom where caught red-handed by irate householders or found quickly by the Edinburgh police, were largely habitual criminals who chose to steal, and hard-tempered women who repeatedly got into fights. Log and M'Dougal differed from most of them in having no previous police records, but they too had chosen their work, even though they both protested that their husbands had given them no choice.[1]

In other words, with these seventeen women, leaving aside Log and M'Dougal, we are seeing something of the people the Edinburgh police referred to as "habite and repute" criminals, women who, with scores of associates, lived with a different map of Edinburgh in their heads. Their map, the underworld map, highlighted, for example, the spot on the North Bridge where strangers waited for their coaches; the room in Little Anderson's Close available for prostitution; the particularly narrow and empty closes that were good places to pick a drunken man's pocket. It included the pawnshops, loan companies, and brokers who would buy an exquisite men's shirt or a nice gold watch from a woman without asking any questions. Ironically, in parts of the Old Town in the late eighteenth and early nineteenth century, the underworld as figure of speech became a reality, as improvements like the Mound, the George IV Bridge, the North Bridge, and the South Bridge linked the Old Town and the New. Between 1784 and 1834, bridges over dry ground literally provided new, direct streets through the Old Town, and extended neoclassical style into, and over, the jumble of early modern tenements, closes, and courtyards.[2]

This University of Edinburgh building, now known as Old College, faced the South Bridge that ran over the Cowgate, creating a wide thoroughfare over the old streets below. Betty McKinnon pawned several stolen shirts at Salt's on the South Bridge.

The Creation of an Underworld

The heart of the Old Town lay atop a volcanic ridge, while many of the tenements, especially the poorer ones, lay on the northern or southern slopes of that ridge. As new streets came to connect the New Town, itself built on high ground north of the old ridge, they were built as bridges over the old neighborhoods. On the north side of the very old High Street, even in the eighteenth century, closes were leveled or covered to become the basements of great new buildings. Mary King's Close was preserved intact within the basement of the Royal Exchange. On the south side of the ridge, where the Cowgate and the South Back of the Canongate ran parallel to the High Street, the old wynds and closes were still in use. But by 1834 the South Bridge and the George IV Bridge ran above the Cowgate, adding a new dimension to life there, a forced awareness of those grand wide streets overhead, which, if followed north, took one directly to the New Town. The head of the Cowgate, where it joined the Grassmarket, became a darker spot between 1828 and 1834 as the George IV Bridge, several times wider than the Cowgate, was built over it.[3]

Margaret Veitch

At the other end of the Cowgate, to the east of the Grassmarket and somewhat south, on Davie Street, we find the household of Margaret Veitch and her husband Thomas Low, and their two children, a son, and a daughter Barbara. It was a neighborhood not unlike the West Port—not formally part of the Old Town, but attached, comprised of newer buildings as the city grew, and chiefly inhabited by working people. Veitch, then in her second marriage, had moved to the city from Selkirk in 1825, and the family had apparently settled into a comfortable business by 1828, resetting stolen goods. In the particular instance that led to her questioning in 1828, she had bought some clothes from a boy of fifteen, John Brown, a neighborhood lad from Bristo Port, about a quarter of a mile to the west.[4]

Their system was simple. Veitch would buy clothes from thieves, sending her daughter to pawn or sell women's clothes, and her son to dispose of men's. Her husband Thomas bought watches, presumably stolen, and sold them to other dealers. In this case, the clothes, which had been stolen outside Edinburgh proper, in Morningside and Tranent, were taken to the Equitable Loan Company in Keir Street, just south of the West Port. But Veitch was either new to this business or very enterprising, because she also tried to sell the clothes to her sister in Selkirk, and to a woman keeping a public house in Leith Street. That a young thief like Brown would go through such a roundabout system to dispose of goods suggests that a simple and old system still governed social relations among criminals. Rather like an extended family, young thieves may have often relied on older resetters to redistribute their goods, placing them back in circulation in the accepted economy. This was practical, since Veitch and Low, with a household of their own, and growing children, could plausibly claim to have goods of which they might dispose. This family enterprise would have been perfectly familiar to Log and Hare, and Burke and M'Dougal—to a point.[5]

Elizabeth Paterson

Elizabeth Paterson, questioned by the police after she was caught running from a house with a bundle and a young boy, insisted that she had been mistaken for some other young woman. She had been working, she said, collecting "bones in Musselburgh," which she had sold to a woman in Leith. She was then walking home, she said, when she was grabbed by a young man in the neighborhood of Gayfield Square, which is near the east end of Princes Street in the New Town. The police were not inclined to believe her, since the young man and his sister had just chased Paterson and the boy from their house, and because Paterson and her family were well known to the police. As a sergeant with the Edinburgh Police Establishment put it,

> She is a very bad character, and associates with thieves and her mother, and her Sisters are Considered thieves by the Establishment... the prisoner gains her livelyhood [sic] chiefly by stealing or resetting stolen goods, but as she sometimes goes round the town with a basket selling eggs, and resides at home the Declarent can hardly say that she is habite & repute a thief; that he had no doubt she Carries the basket of Eggs as a Cloak or cover for her stealing what she can lay her hands on.[6]

Paterson, along with her mother, sisters, and an absent brother who had already been transported, made up another household like the one of Margaret Veitch and Thomas Low. But this one had a female head, for Paterson's father, James Paterson, had nothing to do with them, although Elizabeth insisted that she often met him in the street. Elizabeth's mother, Mary Ross, may have been something of a matriarch, with her daughters on the street, and Elizabeth using, in this case, an even younger boy to climb through a window to steal. There was order and loyalty to be found in the old household, and it undoubtedly worked as a means of organizing criminal enterprise.[7]

Old Mrs. Burrows

Margaret Stewart was the wife of William Burrows, a weaver from Glasgow. They married in 1805, had two daughters, Margaret and Mary, and moved to Edinburgh around 1813. By 1828 Mary, who was then twenty, and her mother, then known as the Old Mrs. Burrows, were resetting stolen clothes in the Old Town. The family lived in Hastie's Close, off the Cowgate, and regularly sold clothes to Mrs. Tonner, in Libberton's Wynd, off the Lawnmarket. Mrs. Tonner said that it was Mary who appeared carrying both a bundle of men's clothes—an olive-colored coat, black trousers, and a "camblet cloak"—and her child, in her arms. Mary, she said, claimed that the police had been around, at which point her mother joined them. So, we know that Margaret Burrows and her daughter Mary were selling stolen clothes, and that her husband and other daughter may have had little to do with this.

When Mrs. Burrows was questioned by the police, who were anxious to have her identify the person who had sold or given her the clothes, she at first said very little, but finally admitted—or lied—"it was Davie." At that, David Stark, who was in the same room, blurted out, "Oh you rotten hearted Bugar [bugger]." Stark claimed that he was in her house because Burrows wanted to sell him clothes, but that he was afraid to buy from her. But he also admitted knowing "that Burrows' house is a receptacle for thieves and women of bad character." Stark was nineteen, a shoemaker who lived in Shoemaker's Close, off the Canongate, with his widowed mother. What we have here may well have been a classic pattern, in which a household reset goods, taking on the extra labor it needed for thieving in the form of young men or children, much as an old agricultural or crafts household would take on young servants or apprentices. Three men, two of them in their early teens, were mentioned in connection with Margaret Veitch; Elizabeth Paterson had a young boy creeping in windows for her; and the Burrows had, no doubt among others, Davie Stark.[8]

Betty McKinnon

But not all women were so safely established in households. Betty, or Elizabeth, McKinnon was a twenty-eight-year-old Irish woman who had lived in Scotland, and possibly in Edinburgh, for eleven years, since approximately 1817. She had no fixed residence, probably staying in places like Log's Lodgings when she had the pennies; she had been in the Bridewell, or local jail, four times for minor infractions, and was considered to be "habite & repute" a thief. When she appeared before the police in 1828, she had been caught in a pawnshop or old clothes dealer called Salt's, on the South Bridge, disposing of two very fine linen shirts. She was seized by the woman from whom she had stolen the shirts, an old laundress who washed in her own home for the household of a gentleman, Thomas Boswell of Blackadder.[9]

The laundress was Janet Lawson, whose daughter was in service to Boswell, and she lived just off the North Back of the Canongate, on a set of steps known as Crawford's Close. The close, really a narrow stairway, led to Calton Hill, where Lawson had clothes drying. When she went out to collect them, she was careful to remove the lifter from her door latch—she took the "lifter of the Sneck"—probably because she had "Nine Linen Shifts," still damp, in the house. She was gone no more than fifteen minutes, but when she returned, the shifts, or shirts, were gone, and neighbors told her they had seen a girl leave with a bundle. Lawson immediately went to the nearest watch house to tell the police, and then began making the rounds of the pawnbrokers, looking for her still-damp shirts.[10]

Janet Swanston and her husband Robert Sinclair were grocers and spirit dealers in Scott's Land, on the north side of the North Back, very close to the North Bridge. Their shop was fourteen paces from Crawford's Close, and she had clearly seen McKinnon come down the North Back, carrying the linens, and she left a particularly striking description of the twenty-eight-year-old thief. Swanston was "standing at her own shop door" when "she observed a miserable looking dirty woman coming up the side of the street with some linens, and when she had passed [Lawson] saw them more distinctly hanging under her arm and thought it strange that a woman of such an appearance should have such beautiful linens under her charge . . . she walked quickly and kept her shawl drawn over her head."[11]

But McKinnon, however suspicious she looked to Janet Swanston, nonetheless walked to Salt's, about a quarter of a mile southwest, and pawned the shirts with no trouble. Had she not lingered in the shop on the South Bridge, she might well have gotten away. She was no fool; she plainly knew something of Lawson's habits, and she knew where "a miserable looking dirty woman" could pawn fine clothes with ease. When the police questioned her, she had a story to tell them. She claimed that she had been north of Edinburgh, in Queensferry all week, selling matches, and that on Friday morning as she made her way back into town, she fell in with another woman, they had a dram, and she was quite "tipsy" when she reached Edinburgh. So, she said, she sat down on some steps in the Cowgate, at the bottom of Niddry Street—where the South Bridge passes over the Cowgate—where another woman came up to her. This woman offered her a sixpence and a dram to take the shirts up to the South Bridge and pawn them, so she did, without knowing they were stolen.[12]

McKinnon was twenty-eight, and obviously had been supporting herself for some time, probably for at least the eleven years that she had been in Scotland. She had neither starved nor spent a great deal of time in the Bridewell, so her skills in locating goods, taking them, and disposing of them were sufficient, although she was plainly quite poor. Janet Swanston had described her as wearing "an old striped gown, & a cast second mourning shawl," which sounds much like what Docherty wore, and she may well have lingered in Salt's shop because she was looking for better clothes. Of course, she may well have thought to hide herself in the shop for a while, suspecting that Lawson or the police would be looking for her, but then a pawnshop seems like a poor place to hide. McKinnon was not doing well as both thief and resetter, with neither house nor family, but her miserable attempt to steal shirts appears businesslike in comparison to the work of Jean McBeath.[13]

McBeath apparently stole the pinafores off two young children while they were playing in King's Park, or St. Ann's Yards. Earlier, she had stolen a quart of small beer from a baker's in Gilmour Street, near Simon's Square, which was probably quite near where she lived in Hardwell Close, off the Pleasance. At first glance this story of a woman who might have been seventeen or seventy, downing her bottle of small beer and then tugging the pinafores off small children seems little more than pathetic. But it forces us to consider under what circumstances women would act alone, and it raises the question of whether women and men habitually drank before committing crimes.[14]

The small beer might of course have been her usual breakfast, or dinner, and it was hardly a potent spirit, but it brings to mind McKinnon's insistence that she was "tipsy," and unable to recall much about the shirts. Whether that was purely an alibi, or an alibi largely drawn from truth, we do know that Burke, not to mention his three companions, drank heavily before and during a murder and sale. But in a society where drinking was unregulated and fairly common this may not mean much, and we should probably remember that most Western people went about their business in 1828 while consuming a fair amount of alcohol.[15]

Hannah Barton

Women acting alone depended on what they could carry, and carry without suspicion. For McKinnon, McBeath, and especially Paterson, running with a young boy in tow and a bundle of blankets and clothes, that was a very real limit. But Hannah Barton, an English pickpocket who specialized in removing money and watches from gentlemen's pockets while posing as a prostitute, chose to carry off goods that were both small and valuable. Barton had been in Edinburgh since 1822 or 1823, and had been in the Bridewell once or twice, and she may well represent the best a woman could hope to do for herself on the streets. Barton was twenty-five years old and lived with a laborer, Thomas Nudgent, in Hyndford's Close off the High Street. Her husband, whom she accounted for as a tailor, had been transported, or so she believed, and Serjeant [sic] John Stuart of the Edinburgh Police Establishment reported that he considered her to be "habite and repute" a thief. Somewhat more of her story survives, so we can consider just how she worked, and how she differed from McKinnon and McBeath, and perhaps, resembled Lucky Log.[16]

Her victim, an Edinburgh brushmaker named John Thomson who had moved to the village of Portobello, was pacing back and forth on the North Bridge waiting for a coach, holding his new shoes in a neatly wrapped parcel. He was careful to tell the police, or they were careful to find out, that he was also "perfectly sober." He told police that a woman came up to him, and "taking hold of the breast of his Coat with both hands in rather a gentle manner, said 'My Dear, what are you going to give me to night' or some words to that Effect." He sent her off, but as she left he felt his watch being pulled out of its pocket and he grabbed her. Her manner immediately changed, and she "gave him a great deal of abusive language," a crowd gathered, she threw or dropped his watch, he let go of her to grab the watch, and a younger man stepped forward to take hold of Barton.[17]

Thomson must have been somewhat distracted by her approach and certainly by her touch, since he remembered the touching so well, but was not as sure of her exact words. But perhaps his memory had as much to do with suspicion as with desire, since he promptly sent her away, and then felt the watch slipping away—a sensory rather than altogether rational experience. No doubt Barton had picked him as a well-to-do older country man, visiting Edinburgh to buy, and old enough to be flattered by her, or at least surprised. But she got a man who had lived in the city for many years and had seen women like Barton on the streets. One need only recall how Burke harangued a prostitute who approached him for wearing too much makeup, until he had passers-by laughing at her, to understand something of the struggle between men and women, and between those a step above or below poverty. For lone women, the obvious source of wealth was men, but only if they could master that struggle, either as a prostitute or a thief. If they could not, or chose not to do so, they could steal clothes and blankets, probably often from other women.[18]

Barton had her own version of what had happened: she and Thomson had been drinking together earlier, and when they argued on the North Bridge, his watch fell from his pocket. But she did not say much, perhaps because she had some record of stealing watches, knew it was pointless, and did not really want to deny her profession. Barton, like Log, was not a woman to appear pathetic. Ultimately, Barton and Log and Veitch may have had more in common with each other than with McKinnon.

The Gangs

Some women worked from criminal households, some women worked alone, and some worked in gangs that were not chiefly defined by family or household relations. To begin, we have the story of Barbara Kerr, aided by her friends Janet Taylor, Ann Brooks, and the resetter William Baslar.[19] Then we have the similar but far more ludicrous annals of Janet Morrison and her friends. In both instances, one or more women drew well-off gentlemen into dark corners, and proceeded to remove the contents of their pockets. Kerr required little help, while Morrison's machinations verged on comic opera.

Kerr described herself as an unemployed servant who had been in the Bridewell twice, once about a watch. She lived with her mother in a close near the east end of the Grassmarket. At eleven o'clock one night she met up with Ann Brooks, apparently a prostitute walking with Janet Taylor. Brooks was standing around in the Grassmarket, near Candlemaker Row, waiting for Janet Taylor and a gentleman who was "worse for liquor" to come out of Mrs. Harper's public house. He asked Taylor and Brooks to go in with him and get a dram, and after leaving, asked Taylor to go back in with him. While she waited outside Mrs. Harper's, Brooks told Kerr about him: that he was drunk and that he had a fine gold watch. When Taylor and her gentleman came out, Kerr turned to Brooks and said "Stand you back and I will take the gentleman's watch from him, as I am better acquainted with doing it tha[n] either you or Taylor."

Kerr took him down the close where her mother lived. Brooks reported seeing Taylor and Kerr leave together, probably, as Kerr half-

Common Thievery in the Old Town in 1828

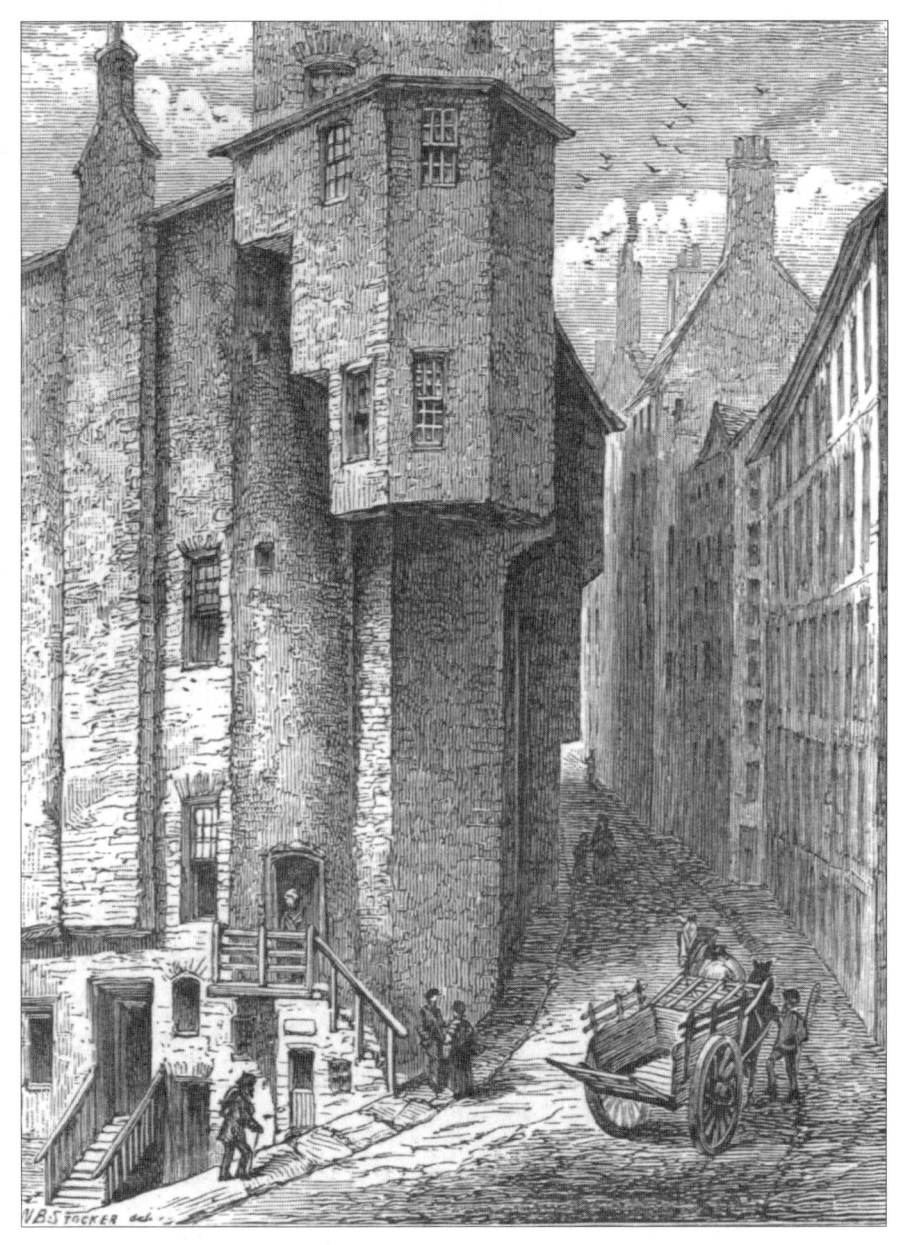

This respectable building at the top of the West Bow, used for public gatherings, was a stone's throw from the east end of the Grassmarket (on the left), where Barbara Kerr stole gentlemen's watches and William Baslar sold them.

way admitted, to run from the scene, only to reenter the Grassmarket through the West Port, and then go to a public house in the West Bow, and give the watch to William Baslar. Baslar, who was reported by the police to live in "a ruinous Garret" in East Smith's Close, off the Grassmarket, was indicted along with Kerr. But he got only the watch; the seal and chain went to Kerr's sister, who lived opposite East Meal Market Stair in the Cowgate, and she was able to sell it to Christian McKay or Divine, in Big Hamilton's Close, in the Grassmarket. Taylor also lived nearby, in John McDonald's lodgings in the Grassmarket, so we can see that none of these people, except the victim, was far from home that night, and they had seen each other here and there during the evening. Nor were they ever far from Log's Lodgings.

One can step back and see the evening's progress fairly clearly. The gentleman in question has wandered down Candlemaker Row from the new George IV Bridge, into a neighborhood that was fairly rough well after dark, knowing what he would find there. He takes two women into a small public house, and then returns to it with one while the other waits outside. The one who waits tells Kerr, perhaps because she is known to be good at taking watches, about him, and when he comes out, two or perhaps all three women escort him down a close with promises of some sort. He loses his watch and chain, his glasses, and his silk handkerchief, and has to tell the whole embarrassing story to the police. Meanwhile, his watch has gone in one direction, and his chain and seal in another. This glimpse of the Grassmarket after dark, through eyes other than those of Burke or Log, illustrates that their neighborhood was a convenient one for habitual criminals, who, with the exception of the prostitute Paterson, they avoided taking as victims. No doubt the survival of Paterson's partner Brown, and her constant search for some sign of Paterson taught them to avoid resident criminals, likely to have associates.

Just as Log's Lodgings and Brogan's house seemed very porous and open to outsiders, we have here a crime that was one of opportunity, in a porous setting, with a perhaps accidental cast of characters. Without a household, there were still networks of individuals on the streets—prostitutes seem to have worked in pairs, as Paterson and Brown, and Brooks and Taylor did—and Kerr's mother and sister should probably be included in this network. These not-quite-accidental gangs could be fairly efficient, as Kerr and her friends were, or laughable, as the following example shows.[20]

Janet Morrison and Friends

On August 15, a Friday, Janet Morrison and her friend Betty Gibb, who was just out of the Bridewell, invited a drover from Cromdale in Moray, William Macintosh, into a house in Little Anderson's Close. Little Anderson's ran through to the West Bow from the head of the Cowgate, and so we are in very much the same part of town—the east end of the Grassmarket, and the streets running north and east from there—as Kerr, Taylor, and Brooks. What ensued was much funnier, even though in the end seven persons (eight, if we include the drover) were questioned, two of them taken in evidence, and the other five convicted and transported.[21]

Macintosh said he had been buying things in the Cowgate that morning, when he was approached by the women, who offered him snuff from a bit of paper. We do not know what was said, but he claimed that he followed them into the house in Little Anderson's Close because he thought they had something to sell, and that "he was no sooner in than he was anxious to get out again as he did not like the look of the place." The house consisted of two rooms belonging to William Paterson, a twenty-eight-year-old tailor who had been in the Bridewell twelve times, and was considered, along with Morrison and Marion Campbell, a "habite and repute" criminal. When the drover walked in, there were several other people in the room besides Paterson: Robert Donaldson, a tailor who lived upstairs; his wife, Bell Anderson, who was twenty-two; and Marion or May Campbell, who was forty. Morrison seems to have ordered them all out of the room, if May Campbell, who had been in the Bridewell forty-one times, is to be believed, and then gotten into a bed with the "Country looking man." Campbell claimed to know this by looking through a hole in the wall, since she and Donaldson and Paterson had not left the house, but merely gone into the next room when Morrison and Gibb and Macintosh had come in.[22]

While Macintosh emphatically denied using "any improper freedom with them," sex is really the only explanation we have for what happened in that room, as shouting began and tempers flared. It is possible that the women hoped to rob him once he was in the house, with the help of Paterson and Donaldson, but to rob a drover who has just brought cattle down from Inverness, who is quite sober in mid-morning, seems like a very bad idea. On the other hand, whether sex was involved or not, that is what they tried to do to Macintosh. As Campbell put it, she "saw Janet Morrison and the Country man lying in a bed, and after they came out of it, she heard Janet Morrison and Betty Gibb demanding money from him but he said he had no money. That upon this Janet Morrison called upon William Paterson by a feigned name and as she thinks Jankisson to come into the room."

Once Paterson went in, he called for Donaldson, and Campbell, still in the other room, heard "loud speaking and quarrelling amongst them." That seems to have been the signal for everyone to join in, and Betty Duff, a young woman who seemed bemused by it all, Bell Anderson, and Campbell all went in to see what there was to see. The country man was "fixed up in a window," with Morrison and Gibb "rifling his pockets" while the two men held him by the neck. How exactly he was in the window is not clear, but during this Morrison yelled out that she had gotten the watch, and she gave it to Bell Anderson, telling her to take it out of the house. Then the drover, apparently down from the window, got between Bell and the door, claiming that she had his watch. At this, Robert Donaldson "damned the man and said will ye prevent my wife Bell Anderson from leaving the house." With this, the two men, Morrison, and Gibb, "laid hold of said Countryman" and pulled him away from the door, and Anderson left.

At this point, bleeding from the mouth, the drover repeated that his watch had been stolen, and that he would give them "any money" to get it back. Still fighting—Campbell said "they were all tearing at

Common Thievery in the Old Town in 1828

him"—the group moved downstairs and out into the street, and "there was a scuffle in the close betwixt Donaldson, Paterson and the Countryman." Then the police arrived, and Donaldson and Campbell were taken into custody. The others made themselves scarce, only to be taken later.

This form of stealing, in which two women would approach a man, acting as prostitutes, appears to have been common in the early nineteenth century, as several English accounts survive. Ellen Reece and her companion Jane Doyle reported picking a man's pocket while his pants were down, and Reece said that "none of the girls thinks so much of prostitution but as it furnishes opportunities of robbing men." Reece was twenty-four in 1837, had been stealing in this fashion since 1827, and insisted that she earned seven times as much by robbing men as by prostitution, which was clearly a second choice for her and for other women she knew. In other reported variants, the women would call for male or female help once the victim's watch had been taken. So it would seem that Morrison and Gibb, and Kerr were practicing a sort of theft that was widespread in the early nineteenth century. Women like them, and Barton, were caught up in what would seem to be a timeless relationship—a man and a woman on the street—unless one considers how the number of men carrying pocket watches must have increased in the course of the eighteenth and nineteenth centuries. For those women, the watch represented an innovation, requiring a system of reset, apparently male, as with the sale of bodies, and the hope of a substantial profit.[23]

What Household?

How did Log, Hare, Burke, and M'Dougal avoid such scenes? Only on the evening of Docherty's murder, and on the subsequent Saturday night did their lives, with the neighbors questioning them, really resemble Morrison's fiasco. Perhaps the seriousness of murder led them to be cautious, secretive, and careful in selecting victims, but they were probably simply lucky. Janet Brown might have interrupted the murder of Paterson, or Hugh Alston might easily have burst in during the murder of Docherty, instead of listening at an outer door.

They greedily chose anyone who came within their grasp, although after the murder of Paterson they may have avoided criminals, or local people with local friends. But if Morrison and her colleagues were unwise to take on the drover, Log was foolish to invite Daft Jamie in, and Burke equally stupid to think of murdering such a well-known prostitute as Paterson.

The one great advantage that the four murderers possessed was their organization: they were a small group, very tightly bound through the male partnership and the two marriages. Compared with the six people Morrison used to get the drover's watch, at least two of whom seem to have been there for no reason, Burke and Hare worked well together, and Log and M'Dougal supported admirably. But the organization of the two groups was not all that different, if we separate out the serious participants in Morrison's robbery from the accidental onlookers. First, of course, are Morrison and Gibb, both of whom had been in the Bridewell. Gibb had been in at least once, and Morrison apparently thirty-three times. They brought Macintosh to the house of William Paterson, who seems to have worked with Morrison—she called out to him, using a false name, which suggests some arrangement—and may have been a partner of some sort. And then, upstairs, we have the other main participants, Robert Donaldson and Bell Anderson, both of whom were ready and probably experienced assistants. Anderson was a habitual criminal who had been in the Bridewell eight times.

Between these five people, we have two households, one clearly the house of a couple, both of whom had, or claimed to have legitimate trades, as tailor and laundress. In the other house we have Paterson, apparently working with Morrison, who is in turn out on the street with a female partner, Gibb. Morrison and Gibb had both gotten out of the Bridewell almost immediately before the robbery; Morrison was both older, at twenty-nine, and more experienced, so Gibb was probably the new member of the group. If Paterson and Morrison constituted a couple, we have a structure similar to that of Log and Hare, and Burke and M'Dougal, with Gibb as the younger assistant, much like John Brogan, or David Paterson, the doorman for Dr.

Knox. The biggest difference is that Morrison's group relied far more on the women, for obvious reasons. To lure men, women walked the streets. But Burke and Hare preferred female victims, and they most often brought old women home.

The household was clearly an old and a useful means of structuring all kinds of work, urban and rural, legitimate and criminal. If anything was old about the workings of the criminal world, the use of households, which verged on becoming businesses—much as Margaret Burrows's house was "a receptacle for thieves and women of bad character"—was old. But the household was never stable. It was broken by death, especially during famines, by recruitment for wars, and by the marriage of children, among other things. And the criminal household, especially as the Bridewell or prison began to replace old physical punishments, was further broken by the dispersal of household members through prison and transportation. One alternative, of course, was the gang, which had also always been there, from Robin Hood and his merry men in England, to the gangs of smugglers who infested the coast, the robbers on the highways, and the body snatchers who robbed graveyards around Edinburgh. But without knowing more about them, it would be impossible to describe the kinds of relationships that structured them, not to mention the presence of women in them. Women may have been there. In 1829, one woman, Helen Begbie, was taken with a gang of grave robbers that included an anatomist. And Walter Scott, who was generally no fool about the history in his historical fiction, described a roving highway gang of 1736 through its prominent women.[24]

Yet another alternative was to slowly combine the household with some sort of partnership among unrelated individuals—like Burke and Hare, and like Morrison's, Gibb's, and Paterson's alliance of sorts with each other, and with the married couple upstairs. In this way the household might slowly become irrelevant, with the result being a partnership among individuals who simply worked together, like Robertson, Reid, and Adams. But household ties, especially those of marriage, would probably not become irrelevant easily for those who were already married, like Burke, or Hare. It may be that the fear with which the four murderers were regarded stemmed from the tensions within the group. This was a group where the two couples watched each other warily, while the two men and the two women also regarded each other as potential enemies, which kept them on their toes, and made them seem more vicious and calculating than they were.

For Burke, Hare, Log, and M'Dougal partnership could shift at any moment. Clearly both couples had survived as couples for years, but late in 1827 Burke and Hare found some fit between themselves, and all through 1828 their wives must have noticed their own increasing exclusion. Perhaps M'Dougal's feigned jealously over Docherty's attachment to her William—her oft-repeated excuse for throwing Docherty out—stemmed from a very real jealousy of her husband's attachment to his business and his partner. Burke and Hare were, after all, primarily in the business of killing women, sometimes with one of them lying on the woman, while the other held her mouth. Perhaps, as their wives thought about it, it seemed a perverse sort of intimacy between the two men and their victims.

But this is to focus too much on what was problematic and weakening among the four, and they were ultimately too successful to be taken only as a model of self-defeating organization. They also benefited from their double organization. A male partnership dealt with Knox and his people, while the two couples dealt with their victims, looking like familiar, respectable householders. Minus their wives, it might have been difficult for the men to lure all those women and especially the men into a house, while a married couple would have seemed out of place in Knox's rooms, bargaining with the assistants. And so they hit on a perfect combination, even though the competing loyalties must have made their lives harder.

In comparison, what Robertson, Adams, and Reid had in mind, breaking into a warehouse, required no particular social persona, just the ability to carry parcels in the dark, over familiar streets. They had no skills in resetting the goods they stole, but perhaps if they had found the tea for which they were looking, they would have had a buyer. In another case, a woman stole thirty-nine Bibles from the man with whom she sometimes lived. She sold them the next day, to a bookseller, which suggests that resetting was not difficult—but then she may have known with whom her sometimes husband dealt. Robertson and her older friends seemed not to know how to get rid of what they had taken, and the traditional resetters, older women who generally dealt in clothes, may not have been readily able to resell any large amount of food.[25]

In other words, what they needed to take and then dispose of that food was never anyone with a particular social identity, but anyone who could identify a suitable warehouse, anyone who could carry goods out, and anyone with knowledge about selling groceries. No doubt there were other small grocers like Christian McKay,[26] who did indeed take a cheese and a ham without question, but that was hardly a sufficient means of selling off what must have been a small roomful of food. It would seem that Robertson, Adams, and Reid were doing something new, something for which no resetting expertise existed—and a sort of theft that apparently required neither male nor female participants. If indeed, "each society gets the [kind of crime] it deserves, . . . that emanates naturally from its prevailing social relations," then this, along with Burke and Hare's rather contentious male partnership, was the new crime, both more calculated and preferably male as a reflection of the increasingly male world of business. It was a male enterprise because Robertson, a sixteen-year-old young woman, could not hope to lead her gang, and Log, who might have hoped to lead hers, rather quickly lost out to Burke. It was more calculated in that these thieves looked to demand, rather than supply, in the case of the bodies, and perhaps also in the case of the futile search of Rymer's cellar for tea. And perhaps the same was true of watches.[27]

The ways habitual criminals stole, robbed, and cheated to make money changed as the society of which they were a part changed. Nonetheless, change was not absolute or sudden. Paterson, McBeath, and McKinnon could steal and reset a few bits of clothes because Edinburgh possessed a network of dealers and brokers in old clothes, many of them women, used to dealing with women from the laboring classes. For McBeath and McKinnon, living outside the household and the tutelage of an older thief or resetter like Morrison or Old

Mrs. Burrows, there was the hard lone individualism of petty pilfering and inept resetting of the goods. System, organization, and knowledge of a network of resetters—a market—marked the serious thieves.[28]

Those women could climb in windows, drink, find their way all over the city, and knew just where to sell a watch or a pillowcase, but Log and M'Dougal could not go to Knox and sell a corpse, even though they entrapped victims. They did what they could do. They carefully followed their husbands to Surgeon's Square, and to Dr. Knox's house in Newington, and waited outside. Maggie Robertson also survives in the records as a partner, with men, in a gang of sorts, willing to file the keys. Perhaps because she was sixteen, she was simply a thief, working with other thieves, not identified as anyone's daughter, mother, or wife. Whether that pleased her or not, we will never know. Nonetheless she, in conjunction with what we know about Log and M'Dougal, forces us to think about how men and women in the shadow economy worked together, how the larger world impinged on that world, and how permeable the line between the shadow and the larger economy was. These women and their male colleagues were all part of their larger worlds, licit and illicit, and subject to changes in work and marriage, and to beliefs about both that affected all men and women.[29]

There are two final lessons we can take from the escapades of the nineteen women indicted in 1828 who were not Log or M'Dougal. Most of them worked with men. The nineteen women simply offer us a glimpse of the underworld, filled with "habite and repute" criminals, working as best they could, preferably in groups, to take what was not theirs, and sell it. While seducing men would be women's work, the resale of the contents of the men's pockets was not. Sometimes, even the task of searching the pockets required teamwork, as with Paterson and Donaldson holding the unfortunate drover in the window while Morrison and Gibb tore at his pockets. Their world at that moment was one room, and the Old Town. And their world overlapped that of Burke, Hare, Log, and M'Dougal. Most of these crimes took place within, to use old measures, a stone's throw or a gunshot of Log's Lodgings or Brogan's house. These people were some, but not all, of the murderers' neighbors. And when Burke and M'Dougal came to trial—for they were the only two who were tried for the string of murders—many of their neighbors gathered in the streets, appalled, demanding hangings. Some members of the large crowds that gathered during Burke's and M'Dougal's trial and Burke's hanging must have included, if not the thieves discussed above, their friends and relatives. The line between murderers, especially of the neighborhood poor, and petty criminals was quite clear to the people living in the Grassmarket, the Cowgate, and all the other nooks and warrens developing beneath the bridges and the High Street.

CHAPTER 3

The Spectacular "Burke mania" Trial

The public frenzy that ensued after that Sunday in 1828 when the Grays reported Docherty's murder had much to do with the history of spectacular criminal trials and popular fascination with the criminal underworld. But many citizens in Edinburgh saw, or believed they were seeing, a new kind of crime that shocked them deeply. So it seems appropriate to delve into the trial, the riots that followed it, and the fates of four, to pin down what that new quality was.[1]

On December 24, very early on a cold, wet morning, people gathered outside the old Parliament House where the High Court of Justiciary sat. They hoped for seats, but the seats were already spoken for—watching noted trials was an old Edinburgh pastime, and in this case many lawyers exercised their privilege to watch the proceedings. Nonetheless, with great public excitement and fury over the murders, many gathered outside the court, and a good many police were on hand to control the crowd. Just before eight, reporters were admitted; the jurymen were hurried through a side door even earlier. At about nine, lawyers who wished to watch, and a few others with permission from the judges were allowed to take their seats, and at nine-forty Burke and M'Dougal were brought to the bar. They were the only ones accused and indicted, and their indictment and Log and Hare's escape became, after the murders themselves, the second great drama of the notorious and inescapably political affair.[2]

At ten-fifteen that morning the trial began. The room was cold, the day was wet, and the grimness of the proceeding was exacerbated by the judges' order to open a large window, apparently because of the great crowding in the room. The various lawyers who had come merely to watch—advocates and writers to the Signet—had their black gowns and assorted handkerchiefs wrapped around their heads for warmth, and the anonymous editor and annotator of *The West Port Murders* wrote that the bulk of the audience had "such a grim and grisly aspect as assimilated them to a college of monks or inquisitors, or characters imagined in tales of romance." Regardless of the men in the audience, the men at the bar must have made quite an impressive sight. Four judges, including the lord justice clerk himself, the Right Honorable David Boyle, and three ordinary judges, Lords Pitmilly, Meadowbank, and Mackenzie, were in attendance. Prosecuting was Lord Advocate Sir William Rae, along with three advocate deputes: Robert Dundas, scion of the old Dundas despotism in Scotland; Archibald Alison; and Alexander Wood. And volunteering their services for the defense were a number of talented men. Burke was defended by the dean of the faculty of advocates, the elected head of Scots lawyers, Sir James W. Moncrieff, along with three junior men: Patrick Robertson, David Milne, and Duncan M'Neil. M'Dougal had the noted Whig advocate, and distant relative of Dundas, Henry Cockburn, along with Mark Napier, Hugh Bruce, and George Patton. These men were smart, well known, and practiced in the courtroom. In keeping with Scottish tradition, the best men volunteered their services for the poorest pannels, or accused persons. Given the great hysteria over the case, and the Scots passion for legal argument, it is no surprise that every lawyer who could get a seat came to watch the trial as it continued for twenty-four hours, through Christmas morning.[3]

Burke and Hare had always been careful, as Burke later confessed, to make sure that no one, not even their wives, had ever seen them kill. They knew enough about Scots law to comprehend that a conviction on a capital charge was difficult without direct evidence. In this case, that meant that one of the two men would have to testify against the other; had both remained silent, it is possible that a Scots jury would have found the indictments against all four not proven, and they would have been set free. Lord Advocate Sir William Rae was unwilling to lose, and decided not to try all four with the evidence he had from other witnesses, none of whom could have seen the murders. This set the stage for a political fiasco of stunning proportion, as the lord advocate, representing a conservative government, appeared to deal with this great crime by taking Hare and Log as king's evidence sometime between November 19 and December 1. This guaranteed that they would be immune from prosecution for any of these murders. The Whigs were quick to step in. Henry Cockburn and James Moncrieff volunteered their services for the defense of Burke and M'Dougal. Later, Francis Jeffrey would prosecute Hare for the relatives of Daft Jamie Wilson. As the case progressed, not only did the public's horror increase, their outrage grew as M'Dougal was acquitted, and Log and Hare were set loose. From November 1828 until well into March 1829, a battle raged in the newspapers between those defending or attacking Rae, and ultimately the government, for inadvertently saving Hare, Log, M'Dougal, and finally and most problematically Dr. Knox, from the gallows.[4]

The attack on the government came to rest on a defense of Burke and M'Dougal as the least guilty of the four. It was far more effective to pillory the lord advocate for accepting Hare and Log as protected witnesses if they could be made out to be the real villains, and Burke and M'Dougal presented as their somewhat hapless assistants. Indeed, Cockburn went so far as to say during the trial that "if [Hare and Log] were the pannels, and Burke and M'Dougal the witnesses, then would the true state of the case appear and the present witnesses would be proved the guilty perpetrators." Cockburn cross-examined Hare into looking bloody and perjured, repeatedly asked him questions about other murders that he, with the court's advice, refused to answer, incriminating himself and Rae in the public's all-too-anxious eye.

But the bigger question that lurked behind public argument over which couple was most guilty was the suspicion that Burke, M'Dougal, Log, and Hare represented only the tip of the iceberg. The rest of the iceberg, of course, would have been not only Knox, but the entire respectable Edinburgh medical establishment, along with most of Burke's and M'Dougal's friends and relatives. It is no great leap to imagine citizens of a city much plagued by resurrectionists quickly imagining vast conspiracies of anatomists, students, and criminal gangs preying on unsuspecting persons, and then fearing, at every step of this criminal procedure, that the government was acting to hide the horrors. In 1828, it was.[5]

Conspiracy

In the twenty-first century, we live with the labyrinthine truth of the Holocaust behind us. But in 1828 this fear of conspiracy was a newer problem, and the Whigs dutifully played their part in embarrassing a conservative government chained by the limits of evidence and legal rules of proof. Nor was Scots law prepared for the advent, much less the desirability, of the kind of privacy for the poor, within which Burke and Hare worked. The law assumed community, or at least proximity, thus assuming that witnesses to capital crimes would and could be found, and that a case without such a witness should be seen as weak. That murders in privacy were possible had been demonstrated in late seventeenth-century infanticide prosecutions, and had resulted in a law specific to infanticide that rested entirely on circumstantial evidence. But for adults, and in the absence of modern forms of evidence, like blood tests and fingerprints, direct witnesses were still preferred unless absolutely damning circumstantial evidence could be shown.

Not that this would have mattered to Whigs like Cockburn, Moncrieff, and Jeffrey in the 1820s. They probably thought, by way of explanation for their success in rallying many citizens to criticize Tory leaders, that they were smarter than the prosecutors. Those leaders, especially Rae, were after all placeholders, men appointed by London because of their connections and loyalty, not their talent. Yet Cockburn's intelligence, in his defense of M'Dougal and his cross-examination of Hare, which laid the foundation of Hare's immunity, served the Whigs more than it served the people of Edinburgh. The government was doomed to embarrassment, the Whigs were doomed to profit by this—and the fear that plagued the people of Edinburgh ultimately left questions of party far behind.

The Hysteria

It is hard to calculate hysteria from a distance of nearly two centuries, but rumors abounded. The trial itself supplied the first hard-and-fast knowledge about Docherty's murder. But news had begun to leak out promptly on Monday, November 3, when the *Edinburgh Evening Courant* carried a brief story about the disappearance of an old woman, and the discovery of her body in a dissecting room. It was on that day that Burke and M'Dougal, and probably Hare and Log, and Brogan, who was also in custody by then, gave their first declarations, or statements, to Sheriff-Substitute George Tait, and some sense of these must have reached the *Courant* quite quickly. Those November 3 declarations from M'Dougal and Burke do survive, but nothing survives from Log, Hare, or Brogan, other than their testimony at the trial. Burke began the initial dissembling by telling a remarkable tale about a strange man who left a big box in his house, and Hare apparently claimed that Brogan hit Docherty and killed her.

Whatever they said, by November 19 a warrant had been requested to "apprehend" all four for the murder of Daft Jamie, so the investigation was making progress, but it was apparently not enough to satisfy Rae. If the old historian of this case, William Roughead, was correct, Rae was anxious "to obtain a full disclosure of further similar crimes," and "did not underestimate the chariness of Scots juries to convict in capital cases on circumstantial evidence." In that light, Rae got what he wanted by taking Hare and Log as king's evidence on December 1, because on the fourth Archibald Scott, the procurator-fiscal, was again petitioning the sheriff for a warrant, this time to apprehend only Burke and M'Dougal for the murder of Mary Paterson. When the indictment was written, Burke and M'Dougal would be charged with three murders. The citizens of Edinburgh paid for the minimal knowledge provided by Hare and Log. The freedom of two of the four or more murderers was traded for information that convinced most of the town that all four, and Knox, and others were guilty. Rae was a good servant of the government to risk his own infamy for this devil's bargain.[6]

"a new species of assassination..."

With the indictment written, containing a list of fifty-five witnesses, and the trial scheduled for Christmas Eve, public discussion became frenzied. The *Courant* and other papers had told the story, as it then stood, to the public on December 6, and on the eighth Burke and M'Dougal were formally served with the indictment. On the night before the trial, December 23, troops in Edinburgh Castle were put on notice, and the number of police increased by three hundred. During the week of the trial, some eight thousand extra copies of newspapers were sold, and the *Caledonian Mercury* reported on Christmas Day that the West Port murders were "a new species of assassination, or murder for hire." The day before, Rae had begun his remarks to the jury by saying "that this is one of the most extraordinary and novel subjects of trial that has ever been brought before this or any other Court, and has created in the public mind the greatest anxiety and alarm." At sentencing, only a few hours after those closing remarks, Lord Meadowbank, Alexander Maconochie, said that

in the whole history of the country—I may say, in the history of civilized society—nothing has ever been exhibited that is, in any respect, parallel to this case. Murders have been committed before now; crimes of all descriptions have unhappily been too common; but we flattered ourselves that our country was, in a great measure, free from the stigma of any great or heinous atrocity committed within its bounds. That there should have been found, therefore, not one but many leagued together, in order to sacrifice their unoffending fellow-creatures, for the wretched purpose of disposing of their bodies, is, to the last degree, humiliating.[7]

And the editor of *The West Port Murders*, a hurriedly produced transcript of the trial cobbled together early in 1829 with bits from the papers and other accounts that came to hand, had much to say:

The intense sensation which has been excited among all classes by this extraordinary case, far exceeds what we have ever witnessed on any former occasion. The story, when it was first rumoured, created the deepest agitation. But it was treated by many as an idle tale, framed to feed the vulgar appetite for the marvellous, and too horrible to be believed. Nor need we wonder that the most credulous should have been startled by the recital of such atrocious cruelty, which far surpasses any thing that is usually found in the records of crime. The offence of murder, dreadful as it is, is unhappily too familiar in our criminal proceedings; but such an artfully contrived and deliberate scheme, such a systematic traffic in blood, was certainly never before heard of in this country. It is a new passage in our domestic history.[8]

The sense of cataclysm sometimes outweighed the legal and political squabbling that also occupied reporters, especially after the excitement of the trial was over. But as new information appeared, and the alleys of the West Port were searched for individuals willing to supply accounts of anyone or anything related to the murders, familiar legal and political questions comfortably framed public discussion.[9]

Legal questions arising during the trial—Could Burke be tried for three crimes at once? Was M'Dougal's case prejudiced by Burke's possible guilt in two murders for which she was not charged? Could Cockburn ask Hare questions alluding to other murders, beyond the three raised in the indictment, or the one for which Burke was on trial? If Cockburn could ask, did Hare have to answer?—no doubt held the attention of the lawyers present, and more readers than we would credit. But the great popular issue was the verdicts. In response to the defending lawyers, the trial proceeded only on the third charge, that of the murder of Docherty, in which both Burke and M'Dougal were named. Twenty-four hours later, before an exhausted and weary court and crowd, after fifty minutes' deliberation, the verdicts were read by John M'Fie early on Christmas morning:

The Jury find the Pannel, William Burke, Guilty of the third charge in the Indictment; and find the Indictment Not Proven against the Pannel, Helen M'Dougal.[10]

On that verdict, the court promptly freed M'Dougal, although she was kept in the jail for a day to protect her from the crowd, and sentenced Burke to be hanged on January 28, and "publicly dissected and anatomized." In pronouncing sentence the lord justice clerk also suggested that Burke's skeleton be preserved, "in order that posterity may keep in remembrance your atrocious crimes." All that was done, and more: Burke's body was also flayed, and the skin tanned and sold in small bits, as souvenirs. As the only victim Edinburgh would get, Burke was not only hanged, but shamed and virtually consumed by the populace. Although in 1828 he would not be tortured or hung in chains after death, he was literally commodified, and turned into tobacco pouches and wallets for those who could afford to buy.[11]

Burke's conviction was not enough to satisfy the public outcry and mounting anger, as more and more came to light about the murders. His conversations were reported, and as these leaked out, Burke seemed human after all. But this merely aggravated the government's discomfort, by making Hare look all the worse—a process much accelerated by Burke's two post-conviction confessions. Rae greatly underestimated the poor impression Hare would make as king's evidence, especially in the face of Cockburn's cross-examination, which revealed more about Cockburn's contempt for Hare and Rae than about Burke. The *Caledonian Mercury* printed a virtual indictment of Rae on December 27, as if giving notice that the outcry would not abate:

The conviction of Burke alone will not satisfy either the law or the country. The unanimous voice of society in regard to Hare is, *Delendus est;* that is to say, if there be evidence to convict him, as we should hope there is. He has been an accessory before or after the fact in nearly all of these murders; in the case of poor Jamie he was unquestionably a principal; and his evidence on Wednesday only protects him from being called to account for the murder of Docherty. WE TRUST, THEREFORE, THAT THE LORD ADVOCATE, WHO HAS SO ABLY AND ZEALOUSLY PERFORMED HIS DUTY TO THE COUNTRY UPON THIS OCCASION, WILL BRING THE "SQUALID WRETCH" TO TRIAL, AND TAKE EVERY OTHER MEANS IN HIS POWER TO HAVE THESE ATROCITIES PROBED AND SIFTED TO THE BOTTOM.[12]

The phrase "squalid wretch" was Cockburn's, from the trial; that it should reappear in print two days later means that his characterization of Hare had worked, and was refocusing the public's horror on the other actors "leagued together," as Lord Meadowbank, above, had put it.[13]

William Roughead, writing in 1921, regretted that Rae chose to try Burke and M'Dougal for the one murder in which Knox and his associates had not seen the body. They would not be called as witnesses, even though they were in court that morning, and they had certainly seen the bodies of Wilson and Paterson, along with many others. Knox, along with David Paterson, his museum keeper, and his three assistants, Thomas Wharton Jones, William Fergusson, and Alexander Miller, were indeed on the Crown's list of witnesses that formed a part of the printed indictment. But, according to the copy that survives in the court records, and was presumably annotated by one of the prosecuting lawyers, Knox was "not precognosed." In other words, he was never questioned before the trial, which suggests that Rae had no intention of calling him. There is one good explanation for the Crown's failure to question Knox, who was no favorite of the medical establishment in Edinburgh. Any protection he received must have been motivated by a desire to keep all discussion of resurrection, never mind murder, out of the ken of the public.

Lord Advocate Rae's Role

The resurrection of bodies for anatomists continued as long as it did because the bodies recovered were often those of the poor, dying in public hospitals, and buried, if at all, in unguarded mass graves. In the 1820s, perhaps in response to rising prices and the complaints of anatomists and universities, the home secretary, Sir Robert Peel, added to the supply by offering bodies from prisons and army hospitals. This awkward and slightly conspiratorial policy could not hold in the face of murder in Scotland. Nonetheless, Lord Advocate Rae certainly tried to maintain it, as his letter of November 1828 to the home secretary shows. Written just as the investigation of Burke, Hare, Log, and M'Dougal was warming up, Rae complained that a shipment of bodies from Dublin, intended for Professor Monro at Edinburgh University, had been seized by customs men at Greenock. He wanted Peel to order customs officers to keep their hands off such shipments, and went on to tell Peel that some twelve murders for anatomy subjects were under investigation, and that Burke would be put on trial for only two, "as we are most anxious to conceal from the public the extent to which such crimes have been carried." Rae assumed that it was his job to defend the system, to prevent discovery of the market in bodies, and to protect the well-being of Edinburgh University and the city's private anatomy schools as centers of medical teaching.[14] So Knox was left in peace by Rae and the police, and defended by Cockburn, who went so far as to claim, much later, that Scots "anatomists were spotlessly correct, and Knox the most correct of them all." Odd as it seems, neither Whig nor Tory would touch him, but the ordinary working people of Edinburgh did not share that faith in his moral rectitude.[15]

The Natural and Proper Wife

As for M'Dougal, probably no one other than the jurors, carried away by Cockburn's flattery and manipulation, saw an innocent, anxious, concerned wife when they looked at M'Dougal. The full text of his closing statement for M'Dougal was reprinted in the Whiggish *Trial of William Burke and Helen M'Dougal,* but not in *The West Port Murders.*[16] Cockburn's defense of Helen M'Dougal relied on three arguments. One, M'Dougal was indicted as an accessory to the murder, the definition of "accession" was precise, and Cockburn cited Baron Hume to show that one could act out of affection, or compassion, to protect an accused person, without becoming part of the crime as an accessory. He then went on to argue that M'Dougal was most probably Burke's wife, as they had no proof of "any legal impediment" to their marriage, and that, legal or not, "she was as completely under his influence, as any wife could be to any husband. Great allowance, therefore, must be made in judging her conduct, from the controul [*sic*] which he may have exercised over her; and for the interest which she may naturally, and most properly, have had in concealing her husband's crimes." Cockburn continued his picture by claiming that Burke was no more than a resurrectionist, a man supplying anatomists with corpses taken from graves, or wakes. He then suggested that Hare and Log were the real murderers, and that all that M'Dougal did after the murder might be interpreted as "the natural tendency which she had to hide the delinquency of her husband. Does it go far to implicate a wife in a crime committed by her husband, that she offers money for its concealment; or, on her knees, implores a probable discoverer to be silent?"[17]

Cockburn was very clear in insisting that M'Dougal's actions were, to use his words, natural and proper, and proceeded from affection. It is a very wonderful proposition that a woman who loves her husband cannot be an accessory to murders committed by him, because in acting with him and in his aid, she is acting out of love. Here, absolutely, the notion of a household business, a household economy, a partnership of husband and wife has come to an end. Instead of an active partner, we have a trope, and a new Whiggish trope at that, of M'Dougal on her knees, pleading for her husband's sake. This was strong enough to dilute, if it did not erase, all the testimony that had come from the Grays, Connoway, Law, Brogan, and then Hare and Log, describing her part in keeping Docherty in the house, and drunk. And if affection were not enough to explain all this, we have Burke's "controul" added, to convince the jury that this woman could not be dangerous, for she was natural, proper, and controlled.[18]

The trial delivered sufficient details regarding Docherty's demise to the public to set speculation ablaze, and to trigger much more public and anxious investigation. The witnesses who gave testimony about Docherty left a clear impression—Burke looked for victims, the four were complicit in detaining them, and one of the group killed them. And then they were sold to Knox. But the trial offered not a word about Daft Jamie, or the prostitute Paterson, and that left the public hungry for details, and angry. That anger would be directed toward the dumbfounded Hare, Log, and M'Dougal, the far less naive Knox, the prosecutor Rae, and then continue on as an inchoate fear for years.

M'Dougal's Release

M'Dougal was released on December 26, a Friday, and returned to the West Port, apparently hiding in the house that night. The next

The Spectacular "Burke mania" Trial

The White Hart Inn, whose cellars date to 1516, still operates on the west end of the Grassmarket, within a two minute walk from Burke's and Log's houses.

night, a Saturday, found her trying to get a drink in a public house, where she was recognized and mobbed. The police got her away to the watch house in the neighborhood, but that was then mobbed and its windows broken. M'Dougal was then dressed as a man and either left through a back window, while the police told the crowd that she was "being detained to give evidence against Hare," or was escorted to a jail just off the High Street, in Libberton's Wynd. At this time, or perhaps a few days later, she got a message through to Burke, asking for money, and he sent his watch, and what money he had. On Sunday, she was taken to the west edge of town, and left, apparently for her father's home in Redding, Stirlingshire. Within two days she was back in Edinburgh, and tried to see Burke in the Calton Jail, but was refused entrance. She seems also to have strayed to Newcastle, and further into England, with reports of mobbing and riot following her until she vanished from Britain and existed only in rumors. One rumor reported in 1829 by *The West Port Murders* was that she was living in Glasgow with Constantine Burke. As the same book put it, "It would almost have been a charity to have convicted her along with Burke. Her wretched life is precariously preserved under miseries more horrible than hanging would have been." The last rumor to reach Scotland concerning M'Dougal was that she accidentally burned to death in New South Wales, Australia, in 1868, which would have made her approximately seventy-three.[19]

Meanwhile Burke, now quite sober, but ill, collected his wits. On January 3 he made an official confession, with the understanding that it would be published after his hanging on the twenty-eighth of that month. Besides his official confessions, he spoke with a good many visitors, and his jailers, and virtually every word seems to have reappeared in print. He also saw both ministers and priests, which if nothing else helped him with his religious vocabulary in convincing others of his rediscovered piety. On January 21 he gave another, and somewhat fuller confession to a representative of the *Edinburgh Evening Courant*, and on the twenty-second, he added a postscript to his official confession, intended to exonerate Dr. Knox. On the twenty-sixth, the *Courant* announced that it would publish this confession on the twenty-ninth, the day after his hanging, but because of Hare's dubious legal position at that moment, Hare's lawyers restrained the *Courant*. At four in the morning on the twenty-seventh, the day before his hanging, Burke was taken from the Calton Jail, where he had been chained, to the "Lock-up-house" in Libberton's Wynd, where he was again chained. He had to be helped to walk, apparently because he was suffering from what was generally described as a cancer, sometimes of the stomach, sometimes of the testicles. He hoped to help hang Hare, but he died an ill man, without knowing if his confession would ever be printed.[20]

Facing the Crowd

At ten that night the scaffold was put up by men reportedly volunteering their labor. At 5 A.M. Burke's preparation began in earnest.

Libberton's Wynd, where Burke awaited execution in the "Lock-up-house" and Mrs. Tonner bought stolen clothing, ran downhill from the Lawnmarket south to the Cowgate.

A smith came to remove the leg chains, after which Burke put on the "dead-clothes," the over-large suit of black clothes in which he would hang. He took a glass of wine with his various jailers, had his arms pinioned behind his back, and in company with his two priests, who had been there since six-thirty, began the procession up Libberton's Wynd, and then west on the High Street. He was reported to have walked very carefully, as his arms were tied, and rain was pouring down on the old cobbled streets, making them slippery. What he would have seen as he entered the High Street was the scaffold, and thousands of people, many of whom were cold and stiff because they had been sheltering in alleys all night to get a good spot. Police were there, but the crowd was reportedly quiet, so densely packed it seemed dangerous, and overwhelmingly male, which was unusual. But a number of "ladies" were at the back, and up in windows overlooking the scaffold, viewing spots which had been rented for the morning. If violence was expected, women were keeping to the back edges of the crowd.[21]

Estimates of the size of the crowd ranged from twenty to thirty-seven thousand, an enormous number for a city of Edinburgh's size, 162,000 in the census of 1831. As these people waited, on that "cold raw disagreeable morning," they gave none of the signs of sympathy with the accused that were usual. When Burke came out into the High Street, he was greeted by yells of *"Burke him!"* and "choke him, hangie!" Looking ill, and wearing his shabby black suit and dirty boots, he walked to the scaffold, climbed up, and knelt to pray with his back to the crowd. He then moved to stand on the drop, and was shoved toward it by one of the executioners. He turned to scowl at the man. The hangman tightened the noose, giving it a nasty tug, and put a cotton nightcap on his head, but without covering his face. The crowd began to yell more loudly: "Hang Hare too," and "Hang Knox," and "Burke the ———, do not waste rope upon him!" and "You ———, you will see Daft Jamie in a minute." The call to give him a short rope was meant to make his death slower, since there would be no fall to break his neck; and observers reported that there seemed to be no fall at all. Once the cap was pulled over his face, he quickly gave the signal—dropping his handkerchief—and died quickly, in about ten minutes.[22]

The Dissatisfied Mob

Burke was dead. For some minutes the crowd did not leave, and then some began to cry "to Surgeons' Square," where Knox's rooms were, and to move in that direction. They were met there by police in force, which means that the town fathers expected the attack on Knox's rooms. There was great debate at the time—it was, after all, the decade that led to the English and Scots Reform Acts—over the dangers of this mob, understood by Tories, as usual, as the first sign that every excess of the French Revolution was imminent. The anonymous editor of *The West Port Murders* went out of his way to defend those people who gathered that day, claiming that they had no intention of rioting, and if they showed anger, they were being honest:

> Some of the journals who record such events, appear to have felt very wrathful upon the occasion, and to have lavished every term of vituperation upon those whose conduct ran counter to their fine drawn sentimentality.... we must recollect that ordinary executions are very different things from what this was.[23]

The same writer went on to point out, rather drily, that "many of the populace were of the same rank in life as the massacred victims, and that they naturally felt more deeply on the subject than those whose station and habits removed them from the risk of being butchered." If that were not enough to justify the loudly expressed sentiments of the crowd, the reader was also reminded that no less a personage than that of the lord justice clerk himself, David Boyle, had recommended in passing sentence that Burke's skeleton be preserved, and had regretted that it was no longer acceptable to hang bodies to "bleach in the winds." These comments show the fear of revolution and the anger of the crowd. And we can see the importance of the struggle between Lord Advocate Rae, and the Whig lawyers Moncrieff, Cockburn, and Jeffrey, and the Edinburgh public as it used its voice. In 1828, the Tory government that botched the punishment of the four West Port murderers was a Tory government close to collapse and compromise, facing what an old Scottish historian called "the phalanx of Whig counsel."[24]

Rae vs. the Reformers

The quarrel between Rae and the reformers Moncrieff, Cockburn, and Jeffrey went back many years, and it was as basic as the differences between conservatism and reform, forged during the years of the French Revolution, could make it. In 1817 the Whig lawyers Cockburn, Jeffrey, and John Clerk had defended a number of weavers and other tradesmen accused of sedition: one had gone so far as to call George III mad, and others had taken "treasonable oaths." Had the weavers been tried in the 1790s, there would have been hangings, but the best the lord advocate could do in 1817 was two six-month sentences, with the rest found not guilty.[25]

The Whig and Tory Journals

The conflict burned brightly in 1828 because competing papers and journals had been founded to keep political quarrels alive. In 1802 the *Edinburgh Review* had been established as a Whig journal, and it was followed in 1809 by the Tory *Quarterly Review*, sponsored by Walter Scott. In 1817 the *Scotsman*, a "political and literary journal," joined the *Edinburgh Review* in presenting the views of moderate reform. In opposition, late in 1817, *Blackwood's Edinburgh Magazine* appeared, to be joined in 1821 by a scurrilous paper, the *Beacon*. A libeled Whig soon discovered and revealed that the new lord advocate, Sir William Rae, was one of a small group of Tories who funded and oversaw the *Beacon*. It folded, to be replaced by the *Sentinel*, which was just as scurrilous. By 1822 its pages had provoked a caning, a suit for damages against the editors, and a duel. But reform did not seem imminent.[26]

Burke as Flint, the Mob as Tinder

Struggles for moderate reform were the background to the public debates over Burke, and Hare, and Rae's conduct of the case. In other words, Cockburn's interest and pleasure in making a fool of Rae had little to do with right or wrong, good or evil, or the people in the Grassmarket. Moncrieff, Clerk, Jeffrey, and Cockburn, good Whigs all, probably would have defended Burke or Log, Hare or M'Dougal—just to see Rae embarrassed. Whether the good or not-so-good people of the closes knew this when they mobbed M'Dougal, demanded to see the dead Burke, and yelled for Knox's punishment we cannot know. But scream bloody murder they did. And nervous commentators on the mobs made no secret of their fear and hatred of what they perceived as mindless, or revolutionary, mob violence.[27]

Burke in the Flesh

Burke's death opened the way to more mobbing and more anger. A crowd had gathered at the college after the hanging, waiting for the body to arrive, but they were disappointed, for the body was moved at night. During the next morning, various distinguished persons, all male, along with the regular members of Monro's class, were allowed to stare at Burke, now naked. A sculptor "took a bust," and several young men sketched him. He was reported to be "plump" and "stout" and "sturdy" and to have very large thighs. His face, or countenance, was described as placid, but also as one that "betokened the same meanness and low wickedness which it exhibited at the trial." At one in the afternoon, when the lecture and anatomization was to begin, the official university lecturer, Alexander Monro, "did everything in his power to satisfy the curiousity of those who wished to have a view of the features, by exposing him in the most favourable position." Burke had by now been viewed repeatedly—in jail, at the hanging, after death—and in order to go further with this looking, Monro proposed to give his lecture that day, not on the whole body, which would have been impossible, and pointless to medical observers, but on the brain.

What exactly these watchers saw, since many of them were not physicians, but curious gentlemen, is not clear. One recorded that Monro took "off the scalp to show the muscles of the upper part of the head; these being removed, the skull was sawn through, and the brain with its covering exposed." But having given that description of what was probably an hour's work, he then spent even more space describing the quantity of blood that ran onto the floor. Once blood flowed in this description, the body was no longer plump and sturdy—Burke was then described as a "vile carcass," in keeping, perhaps, with the writer's association of the room with a "butcher's slaughterhouse." By two-thirty in the afternoon, when the lecture was over, other students had gathered outside, demanding to be let in. They were met by the police and another petty riot ensued, until a professor made arrangements to have them admitted to see the remains in small groups.[28]

On the next day, Friday, the public was admitted, and "an unceasing stream of persons" tramped by the body, which had altered considerably during the night. The head had been put back together, but the face was puffy, and pale, and bloated, and "no longer presented the countenance of Burke." For their trouble, it seems, the ordinary folk got to see quite a different icon—the face of someone no longer placid, but well and truly mangled, looking much like someone who had been strangled. Some twenty-five thousand men may have seen Burke on Friday, an enormous number for the time; seven women found their way into the classroom to see the body, although they were heckled by the men. Others started up the steps, but turned away. Presumably they were deterred and heckled because Burke was naked.[29]

Log and Hare Released

Shortly before the execution, another controversy began, this time focusing on Hare and Log. On January 19, Log was released, signaling that Rae saw no way to bring her to trial. Making her way along the North Bridge to the Old Town, she was recognized, surrounded, and "pelted unmercifully with snowballs, mud, and stones." She may have escaped death because she was carrying her child, or simply because the police came to her rescue. Within days she had walked to Glasgow, hoping to get a ship for Ireland, but she was discovered there, and stoned and chased through the streets. Either she was known in those neighborhoods, or the sketches of her in the popular press were accurate, since she had to be rescued by police, and probably stayed in a jail until she sailed for Belfast. She had money in her pocket, enough to pay her own passage to Ireland. She found someone in Edinburgh to take her other child, so she was not doing badly, especially since

The Spectacular "Burke mania" Trial

she disappeared from the popular record at this point, after giving one farewell interview in the *Glasgow Chronicle*.[30]

Hare had other excitements in store. Three days before Log was released, Mrs. Wilson and her daughter had petitioned the sheriff to prosecute Hare privately for the murder of James Wilson, or Daft Jamie. Private prosecution was possible under Scots law, but raised a difficult question in this case: Did the lord advocate's offer of immunity to Hare protect Hare only from prosecution by the state, or from private prosecution as well? If the immunity covered all prosecution, then the lord advocate had, the Whigs would argue, the power to pardon, a power understood, at least by Whigs, to reside only in the Crown. Francis Jeffrey, Whig leader and editor of the *Edinburgh Review*, offered his services to the Wilsons. Indeed, it seems possible that Jeffrey or some other Whigs had encouraged the Wilsons to take this action, for they were not wealthy and had played no public role up to this time.[31]

The Wilsons, through Jeffrey, had begun their private prosecution on January 16. Hare must have been alarmed, for he was suddenly treated as a prisoner, and examined as if he were about to be charged. How Log behaved in all of this we will never know, but presumably she said nothing useful—no statements from her survive, other than her courtroom testimony—and she was released on the nineteenth. On the twentieth, Hare petitioned the sheriff to stop the proceedings against him. The sheriff saw no reason to stop the Wilsons, seeing a private prosecution as unconnected to the lord advocate's dealing with Hare, but proposed an appeal to the High Court of Justiciary. On the twenty-first, someone took down the *Courant* confession from Burke, who was to be hanged in a week, and who might have given important evidence against Hare. It was certainly his desire to see Hare hang. On the twenty-second, someone representing the sheriff took down a postscript to Burke's previous official confession. Burke must have been somewhat hopeful by then that Hare was about to be indicted. On the twenty-sixth the High Court of Justiciary took up the Bill of Advocation for Hare, but did not decide it until February 2, so Burke went to the gallows not knowing what would become of Hare.[32]

On the second, before yet another packed courtroom, Jeffrey lost, and Rae had a chance to vindicate his handling of the case. General opinion seemed to be that the lord advocate, faced with an unprecedented case, had to take a new step—extending immunity to Hare for all the murders, even though he gave public evidence only in the case of Docherty. This, Rae could plead, assured him of one conviction, and more importantly, of getting at the truth of the matter, for it may have been Hare who told him about Daft Jamie, and perhaps about Paterson. But Hare's complete immunity had no precedent in Scots law, and the practice of king's evidence was itself a recent English import. Scots law did not, before the eighteenth century, recognize the novel proposition that those involved in a crime, with every interest in seeing someone else hang for it, would tell the truth.[33]

But Francis Jeffrey, continuing the attack on the lord advocate's powers begun in 1822, also made his point,

> that it rested entirely with the Lord Advocate to enter into any compact, and to extend immunity to any number of cases without the control of the judge; in short, that the Lord Advocate possessed the uncontrolled power of exercising the Royal Prerogative.... Such a prerogative would be investing the Public Prosecutor with a power of pardon, which belonged only to the Crown, and this too without a tittle of authority, and totally different from judicial authority, amounting to an assumption of the prerogatives of Parliament.[34]

The murders at this point became much more obviously an opportunity for Whigs to attack Rae. When sixteen murders were revealed by Burke's confessions, it became foolish to claim that Hare exposed "what crimes of this revolting description had really been committed." And his testimony at the trial, and Log's, may or may not have been believed after Cockburn got through with him, and may have damaged the case, rather than secured the conviction. In Scots law, Hare's testimony as "socii criminum," one of the associates of criminals, had no standing unless it was corroborated by a respectable witness. There was no corroboration, as one writer in the *Caledonian Mercury* pointed out.

The lord advocate's work was defended by the *Edinburgh Advertiser* and the *Edinburgh Observer*, and the little evidence he uncovered by taking Hare and Log as witnesses was enough to begin a prosecution. But the need to get at the truth of the murders for the sake of "the public interest" did not drive Whigs or Tories as much as it did carters and saltwives. Discoveries had come because the Grays had gone directly to the police; because the prostitute Janet Brown and her friend Mrs. Lawrie had the wit and relative sobriety to be suspicious; and because the political state of Scotland forced the lord advocate to act. Facing the furious, frightened people, the Whig newspapers, and the "phalanx of Whig counsel," Rae had to prosecute. And the consequences were not bad. The murders were revealed, Burke was convicted, and the lives of the other three were so disrupted that it seems impossible that they murdered again. Others, like Constantine Burke and David Paterson, lost their positions and had to move on. Whigs and Tories, at a crucial period in political development, got to make claims, do some public posturing, and defend different members of the gang. And the general public got to examine something that was new, and to express their fear.[35]

But Hare was not free yet, even though the High Court decided in his favor, because on that same day the Wilsons made one last attempt to try Hare. They notified the sheriff of their intention to begin a civil suit for payment, an assythment or blood money in Scots law, and requested that he be held to prevent his leaving the country before the suit could be taken to court. Hare was locked up again, and questioned repeatedly over his intention to stay in Scotland, or to leave. The scene was particularly memorable. Hare was described as

incomparably more gruesome and growlish; for in order to facilitate the operations of some Phrenologists, who had just finished taking a cast of his head, his hair had been mown down to the very sconce, with the exception of a fringe bordering the scalp all round, thus blending in his appearance the ludicrous with the horrid in a way and manner that defies all description.[36]

But he said little, and on February 5 the Wilsons gave up, perhaps because Hare had no money, and they had no evidence of his guilt other than the confessions of Burke, which were as open to criticism as Hare's testimony had been.[37]

Hare's Release in February

Hare's release, after all this, was more dramatic and abrupt than M'Dougal's or Log's had been. On the evening of the fifth he was immediately rushed out of the jail in a cloak, and put on a mail coach headed south. Unfortunately for the authorities, one of the men who had a seat inside the coach—Hare was on top, no doubt freezing—was a lawyer named Sandford who had been one of the junior counsel for the Wilsons. Sandford recognized him at an inn, and when the coach reached Dumfries, the news that Hare was coming had also arrived. Hare was hidden, or trapped, in a taproom where various gentlemen asked him questions, and gave him quite a bit of ale. Eventually the crowd gathered outside, which numbered in the thousands, broke into the room, and Hare was threatened. One old woman, reported to be the only woman in the crowd, tried to get at him, to hit him with her tattered umbrella, but was unable to get through the crowd. Police came to his rescue, and with the mob likely to kill Hare if he fell into their hands, they kept him in the tavern. Again, visitors were allowed in, and they abused him mercilessly. One woman grabbed him by the collar and tried to strangle him. An innkeeper, in a truly Scots form of abuse, was reported to have said to him: "Whaur are ye gaun, or whaur can ye gang to? Hell's ower good for the like o' you—the very deevils, for fear o' mischief, wadna daur to let ye in; and as for heeven that's entirely out o' the question." Eventually Hare was taken out a back window, to a hidden coach, and driven to the Dumfries jail as quickly as possible, while crowds threw stones.[38]

He was thrown out of Dumfries at one that morning, without his belongings, to make his way south on foot. He was seen around Carlisle, and then reports of him stop, although a few men unlucky enough to look somewhat like him were mobbed and attacked. Rumors spread. He was thrown into a lime pit and blinded; he lived on as a blind beggar in London's Oxford Street, pointed out to small children for many years.[39]

Knox, the Boy Who Buys the Beef

On the day after Hare crossed into England the confessions of Burke were published. These, together with the transcript of the trial, gave the public good knowledge of the complicity of the four, the list of sixteen murders, and the information that these people were not criminals before they stumbled on murder as a source of income. This knowledge underlined the role of Dr. Knox, who had escaped questioning, and whose records had not been investigated. He was attacked in the papers, but only one mild punishment had been administered to him. The Fellows of the Royal Society had refused to hear a paper he proposed to read to them on January 14. In February a professional committee of inquiry was appointed by Knox, although the chairman resigned shortly thereafter. The day after it was created, a mob gathered on Calton Hill and proceeded to march to Knox's house in the suburb of Newington, where they burnt him in effigy in view of his front windows. Knox, not one to cower, appeared on his back doorstep, armed to the teeth. While Knox escaped, a similar mob collected in Surgeons' Square at his offices, keeping the police busy.[40]

Nothing was ever resolved. Knox moved further out of town, to Portobello, and was mobbed there in early March. On March 17 he sent a letter to the papers, claiming that he had been libeled, and thought of suing. On the twenty-first, his committee exonerated him, which prompted his current students to present him with a gold cup in celebration. And then nothing happened. Slowly, his career declined throughout the 1830s. He was denied two professorships in Edinburgh for which he was qualified, and students became less and less willing to tie their careers to his. He left Scotland for the East End of London in the 1840s, practiced medicine to support himself, and may have died there of apoplexy in 1862. Whether he was discreetly punished by the city fathers we cannot know.[41]

Knox Primus et Incomparabilis

Ironically, the 1828–29 season had been the year of Knox's greatest success. He had almost too many students, who referred to him as *primus et incomparabilis*, a phrase which probably haunted him as he ended his life in poverty in London. At three hundred, four hundred, and in 1829 over five hundred students, he lectured to roughly two-thirds of the medical students in Edinburgh, leaving a much smaller number for the official and notably inept lecturer, Alexander Monro. He was not only driven by numbers, but by his position as successor to his talented mentor, John Barclay. He had taken over from Barclay in 1825, as a favorite student who would be about ten years older than his new students. As one of them wrote, he "placed himself en rapport with his class, sharing in its enthusiasm and scientific ardor, and, to gratify these aims, thought nothing of the trouble or expense he might incur in furnishing his anatomical rooms.... hence No. 10, Surgeon's Square, had a supply which no other establishment possessed." These words come from Henry Lonsdale, Knox's student, biographer, and earnest defender. In naively discussing his mentor's anatomical zeal, he has told us that Knox spent too much, outbid his colleagues, and "in one session lost the almost incredible sum of £700 or £800 by 'subjects' alone." If Lonsdale's boasting is true, it would seem that Knox, who paid Burke and Hare between eight and ten pounds for a body, sometimes paid resurrectionists fifteen pounds, and once paid twenty-five guineas. He bought, by Lonsdale's account, something like ninety-six or more bodies in the 1828–1829 session.[42]

Here we have, cloaked in his own silence and Rae's unwillingness to prosecute, the founder of Burke's, Hare's, Log's, and M'Dougal's feast: the anatomist who strove the hardest to teach well, the man who had no claims by birth to position in the Edinburgh medical establishment. Not one word of regret or apology escaped from him, nor did he in any way acknowledge that he had done anything wrong. His silence was all the more remarkable in that he was a voluble and outspoken man at other times, notably in the classroom. But on the question of the bodies that came into his rooms, both the murdered and the merely resurrected, he was utterly silent, and anyone who writes about Knox can only speculate on what that meant. He was not the sort of man who would have given the public the contrition it demanded; he was not contrite, and he was not a liar. He was perhaps speechless in the way that a person who has come to an unexpected turning in the path can be.[43]

The West Port, seen here in the foreground, led directly into the Grassmarket, virtually all of which is visible in the background. Apparently a civil enough neighborhood in this 1825 engraving, the Grassmarket and adjoining streets sheltered a thriving shadow economy.

CHAPTER 4

The Criminal Household

The household of Burke, Log, Hare, and M'Dougal was as makeshift as the neighborhood that housed them, and it is with that neighborhood that we will begin. The West Port, bordering the old western entrance to the city, was a newer addition to Edinburgh's Old Town, separated from the Grassmarket by a few yards and three hundred years.[1] Early modern building had bequeathed to the Grassmarket a central square surrounded by a rabbit's warren of closes, courtyards, and passages, but the building along some of the West Port was newer, and in better repair. Even so, Alexander Wood, the advocate depute who indicted William Burke and Helen M'Dougal, struggled to describe their house,

situated in that street of Portsburgh, or Wester Portsburgh, *in or near Edinburgh*, which runs from the Grassmarket of Edinburgh to Main-Point, in or near Edinburgh, and on the north side of the said street, and having access thereto by a trance or passage entering from the street last libelled, and having also an entrance from a court or back court on the north thereof, *the name of which is to the Prosecutor unknown*[2]

Wood did not know the name of the back court, or whether Wester Portsburgh was within or without the city. Nonetheless, this was a hopeful neighborhood, sitting at the nexus of western roads into the city, and including the terminus of the Union Canal.[3]

Understanding Burke's "murdering system" and the shadow economy of thefts, scams, and robbery in the Old Town without melodrama means comprehending Burke, Log, Hare, and M'Dougal as ordinary residents of their neighborhood, which they were until 1828. They would have walked by the warehouse where Robertson, Reid, and Adams stole hams; the house where "Old Mrs. Burrows" bought stolen clothes and possibly housed prostitutes; the close where Hannah Barton lived, and the North Bridge, where she attempted to steal the brushmaker's watch.[4]

Burke

Burke, perhaps because of his voluble, cheery manner and his month of incarceration after the trial, left the most detailed portrait, although whether he is to be believed remains a question. William Burke was thirty-six at the time of the trial, Irish, sometimes Catholic, literate, and possibly "afflicted with a cancer." By his own account, he had been born in Orrey, Tyrone, in 1792. He chose to leave his wife, children, and her father's land around 1817 to look for work in Scotland with many other Irish men as a laborer on the Union Canal, which was then being cut to join Glasgow and Edinburgh. He met Helen M'Dougal in Stirling, as he and hundreds of other navvies dug their way through the shire, and after the canal was finished, the two stayed together.

They moved to Edinburgh and "engaged in the petty trafficking of various sorts of merchandise," while living in various "beggar's hotels" in the Grassmarket. In 1825 they shifted to Peebles, south of Edinburgh, and then to Penicuik for two years before moving back to Edinburgh late in 1827. Some rumors were printed suggesting that Burke developed bad habits in the country, because agricultural laborers, especially those working in seasonal gangs, were not noted for sobriety and civility. Burke seems to have worked on roads in Peebles, and both he and M'Dougal had worked in the harvest of 1827, after which they returned to Edinburgh.[5]

When he and M'Dougal returned to Edinburgh that fall, they settled into Log's rather dirty boardinghouse, and he took up cobbling in the small back room. The use of the room was a mark of Log's and Hare's favor, for both seem to have been fond of Burke. Burke parlayed a modest talent for cobbling old shoes with bits of scrap leather into a trade. Log's Lodgings, in Tanner's Close, was near a tannery yard, and leather scraps were available from scavengers. Effie, the murdered cinder gatherer, had been selling Burke scraps of leather that she collected from the grounds of a nearby coachworks. M'Dougal peddled the shoes some of the time, taking them as far afield as her home county of Stirling, and selling them to colliers there. Their household, shared and public, presents a pretty good picture of the way in which the working poor survived dislocation, working for others for years when necessary, sharing rooms, buying, selling, and scrounging from among the various scraps and castoffs at their far edge of the larger economy.[6]

Burke was well-known. He was building a reputation for himself as one of the notable persons in his part of town, probably much as Log was known, if only from her public role as a lodging house keeper. He liked children. He liked music and singing. Neighbors remembered his pranks and jokes and habit of hiring "minstrels" for dancing. That he beat M'Dougal senseless and eyed "loose women" and a relative of M'Dougal's was not exceptional enough to make the neighbors dislike him. Even his jailers liked him, and M'Dougal's advocate, the smart Whig lawyer Henry Cockburn, found him "sensible, and what might be called a respectable man; not at all ferocious in his general manner, sober, correct in all his other habits."[7]

Yet Burke was a murderer. He probably ingratiated himself with Docherty much as he managed to impress his betters once he was jailed. And he had undoubtedly learned to use the education he had, both in reading and writing, and in service to one or more gentlemen, to his advantage. Whether he was to be believed or not was a problem for those who went to see him. Professor John Wilson, writing as Christopher North in *Blackwood's Edinburgh Magazine* in March of 1829, called him "impenitent as a snake," and went on to add "steeped in hypocrisy and deceit" to his list of adjectives. But then *Blackwood's* was a Tory journal, and Wilson a cynic who no doubt wrote against a tide of mildly evangelical, as well as Whiggish sympathy for Burke, who made an effort to appear suitably reformed, penitent, and prayerful in jail. Wilson, to his credit, was not particularly interested in the religious cant of the period, and his description of Burke is worth noting, especially as he visited Burke in jail.

[Burke was] a neat little man of about five feet five, well proportioned, especially large in his legs and thighs—round-bodied, but narrow-chested—arms rather thin—small wrists, and a moderate-sized hand—no mass of muscle any where about his limbs or frame—but vigorously necked—with hard forehead and cheek-bones—a very active but not powerful man—intended by nature for a dancing-master. Indeed he danced well—excelling in the Irish jig—and when working about Peebles and Inverleithen he was very fond of that recreation. In that neighbourhood he was reckoned a good specimen of the Irish character—not quarrelsome—expert with the spade—and a pleasant enough companion over a jug of toddy. Nothing repulsive about him, to ordinary observers at least—and certainly not deficient in intelligence. But he "had that within which passeth shew"—"there is a laughing devil in his eye," . . . and in his cell he applied in my hearing over and over again the words "humane man," to those who had visited him, laying the emphasis on humane, with a hypocritical tone, as I thought, that shewed he had not attached its appropriate meaning to the word, but used it by rote like a parrot—[8]

If Wilson was inclined to repeat the accepted views of Irish immigrants, dancing and drinking, his insistence on Burke's hypocrisy must be weighed against another standard. He was willing to grant that Burke was intelligent. But Wilson was a scholar, a professor with an ear for educated speech, and it is up to us to judge whether he had truly spotted hypocrisy, or merely heard a commoner, and Irish to boot, use an unfamiliar word awkwardly. Burke was, for all his street wisdom, a man largely unprepared for the visitors he had in his last few weeks, many of them the best and brightest of the city that called itself the modern Athens. What we are left with is the information that Burke could impress some of them, like Henry Cockburn, but not Wilson, and this may tell us more about Whigs and Tories, and their varying willingness to listen to a ragged and disgraced man, than about Burke.

The Criminal Household

Burke was not born a criminal, although he died one, and had lived an unthinkable life for nearly a year, if we do not count M'Dougal's beatings, and his first wife's abandonment in the list of horrors. But he was also a man capable of some presence, and of impressing others favorably and he no doubt relished that approval. And he was a penniless laborer, getting on toward his fortieth year, when physical labor starts to tell on the body. The rewards of dealing with Knox must have been attractive: little physical work, much more money to spend in the neighborhood, better clothes, better food. He told "the wife of an old acquaintance" that he had spent fourteen pounds in a fortnight, and "if he had known where her husband lived, would have been glad to come and spend three or four pounds in company with him." After the murders began, Burke and M'Dougal were noticed in the neighborhood, because they "appeared well dressed, and spent money freely." Burke even had credit at Rymer's grocery and spirit shop, and confessed that he used to "get better victuals unknown to [M'Dougal]." He explained all the money to neighbors, and to his wife, by insisting that he and Hare were resurrection men, and that they smuggled whiskey. The money suited him, even if, as he later claimed, the murder did not.[9]

Yet he must have been balancing awkwardly throughout 1828, as perhaps he had been for much of his life. Even as a soldier, he had moved beyond Catholicism to attend Presbyterian, Episcopalian, and Methodist services, an ecumenicism that he would carry to Scotland with him. And it is hard to escape concluding that he left his Irish wife, and her cottar parents, not out of desperation, but out of impatience, because he intended to make something better of his life. He and M'Dougal might have lived decently on his cobbling in the city of Edinburgh, but that was clearly not enough for this man who was up and out on the streets at four in the morning, and sometimes out all night, drinking and carousing. And so he took to murdering. But "when he slept he had frightful dreams." And he could not even sleep "without a bottle of whiskey by his bed and a twopenny candle to burn all night beside him." We can perhaps believe this, since he continued, in his confession, to pour out the sort of memories that would haunt one:

> Burke declares, when they kept the mouth and nose shut a very few minutes, they could make no resistance, but would convulse and make a rumbling noise in their bellies for some time; after they ceased crying and making resistance, they left them to die of themselves; but their bodies would often move afterwards, and for some time they would have long breathings before life went away.[10]

He was ultimately out of his depth, a small figure in an over-large black suit, glaring but still trembling on the scaffold. And he was probably a man who had seen himself, for many years, as one cut out for something better.[11]

Helen or Nelly M'Dougal

Helen M'Dougal came from Maddiston, in the parish of Muiravonside in Stirlingshire, where she had fallen in with a married man, a sawyer, had a child with him, and then moved to the Edinburgh port of Leith with him after his wife's death.[12] After his death, she returned to her family in Muiravonside, where she met William Burke while he was working on the Union Canal in 1817. Whatever they had between them was sufficient to keep them together for the next ten years. M'Dougal was clearly capable of committing herself without the formal tie of marriage, and of recognizing men equally willing to do so. The sawyer did not run out on her, and neither did Burke.[13]

It was a hard life. She and Burke were outdoors more often than in, and if it was to be preferred to life in Muiravonside, that rural parish must have had very little to offer. She drank, Burke beat her, and she seems not to have fought back, although she was once described as the "aggressor." James Maclean, a neighbor, remembered her as morose, and dull, and "everlastingly quarreling" with Burke, often over other women. We glimpse M'Dougal only occasionally at work, in the harvest of 1827 with Burke and Hare, carrying Burke's cobbled shoes back to Stirlingshire to sell, and at the end, sweeping and washing and cooking pails of potatoes in the small but decent room that had been the Brogans'. It is hard to know, when an anonymous editor described her "drunken dissolute habits," whether she was much different from her neighbors, some of whom must have lived on the same potatoes, whiskey, and tea that seem to have been the staples of M'Dougal's household.[14]

M'Dougal appears to us, well lit and thoroughly examined only once, at the trial on Christmas Eve. If Burke's clothes were shabby, and his expression both "wauf" and hard, M'Dougal became the figure of poverty and misery.

The female prisoner is fully of the middle size, but thin and spare made, though evidently of large bone. Her features are long, and the upper half of her face is out of proportion to the lower. She was miserably dressed in a small grey-coloured velvet bonnet, very much the worse for wear, a printed cotton shawl and cotton gown. She stoops considerably in her gait, and has nothing peculiar in her appearance, except the ordinary look of extreme poverty and misery common to unfortunate females of the same degraded class.[15]

The reporter for the *Caledonian Mercury* who wrote this neglected to mention something that C. K. Sharpe added to his account, namely that M'Dougal looked to him to be ten or twelve years older than Burke. She claimed to be thirty-three, which would have made her suitably younger than Burke, and which may have been true. Sharpe may have been seeing the effects of age, or the effects of labor; he was after all looking at a woman who worked in harvest gangs and peddled in the streets. To bourgeois observers, laboring women must have looked poor, bent, disfigured, old for their age, and often, masculine, while working men looked determined, and could still inspire that bit of fear that the reporter noted as a demeanor "far from inviting" about Burke. Marks left by hard work out of doors enhanced masculinity, but eroded femininity, which must have been increasingly seen as inseparable from life indoors, surrounded by children.[16]

Burke apparently cherished an idea of her as a proper woman, although exactly what that meant to either of them is not clear. It may also have mattered to him that she was Scots, and some sort of

Protestant, and rather cheerless. She did not leave him, and he did not leave her; they were survivors, and she was even more grimly determined to succeed than he was. She would have been familiar with Edinburgh before Burke had ever been there, and may have led them there when work on the canal was finished. And her attachment to the married sawyer M'Dougal may have been dictated by survival, for she may well have been faced with eternal agricultural service in a small village in which, during the French wars, there may have been few men of marriageable age. And after the wars, with unemployed men everywhere, Burke may well have looked cleverer and more ambitious than many. M'Dougal should not be read as a miserable creature, taken in by an abusive Burke and his twinkling grey eyes. She was far tougher, and probably shared Burke's hope of some success.[17]

As we get beyond the great dominating figure of the endlessly prodded and questioned Burke, we move into the real subject of this chapter. That is the way in which the household he established with M'Dougal, and the very porous household established by Log, and then Hare, served the needs of this murdering business, and fit within the community. Burke and M'Dougal worked together, and when they threw in their lot with Log and Hare, they created a new household that was also a business. And when we use the word *business* here, we are not grafting on a modern and inappropriate description, but using a word that, along with the word *system*, was repeated endlessly in 1828, and in subsequent accounts of the murders.[18]

Willie Hare

Willie Hare was a twenty-five-year-old Irishman from Armagh. His father was Protestant, his mother Catholic, and he had been living on his own since he was fifteen or sixteen. Wherever he had been, he spoke with a combination of Irish and Cumberland accents that must have made him nearly incomprehensible in Edinburgh. He claimed to have worked on the canal and on canal boats for seven years, to have spent two years with a quarryman, and to have peddled from a barrow. He also kept pigs, which he seems to have driven out of town to feed, on days when that was not done by his, and Log's, young servant girl. He had met up with Log's previous husband on the canals, stayed at Log's Lodgings for a bit, and then moved in when Log's husband died. No doubt he too, like all of the four, had his eyes open for his best opportunity.[19]

Hare was universally despised; he was "the *beau ideal* [*sic*] of a drunken, ferocious, and stupid profligate," as the anonymous editor of *West Port Murders* put it in 1829. Cockburn described him as a "squalid wretch," and "a monster," but that was mild. He was also described as "a perfect pest" in the neighborhood, "incapable of comprehending anything of moral rectitude," and Wilson described him as "a perfect fool." Adjectives flowed over him, almost endlessly: "squalid-looking wretch" was accompanied by "ghoulishness, squalor, and ferocity;" and then "apathy, vacancy, and mental imbecility." No one liked Hare except Burke, the man almost everyone liked. He was an ill-tempered drunk, but both Log, a woman of a bit of property in a neighborhood where that was rare, and Burke had chosen to like him.[20]

Only once was he described with less fear, as "a poor silly-looking body." He could neither read nor write. He appeared hollow-cheeked and thin, gazing fixedly in courtroom sketches; in Thomas Ireland's he is almost handsome, but in Nimmo's he is bestial and demonically cheery. It would seem that, in captivity, he was rude and unrepentant, but for a stupid man, he was quick enough to turn king's evidence when the chance was offered. His "imbecility" seems to have consisted of saying little, and expressing what the men around him found to be inappropriate emotions, particularly glee. He was not the literate Burke, and emotions burst out of him unpolished. Described as "a perfect fool," he was in fact a fish out of water, refusing to recognize the roles offered him. His testimony condemned Burke, yet he stubbornly continued to describe the friend with whom he had spent much of the last year as "one of the best men in the world." Hare was castigated for this, even though the gentlemen who castigated him almost agreed.[21]

Hare and Burke were Irish in Britain at a time when that was no advantage. Yet they made rather awkward Irishmen, for Hare had a wanderer's jumbled accent, and Burke a penchant for Protestant churches. But differentiating between the two occupied many observers, and the crowds that howled for their Irish blood also howled for the blood of the implicated anatomy lecturer, Robert Knox, and M'Dougal, who were both Scots. Insofar as they were part of an Irish immigrant community, as well as the general community of the laboring poor in Edinburgh, being Irish helped them far more than it hurt them. They identified Irish newcomers who could be killed easily, and on the road to self-improvement, they preyed on the poor, both Irish and Scots, above whom they hoped to rise. To argue that they were hated because they were Irish is to assume that the working people of Edinburgh, from the very poor to the rather respectable, were quite stupid.[22]

Lucky Log

Lucky Log, born Margaret Laird, had left Ireland in 1812 for Glasgow, possibly to work in the Tureen Street power loom factory. She may have lied about working the power looms, but she did work on the Union Canal beside her husband, James Log, who seems to have headed and contracted for a gang of Irish navvies, or laborers. She wore a man's coat, dug ditches and hauled rock, and was repeatedly described as "chiefly remarkable for her masculine and bold habits." Whatever her failings, she "showed no want of industry," which seemingly pleased the compilers of accounts of the trial, although they did not follow this information to its logical conclusion. Log was physically capable of suffocating a struggling adult. If she did not do so, it may have been because she and Hare agreed that killing was man's work. Or she may have simply evaded such work when she could get Hare to do it for her.[23]

When the canal was completed they settled in Edinburgh, near the canal's endpoint, and opened a lodging house, first behind the well in the West Port, and then in Tanner's Close, where Mr. Log died. Hare was already on the scene, although there was a rumor that

Log had taken up with a nice young man whom she left for Hare. Whether or not the young man existed, Lucky Log was quick enough to find herself another companion. According to *The West Port Murders*, Log was "a short, stout, round-faced and fresh-complexioned personage, but withal has a look of coarse and determined brutality." As well she might, one could add, after digging the Union Canal. She was also given to "tyrranizing [sic] over those under her sway.... She had the last word and the last blow," according to the ever-present James Maclean. No doubt her time on the canal with her contractor husband had taught her something about how to give orders, and she was tough enough to carry on the lodging business while Hare continued to work unloading boats and peddling. If she was short, the porter M'Culloch described her as "a big woman," which suggests that she had a way of taking up space, perhaps what we would call presence.[24]

If we believe Burke's confessions, Log was industrious in finding subjects. No doubt she had acquired some skill in spotting the homeless and inviting them into her lodgings. Those available beds gave her great power in bringing people together, creating a household as she chose. She had invited Burke and M'Dougal to stay at Log's Lodgings, offering them the little inside room. She would charge Burke one pound of his share from each body sold for the use of her lodging house in the murder, and perhaps for the loss of customers. We have no way of knowing who first thought of selling the body of Old Donald, the pensioner who died naturally. But we do know that Hare and Log, according to Burke, "decoyed" in the first woman killed, Abigail Simpson, and that Log played an active role in keeping her in the house. The third victim, a woman, was brought into the house, given whiskey, and put to bed by Log, and suffocated rather carefully by Hare, who put a bit of bed tick over her while he was home for lunch, and left her to die.[25]

Log's position between 1827 and 1828 is curious, for she had, by the available accounts, dominated her household. And while some thought of Hare as the more sinister of the men, "the more deeply designing," as one writer put it, and the "author and principal actor in so many murders," others, particularly as time passed, thought that Willie Hare was not capable of much. Wilson described him in jail as "at first look seemingly an idiot." And the anonymous writer in *The West Port Murders*, at the end of the book, by which time Hare had been examined repeatedly, and much written about all four, concluded that

> it was assumed, that [Burke] had been made a tool of by Hare, and that he was the tempter and arch-fiend who had lured him on to his destruction, and instructed him in the hellish arts; and Burke's language favoured the idea. But Hare has since exhibited, along with his hardened indifference and callousness, such a mental apathy, such gross and unconceivable stolidity in his conduct and estimation of his crimes, as to force us to the conclusion, that, however inclined he might be to reach the climax of atrocity, he was not capable of leading or directing any one, far less Burke, or initiating him in the barbarous trade.[26]

The business began in Log and Hare's household, and if Hare was such a fool, and Burke still busy with his shoes at the beginning, it seems more than likely that Log was the initiator that everyone was looking for and failing to see. But Log had become considerably less conspicuous by late in 1828, as the partnership shifted its configuration. The change is apparent if we reexamine two of Burke's anecdotes, the first from the murder of Daft Jamie, and the second from Docherty's demise. When Log had brought Jamie "into her house," as Burke put it, "and left him with Hare, she came to Rymer's shop for a pennyworth of butter," and also a dram, which she drank with Burke; "and in drinking it she stamped him on the foot. He knew immediately what she wanted him for, and then he went after her." If he was something of an obedient son in this story, by the time Docherty was killed, he had become the one giving the orders. He ordered a box from Rymer's, and he sent Log, like a servant, to fetch it on the Saturday afternoon that they packed the body up. Dynamics within the gang were far more complex than observers at the time probably suspected, although the readiness of Hare and Log to turn king's evidence and testify against their partners, along with later impressions of Hare as a fool, might have given the observant a clue.[27]

Log was a quick and enterprising woman who may well have seen herself as acting "art and part" in the murders with Hare, and then with Burke as well. She bullied Hare, and she "had the last word and blow" when they fought. She helped both men stuff the bodies of their victims into barrels, tea chests, and trunks. Her previous husband, James Log, had died somewhat conveniently not long after she met Hare, which suggests either poison or great alacrity in replacing the ailing Log. She was described as boisterous and tyrannizing, and she was nobody's fool. She had distinct ideas about the shape the household should take, and she no doubt viewed her own role, much diminished by the growing partnership between Hare and Burke, with dislike, and as we shall see below, some alarm.[28]

Households, Partnerships, and "she-devils"

The trial focused public attention on the house where Docherty died, and on Burke and M'Dougal, but the powerful defense made for them had in turn brought Hare and Log into view, bathed in the garish light of rumor and fear. At the time most people assumed that Burke and Hare were the murderers, but that, as the writer for the *Caledonian Mercury* put it on December 27, "these she-devils were familiar with the work of death." This hardly captures the brittle and explosive relations between all four, for they quarreled, and separated, and both Hare and Burke had each murdered and sold a body without telling the other.[29]

As George MacGregor suggested in 1884, something happened among the four, probably in June of 1828. Burke related that he and M'Dougal "were on a visit seeing their friends near Falkirk. This was at the time a procession was made round a stone in that neighborhood; thinks it was the anniversary of the battle of Bannockburn." While they were away, Hare took care of his money problems by killing one woman on his own; Burke relates it as Hare's own work, but presumably Log helped in some way. This would seem to mark some sort of falling out, and if we couple another of Burke's stories with it, we can see the first fracture developing in the group. Without ever giving a date to the story, Burke noted in his *Courant* confession,

He was urged by Hare's wife to murder Helen M'Dougal, the woman he lived with. The plan was, that he was to go to the country for a few weeks, and then write to Hare that she had died and was buried; but he would not agree to it. The reason was, they could not trust to her, as she was a Scotch woman.[30]

It was likely that Log had urged this in the spring of 1828, perhaps after the murder in Constantine Burke's house, in which M'Dougal helped, since, as MacGregor wisely commented, M'Dougal must have known something if Log feared trusting her. M'Dougal probably knew what was going on by the time she and Burke had moved to his brother's overcrowded room in the Old Town, since, according to Janet Brown, M'Dougal "requested them to sit still, and seemed anxious that they should not go away." Once the scene had shifted to the Burke-M'Dougal household, Log must have recognized that M'Dougal would see more than she had previously seen.

If Log's proposition to Burke came after this, it suggests that she was trying to control the composition of the group, much as she had when she invited Burke and M'Dougal to live in Log's Lodgings. And Burke's phrase, "they could not trust to her," suggests that M'Dougal was seen as something of an outsider by the three Irish immigrants. If Burke refused to murder M'Dougal, we are left to ponder why they both left Edinburgh for the country, a trip which coincided with Log's plan. Either Burke had thoughts of killing M'Dougal, but could not, or he wished to get her away from Tanner's Close, for fear Hare and Log would kill her. Burke seems to have been consistent in his desire to protect her, and it seems likely that they had lived with Constantine and his wife Elizabeth for a short time in April for the same reason: to keep her away from Hare and Log. Apparently the two couples never formed an ideal partnership, even though all four worked together, uneasily, to kill Docherty.[31]

When Burke and M'Dougal returned from their trip, there was a fight between the two men, since it was obvious to Burke that Hare had a bit of money, and Hare initially denied "doing any business" on his own. Burke visited Dr. Knox, and Hare "confessed." After that, Burke again took up the slightly more dominant role he had first taken at his brother's house, when he had brought home the two prostitutes, gotten them quite drunk, and only then sent for Hare. First, Effie the cinder gatherer was his acquaintance, and probably his find; then came the drunken woman he literally took out of the arms of the police, promising to bring her to her lodgings. But if Burke was beginning to show a decided initiative, Log was not yet quiet.

The final break came with the murder of Daft Jamie. Burke certainly remembered that murder in greater detail than any other, and was able to recount how Log had come for him, stamped on his foot, and then locked the three men into the small inner room. It would seem that he clearly thought of her as having the upper hand in this, and that may have prompted some of his sympathy for Jamie—"Mrs. Hare led poor Jamie in as a dumb lamb to the slaughter." Perhaps Burke thought that he too had been led in, not quite a lamb, to do the slaughtering. If Burke was angered by Log, and perhaps appalled by the struggle the young man put up, he was quick to assert himself. He claimed the clothes for his brother's children, instead of throwing them away, and he refused to pay Log her one pound head tax out of his share of Knox's payment. For the latter treason, he said, Log "would not speak to him for three weeks."[32]

That silence must have included eviction, for the next murder was carried out by both men in John Brogan's house, whose wife was Burke's or M'Dougal's distant cousin. Hare and Burke continued to operate together, but now they worked in what would become Burke's house, and Log was the chief loser by this shift.

Partnership

Burke and Hare were now working as partners, unrelated by blood or family or household membership. True, these partners were still mainly working out of one household, Burke and M'Dougal's, and consequently with M'Dougal's help. Log's influence had waned and M'Dougal's instrumentality had risen by the time of Docherty's murder. This was probably not what Burke wanted, and the first victim to be murdered in Brogan's was a relative of M'Dougal's. Burke insisted that Hare be the first to lay a hand on her, "as she being a distant friend he did not like to begin." This murder, of Ann M'Dougal, cost them dearly. They had to pay off John Brogan—perhaps five or six pounds—to urge him to move his family out, and to keep silence about the big trunk he had seen in his house. Still unsettled, they then killed Mrs. Haldane in Hare's stable. Then Burke, acting alone, killed her daughter Peggy. The killers had to work carefully while the Brogans moved themselves out. They managed one more victim under these tricky circumstances. And then, at Halloween, the Brogans were gone, which may have been one of the reasons for their celebration that evening.[33]

It may seem ironic that they should be caught just as they tried out the new system of operations from the Brogans'—now Burke's—house, and with Log's influence diminished. Burke was now Hare's partner, and probably boss, and their wives were willing to help, if not to watch. But the partnership was undercut by the persistence of household, with all its loyalties and its implied partnership between Burke and M'Dougal. Certainly Burke and M'Dougal worked well together in finding and keeping Docherty in the house, so much so that the appearance of Log and Hare to dance and drink a little more was nearly superfluous until Burke wanted a partner for the killing. And so we come to Hare, and his place in these arrangements and rearrangements. He had earlier, according to M'Dougal, made a proposal to Burke. As she put it after the trial, the two men were "carousing" on money from "a recent murder" when

> Hare raised his hand, and in a fit of fiendish exultation, stated that they could never want for money, for, when they were at a loss for "a shot,"... they would murder and sell, first one and then the other of their own wives. Being in the adjoining apartment, the females overheard, and were petrified by this horrible resolution, as they had every reason to be assured that the monsters would certainly carry it into effect.... Hare finally persuading Burke to consent, that when the dreaded emergency did arrive, M'Dougal should be the first victim.[34]

If this seems like a ploy by Hare and Log to dispose of M'Dougal, we have some evidence that Log believed it, because she testified—for what that is worth—that while she and M'Dougal huddled in the passage during Docherty's murder, she said to M'Dougal "perhaps it might be the same thing with her and I." Hare had his own vision of the partnership, probably conditioned by the many fights with Log that he had lost, and it was a male partnership that he envisioned, and something very different from a marriage, or at least his marriage. Unfortunately, the fight between Burke and Hare on that night suggests that the new partnership would be no better than the old.[35]

The material domain of their business, their houses, necessarily included both husbands and wives, and forced these contradictions on them, if not in articulate ways, in the form of jealousy, fear, and perpetual petty struggles. Log might have stood a chance of ruling the business, if it had remained in her own household. But once the killing moved to Burke and M'Dougal's, where Burke was far more clearly in command, Log was out, and Burke was caught between a partnership with Hare, and making a new relationship with M'Dougal, in which he could no longer pretend to himself that she was innocent. Had their murdering not been stopped, M'Dougal might have become another Log, and Hare, facing a new Medusa, might well have put greater pressure on Burke to kill her, or done so himself.

Womanhood

Consider just how well Log and M'Dougal understood the rules of being a good woman in 1828, how Cockburn used those same assumptions to save Nelly M'Dougal from hanging, and how desperately Burke defended M'Dougal's innocence. Burke said early on, "we always put them out of the way when we were going to do it." And in his January 3 confession, he said "that Helen M'Dougal and Hare's wife were in no way concerned in any of the murders." But after a while he became more frank, and more willing to incriminate Log:

They certainly knew what became of them [the victims], although Burke and Hare pretended to the contrary. Hare's wife often helped Burke and Hare to pack the murdered bodies into the boxes. Helen M'Dougal never did nor saw them done.[36]

He insisted almost to the end that M'Dougal was, if not innocent, more removed from the business of killing than the other three.

Nonetheless, he did blurt out in his last confession, the *Courant* confession, that they were "four murderers living in one house." Not long after the trial, an account was taken down from one of the officers who had arrested Burke and M'Dougal, in which the officer reported that one of the neighbors had tried to see what was going on in Burke and M'Dougal's house during the yelling on Halloween. "One of them, however, had the curiosity to look through the key-hole, when he saw M'Dougal holding a bottle to the mouth of Campbell [Docherty], swearing at her for not drinking, and pouring the whiskey into her mouth. Then all was quiet for a little." This probably happened, for Burke reported that a bottle was forced into Docherty's mouth. But he told his jailers that "that he forced the mouth of a bottle into her throat, and poured down whiskey till she was choaked or nearly so." If M'Dougal was so close to participating in the murder herself, kneeling over the woman who was just about her age, both Log and Hare must have seen her as a capable partner for Burke.[37]

Lucky Log came into the courtroom with a sickly infant in her arms, and was drawn with the child for both of the main accounts of the trial, looking oddly fierce in a ruffled cap, and not very maternal. As she testified, she cast M'Dougal as the villain: M'Dougal came to her house, and told her "there was a *shot* [*sic*] in the house," and that Burke "had fetched her out of some shop." But then she described herself and M'Dougal as rather timid, alarmed women. She could not say what exactly had happened to Docherty, because "Mrs. M'Dougal and me flew out of the house, and did not stop in it." When Rae asked if she had cried out in this distress, she replied, "No, sir, I was quite powerless; and neither her nor me cried out." When asked by one of the judges, Lord Meadowbank, why she had not gone to Mrs. Connoway or Mrs. Law, she distanced herself even more. "I dreaded to go there, as I had left my husband three times. The thing had happened two or three times before, and it was not likely I should tell a thing to affect my husband." And in the other version of the trial transcript, which appears to be condensed and more impressionistic, the phrase "not likely I should tell a thing to affect my husband" was given as "it is not natural for a woman to go

The Criminal Household

and inform on her husband." The more teleological word natural was probably added later by someone. But it shows that what she said was easily transferred into the reigning dogma of the naturalness of femininity and masculinity by a court reporter—even given the overall impression Log created, which was neither good nor maternal.[38]

Log was described as a "she-devil" in the *Caledonian Mercury* on December 27, but that hardly rivaled the description of her that Cockburn used to discredit her testimony.

I never saw a face in which the lines of profligacy were more disgustingly marked. Even the miserable child in her arms,—in stead of casting one ray of maternal softness into her countenance,—seemed, at every attack [coughing], to fire her with intenser anger and impatience; till at last the infant was plainly used merely as an instrument for delaying or evading whatever question it was inconvenient for her to answer.[39]

No one was fooled by her, yet Cockburn, in his defense of M'Dougal, said "how can it be expected that the wife, whose interest, as well as her affections, are involved in his, is, merely for the sake of justice, to become the betrayer of her husband?" He then went on to cite "the natural tendency which [M'Dougal] had to hide the delinquency of her husband. Does it go far to implicate the wife in a crime committed by her husband, that she offers money for its concealment; or, on her knees, implores a probable discoverer to be silent?" Thus did Cockburn try to transform M'Dougal into the angel of the house, while the she-devil Log was damned for her lack of maternal sentiment. This tells us little about how either of the women acted, or what they believed. But it does instruct us on some of the shared assumptions about womanhood that linked them to the men of the court, the jury, and their neighbors. And Burke probably knew and shared some of those beliefs about what a natural woman should be.[40]

With Burke and Hare we are seeing at firsthand the disintegration of the working household, with husbands and wives working side by side. The transition to a new male partnership was never finished, but the outline is quite clear. Log was out; the young Brogan was probably in. So was Paterson, Knox's entrepreneurial doorkeeper, and the porter George M'Culloch. Hare's ranting about M'Dougal put her at risk. The demand for bodies, from a respectable client like Knox, was very real. And Burke and Hare imagined a business reaching far beyond Edinburgh, run by men, selling to men. While the women had figured prominently, Burke and Hare were determined to move on. In this specialization, they were becoming more like the almost entirely male gangs of resurrectionists, Maggie Robertson's gang, and the professional watch stealers, Barton and Kerr.

The Business Model

David Paterson, keeper of Knox's collection of anatomical specimens, lived a stone's throw away at No. 26 in the West Port. Paterson was no innocent; he was, rather, a man who knew how to take care of himself. He admitted in his pamphlet, *Letter to the Lord Advocate*, that he supplemented his salary by collecting fees from Knox's students, and he probably offered Docherty's body to another lecturer for £15. He had an eye for a quick penny. The venerable Sir Walter Scott, ill and overworked by 1829, noted in his journal that Paterson wrote to him, proposing that they collaborate on the story of Burke and Hare. Scott was appalled that Paterson, whom he called "the patron of atrocious murderers and kidnappers," would write "to any decent man." But Paterson had been in the employ of a decent man, who was also a daring man, for some time.[41]

Dr. Knox

Knox may well have provided both market and model for Burke, Hare, and Paterson. In his devotion to his science he was like the fictional Dr. Victor Frankenstein, a product of 1816, and another sign of the rise of anatomy. And he, like the fictional doctor whose tale also spawned countless horror stories, must have known about the bodies brought by Burke and Hare. The old evidence against him has become familiar. With the delivery of the prostitute Paterson, whose body was still warm, an assistant, Mr. William Fergusson, and "a tall lad" recognized her and asked Burke and Hare "where they had got the body." Burke was quick to reply that they had "purchased it from an

The Canongate, near Holyrood Palace and once home to nobles and clerics, offered cheap housing and cheap entertainment by 1828.

old woman at the back of the Canongate." Fergusson, perhaps, or another student remarked that "she was like a girl he had seen in the Canongate as one pea is like another." As a well-known and handsome local prostitute, Paterson was no stranger to the students, and there must have been some speculation on her death. Yet Knox allowed them to sketch her, and even called in a painter, so impressed was he with the perfection of her form. Burke reported that "she was three months in whiskey before she was dissected."

Given contemporary fears of sexual violation of bodies by anatomy students and anatomists, it was hardly wise of Knox to create this spectacle out of Mary Paterson's body, for it did attract attention. Another anatomist, Robert Liston—who, like most Edinburgh anatomists, had been insulted by Knox—came to see Paterson's body, thought she had been murdered, and was further disturbed by the thought that she should be dissected by her previous customers. He argued with Knox in front of the students, and hit him, sending him to the floor. Liston took the remains from the rooms, had them buried, and wrote to Thomas Wakley, an English surgeon and member of a Parliamentary Select Committee on anatomy, reporting the incident. Knox was not investigated, but he must have learned from the incident, for shortly after the delivery of Daft Jamie's corpse, again recognized by most of his assistants and students, Jamie's well-known head and deformed feet were removed and destroyed.[42]

Knox's boldness in buying as many bodies during the college terms as he could is all the more remarkable when we see that he bought the bodies of local people who had been seen alive and well a day or two before. Perhaps the nature of the trade hardened him, for if David Paterson's account is at all correct, bodies came in sacks, hampers, and large shipments from all over North Britain, and did not bear close investigation. And his assistants must have been eager to please their chief. Burke remembered both Paterson and an assistant, Mr. Jones, urging him to get more bodies; as he put it, "they were so successful, and always met with a ready market." Burke remembered the sale of the first body, the man who died of his own accord, saying that "getting that high price made them try the murdering of subjects." But we will never know what Knox knew, simply because the medical men who might have told us chose to keep their opinions, for the most part, to themselves.[43]

One colleague, Robert Christison, was inclined to leave a succinct statement for posterity. Christison had testified for the lord advocate at Burke and M'Dougal's trial, speaking as someone more qualified than the police surgeon, Alexander Black. Christison was professor of medical jurisprudence at Edinburgh University in 1828. He would later retire as Sir Robert and as the queen's physician in Scotland, among other honors. More importantly, he was skilled and principled. And he may well have regretted having to give the inconclusive testimony on Docherty's body that he gave—spelling out how the damage done to the body might have come from rough handling after death, as well as before. If so, he wrote Knox's epitaph in his memoirs: Knox "had rather willfully shut his eyes to incidents which ought to have excited the grave suspicions of a man of his intelligence."[44] If Knox blinded himself to suspicion, it must have been a very rigorous sort of blinding that he practiced on himself after Liston flattened him.

Knox was a man at the peak of his career, and that made him dangerous, and the perfect complement to Hare and Burke. He could pay them so well they were probably astonished, he could make them part of a system, and he could even promise them protection. David Paterson reported that Burke once complained to Knox, through him, that he could not bring in a subject, as the neighbors suspected and had a policeman watching their house. Knox "got rather enraged, he remarked that John [Burke] was a coward, and said, that he would write to the authorities and procure a protection for him to carry any package safe to his Lecture Room." This was no hollow promise, for the medical schools of London and Edinburgh were well protected by the state. On another occasion, Paterson reported hearing Burke and Hare arguing with Mr. Fergusson, a surgeon and assistant to Knox, about getting more than their usual eight pounds for a body. The system to which Knox had introduced them was not a polite one.[45]

The "ready market"

Knox provided the "ready market" that lifted the four killers and their hired help above the usual run of petty thieves in the Old Town. At eight or ten pounds per corpse, the price was better than what could be gotten for a watch, unless it was a very good example. Shirts, teaspoons, bed curtains, and boots, much the same things stolen from the dead Scrooge in Charles Dickens's *A Christmas Carol*, would have brought even less from the pawnshops and resetters of Edinburgh. Christian McKay in her small shop, or William Baslar who reset watches, would hardly have been as encouraging as Knox's students, eager for bodies. But quite aside from the price was the sense of connection to a legitimate enterprise—anatomy—that Knox offered. If the money fueled greed among the four killers, the access to Knox's rooms probably encouraged Hare and Burke to think in terms of enterprise and expansion. Remember that Barbara Kerr was proud of her skill in lifting watches: criminal enterprise was common enough. But murder for profit, enterprising, without threat, passion, or revenge was still frightening, and it is instructive to see that in a community where planned and opportunistic theft, most of it petty, was tolerable, murder was not.[46]

The households of common people were not sacred hearths in 1828; they were still synonymous with work. Burke cobbled in his, before he murdered. The ludicrous but violent attempt by Janet Morrison and her six friends to take the drover's watch reminds us of what the inside of a working home might have looked like. Log's Lodgings was not so different, even if the murderers were less inept. Both Morrison and Log knew how the goods reentered the economy. The shadow economy stretched from Knox's rooms, and those of the university lecturer Alexander Munro, to the small network of private resetters and dealers in secondhand goods. Margaret Veitch of Adam Street bought clothes from young thieves, and sold them to a public-house keeper in Leith, her sister in another county, and the Equitable Loan Company in Keir Street. Her husband bought watches, presumably also for reset. Similarly, Old Mrs. Burrows of Hastie's Close off the Cowgate bought clothes from a young man, and sold them to Mrs. Tonner in Libberton Wynd, off the Lawnmarket. Barbara Kerr sold a watch to William Baslar in the Grassmarket, and gave the watch's seal and chain to her sister to sell. Other thieves sold directly to shopkeepers: Salt's shop on the South Bridge; Christian McKay's shop on the ground floor in Blackfriar's Wynd; Sinclair's at the foot of Blair Street; Divine's in Big Hamilton's Close off the Grassmarket; and also Peter Divine, broker at #2 Leith Wynd.[47]

None of these rooms or small shops could have matched the experience of selling to Dr. Knox, and receiving ten pounds from assistants who had been instructed to deal with you whenever you might call. While the market in watches and perhaps in tea may have been inviting, the market in bodies was both lucrative and, for resurrection-

The Criminal Household 125

ists, almost legitimate. That last quality lifted body snatching above the common thievery of the Old Town, and put it in the company of other staples of the early modern economy: smuggling (especially whiskey), privateering, piracy, the slave trade, and the merchant outputting that undercut the textile guilds. The early modern European economy nurtured various forms of enterprise, some of which grew to be called capitalism, and some, theft.

CHAPTER 5

The Transformation of the Shadow Economy

"Hence old crimes have become new"[1]

While the story of Cain and Abel suggests that murder is as old as life, responses to the Edinburgh murders in 1828 suggest something else. As the anonymous editor of *The West Port Murders* put it,

the march of crime has far outstripped the "march of intellect," and attained a monstrous, a colossal development.... Hence old crimes are become new by being attended with unknown and unheard-of concomitants; and atrocities never dreamt of or imagined before have sprung up amongst us to cover us with confusion and dismay.[2]

The editor went on to discuss "the regular system of murder" that was "organised" by Burke, Hare, Log, and M'Dougal, finally calling it "wholly without example." One suspects that, coming on the first page of a hurriedly written popular tract, this was no great insight, but a reflection of one aspect of common discussion in early 1829. The murders forced many people to connect three disparate phenomena: the bleakest sort of bloody crime, the study of anatomy in the tradition of Enlightenment empiricism, and the invisible hand of Adam Smith's marketplace, the law of supply and demand.[3]

The Not-So-Invisible Hand

To see the invisible hand suddenly figured as the hands of William Burke or William Hare was enough to strike fear into the minds of people who saw themselves reduced to the status of objects in a market, with a price on their heads. Rumors had surrounded the teaching of anatomy for a hundred years at least, but fear of the resurrectionist's spade was a far cry from outright murder. And so the working poor and the respectable artisans of Edinburgh had responded to the news of Burke, Hare, Log, M'Dougal, and Knox with anger and fear, rooted in their knowledge of just whose bodies were turning up on anatomists' tables: beggars, peddlers, prostitutes, pensioned soldiers, washerwomen, laborers. Nor could they be fooled into thinking those bodies were the result of bad character on the part of the murderers, when it was apparent that the renowned Dr. Knox's money and the Edinburgh medical establishment underpinned the system. What the Edinburgh and, for that matter, London anatomists had done was to create a market for fresh human bodies, thereby commodifying the body in a way that horribly outreached the excesses that Marx would later catalog for the sale of the body's labor power. Knox, Burke, and Hare, and for that matter M'Dougal and Log, laid bare an embarrassing facet, not of the markets but of the new, and increasingly capitalist, society. This had become powerful enough in Scotland by 1750 to begin to dissolve the social ties and institutions—religious, communal, political—which might have impeded this new, exceptionally pragmatic business in the West Port.[4]

But the developing market in bodies, which appeared to the well-known radical publisher Richard Cobbett as an unwelcome entrepreneurial response to demand, was also interpreted as the result of anachronistic regulation by state and church, which kept the legal supply of bodies ruinously short. Progressive middle-class men preferred to see the murders as the predictable outgrowth of unwieldy early modern regulation, rather than see an entrepreneur at work in the underworld, which was extraordinarily free by its very nature.

They looked to reformed laws and attitudes to free individuals from both legal and traditional attachments to the rituals of death.[5]

But no such rational, reformed, or Benthamite legal solution emerged immediately. Lord Warburton's Anatomy Act of 1832 still preyed on the poor for something as yet distasteful to middle-class men—leaving their bodies to science would come later—and unthinkable for middle-class women. But Warburton's Act was an effective solution that ended the murders and the grave-robbing by offering the bodies of paupers to science. In the same year Jeremy Bentham, the purposeful Utilitarian, left his body for dissection, after which it was reconstructed from his skeleton by workers from Madame Tussaud's waxworks, and left in permanent public view in London. Bentham, attempting to be useful and unsentimental, erred. His bizarre display, which ultimately more closely resembled the mummification of a pharaoh than a selfless act in the name of science, probably repelled more than it attracted to his cause.[6]

Burke's Skeleton

Burke was dissected, then skinned, and then probably boiled to remove the flesh from the bone. Presumably something similar happened to Bentham, although with far more discretion, and Bentham was subsequently padded out with wax, dressed, and displayed to the public, seated at his desk, in a cabinet in the University of London. Burke's bare bones still hang for all to see in Edinburgh.[7] On those bones, it is worth recalling the words of David Boyle, the lord justice clerk who, in sentencing Burke, said

> In regard to your case, the only doubt that has come across my mind, is, whether... your body should not be exhibited in chains, in order to deter others from the like crimes in time coming. But, taking into consideration that the public eye would be offended with so dismal an exhibition, I am disposed to agree that your sentence shall be put in execution in the usual way, but accompanied with the statutory attendant of the punishment of the crime of murder, viz.—that your body should be publicly dissected and anatomized. And I trust, that if it is ever customary to preserve skeletons, your's [sic] will be preserved, in order that posterity may keep in remembrance your atrocious crimes.[8]

Boyle was willing to recognize that a body hung in chains and rotting in public was no longer acceptable, and he was willing to suggest a more sanitary equivalent. That Burke did not hang in chains tells us that Edinburgh was not quite an early modern city any more. But the skeleton in the museum is a two-faced totem, suggesting the sanitary empiricism of Enlightenment science, while recalling the resplendent, sensory, hideous punishments of an earlier world. That Boyle could hesitate between the two means that the early modern city had not been left far behind in December of 1828.[9]

The System

Lord Meadowbank, Alexander Maconochie, another of the judges in Burke and M'Dougal's trial, called the murders "that most sanguinary and atrocious system," "a system of barbarous and savage iniquity," and a "regularly organized and established system of cold and premeditated murder," and spoke of "a number of individuals, both male and female, leagued and combined together." He chose to associate the murders with an earlier period, or perhaps an alien geography, "barbarous and savage." The *Caledonian Mercury*, three days after the trial, told its readers that "murder had been reduced to a system." The editor of *The West Port Murders* repeatedly referred to the murders as a "system of crimes," and as "systematic" on many pages, and finally, as "the work of murder as a trade." It is no surprise that Burke himself ended up, whether he knew it or not, echoing these words in his last confession, where he referred to "this murdering system."[10]

This obsession with systematic crime, so systematic it could be referred to as a trade, tells us as much about how people thought of older criminals: a daring thief, a public performance, a recognizable person. And it betrays a certain longing for the thoroughly romanticized characters of the half-true, half-false pamphlets, ballads, rumors, and confessions by which many people knew about crime before the coming of statistics and commissions in the nineteenth century. Recall what John Wilson, writing as his character Christopher North in *Blackwood's Edinburgh Magazine* in 1829, had to say about the West Port murders:

That the [*sic*; they] were too monotonous too [*sic*] impress the imagination. First ae drunk auld wife, then anither drunk auld wife—and then a third drunk auld wife—and then a drunk auld or sick man or twa. The confession got unco monotonous—the Lights and Shadows o' Scottish Death waut relief—though, to be sure, poor Peggy Paterson, that Unfortunate, broke in a little on the uniformity[11]

Wilson was quick to understand that these murders had nothing daring, heroic, or even very violent about them. Mechanical, drunken, and barely human, the episodes became tawdry and uniform examples of what another Scot, Thomas Carlyle, would call the cash nexus, meaning the connection of human beings by no more than the exchange of money due. As with Burke's bones, the system had stripped away what was human and curious about the murderers and the victims. In that light, it is no longer macabre that some of Burke's clearest recollections of victims were of the few pennies they had clutched in a death grip as they died.[12]

This fear and recognition of criminal systems had been described before 1828. In 1751 Henry Fielding, the famed Bow Street magistrate in London, had written about "a great Gang of Rogues" who had "reduced Theft and Robbery into a regular System" in London. It seems likely that for several decades before 1828 reporters had been differentiating between modern crime and an earlier breed of pistol-waving highwaymen and dangerous women. But they were also acknowledging the implications of a system—a nice fit with the existing economy, and the existence of an impersonal criminal, a stranger who acknowledged no ties to the community. In 1828, the dissolution of village and urban neighborhood ties was well underway, driven by migration in and out of Scotland and population growth, and a shifting economy pulling people toward a central industrial belt that ran from Glasgow to Edinburgh. Strangers were not in short supply.[13]

Facing Burke

Hanging up Burke's bones may well have been an attempt to regain feelings appropriate to old crime: horror, pity, anger, and resolution. If we look at Burke's skeleton in the harsh light of this threatening anonymity, we can better understand the almost obscene intimacy of the repeated public viewing of him, and the great rush to reclaim both the prostitute Paterson and Daft Jamie as mourned citizens of the city. The crowds who came to see all four of the murderers, to speak to them and express their anger, and to look at Burke after death, were very probably trying to reestablish some sort of face-to-face relationship with them, to regain control, as villagers had once resorted to shaming their neighbors before going to court.[14]

But Burke, M'Dougal, Hare, and Log were not inclined to express remorse or even hint at guilt in any way that was not, most probably, calculated and deceitful. Burke did the best job of ingratiating himself with his keepers and his society while he sat in jail awaiting hanging, but we cannot know whether this was a genuine relief to him, or merely a defensive habit. The others, especially Hare, seemed to be utterly unacquainted with remorse. Surely all past crime, stretching back for centuries, had also implied a certain suspension of social relations, an impersonalism between the thief or murderer and the victim. But it is possible to argue that in the past, that suspension had been temporary, and was still open to negotiation—through a fight, a handshake, some shaming ritual, a fine from the kirk, or for witches, through propitiation and a lifting of the curse. But in 1828 the suspension of social relations, that temporary disregard for sympathy and community, was beginning to harden into permanent character for Burke, Hare, Log, and M'Dougal, no doubt as an unpleasant mutation of systematic individualism. Eighteenth-century talk of individual rights, now underpinned by the individual wage and the rented room, also entailed loneliness and distance. This distance, which allowed Burke to kill, may explain why observers at Burke's hanging found the crowd hostile, since crowds previously had been, typically, quite sympathetic to criminals facing the gallows. On January 28 there was no sympathy for Burke, and he returned the fierce looks, as if he and the crowd recognized that a great distance separated him from them, and that it was unbridgeable.[15]

Individuals Both Male and Female

The two women were much like Burke and Hare, hard and fierce, yet it was still possible, despite the crowd's hatred, to manipulate each woman's image as Woman—maternal, subordinate, connected to husband or child—in the courtroom. The crowds in various confrontations after the trial may have howled for their blood, but the men in the courtroom still responded to their shreds of womanhood. Two men in their place might have hanged, or, given the legal problem of direct evidence in the case, the youngest or least criminal might have turned king's evidence and hanged the other three. But Log and M'Dougal were never in much danger, because M'Dougal and Log were still women more than individuals, still the creatures of their husbands in the eyes of the lawyers and the jury. And so they passed beyond the reach of the gallows, becoming hardened, homeless, and alone even as both women's defenders had, in court, played on precisely those aspects of womanhood that made each one seem tied to others, Log to her infant, and M'Dougal to her husband. Log and M'Dougal were, by December of 1828, well-hardened killers, and their marriages, which were the basis of the gang, had brought both women into intimate relations with men even more vicious than themselves. Their husbands had, we must remember, talked of turning their wives into merchandise, and any reference by the lawyers to either woman's marriage as respectable or normal was a terrible joke.

Nonetheless, lawyers and jurors clung to whatever vestiges of Log or M'Dougal as a good wife and mother they could. Not only were these popular views of womanhood in 1828, profoundly rooted in the anatomists' uncovering of the workings of maternity; they allowed some of the men closest to the case to inject a few presumptions of humane normalcy into the "atrocious system." The cultural presumption that women were first and foremost mothers was well fixed by 1828. In 1809, the Scots statute making infanticide a capital crime had been struck down, because prosecutors were increasingly unwilling to bring indictments for infanticide, jurors unwilling to convict when indictments were made, and few people willing to believe that a woman could do such a thing. From there, it is a short step to seeing women—Woman—as unable to kill at all, and innately solicitous not only of her child's needs, but also of her husband's.[16]

The Price History of the Body

If the gentlemen of the court clung to notions of womanhood to alleviate their horror at the coldness of that particular criminal endeavor, or system, we can understand their horror much better by constructing a price history of the dead body as merchandise. The four murderers stumbled into a lucrative trade in a period of recurrent shortages that drove up the prices that anatomists would pay. In Edinburgh between 1822 and 1826, A. J. Lizars published his *System of Anatomical Plates of the Human Body* to aid students who had no access to bodies, and he noted that prices for bodies had risen to "the enormous sum of twenty guineas." Lizars himself intended to make what he could from the shortage, which was sometimes supplied by bodies shipped from London or Ireland, apparently the result of both the growing interest in anatomy and the increasing watchfulness of relatives and officials in the area surrounding Edinburgh. Citizens, cognizant both of the city's reputation as a European center of medical study, and of the difficulty of keeping a relative safely buried, hired guards and bought patented devices to discourage grave robbers. The dead were fenced in like zoo animals, if the family had money. If not, villagers might take turns standing guard.[17]

With this shortage as background, we can begin to understand the magnitude of the market into which Hare, Burke, M'Dougal, and Log had stumbled. The study of anatomy was passing through a crisis; even the Royal College of Surgeons at Edinburgh complained about the resurrectionists, and the astute way in which they profited from various shortages. As Jeremy Bentham's friend T. Southwood Smith put it in 1824, "the medical school at Edinburgh, in fact, is now subsisting entirely on its past reputation; in the course of a few years it will be entirely at an end, unless the system [resurrection] be changed." And the crisis was certainly broadly British, for London anatomists also struggled with their resurrectionists, with both sides

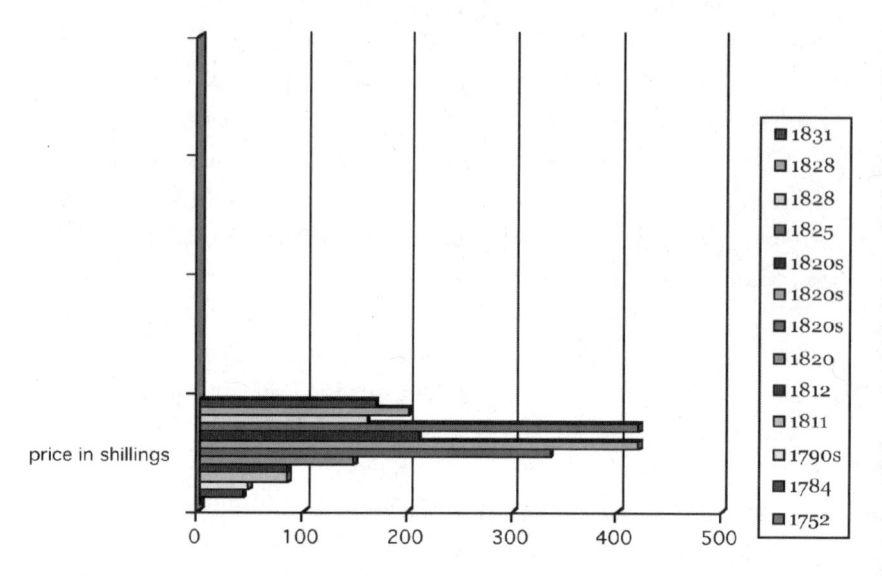

Recorded Prices Paid for Bodies between 1752 and 1831

price in shillings

■	1831
□	1828
□	1828
■	1825
■	1820s
□	1820s
■	1820s
□	1820
■	1812
□	1811
□	1790s
■	1784
■	1752

Figure 1. Chart shows prices, drawn from memoirs and Parliamentary Committee testimony, increasing in the 1820s from much lower rates in the late eighteenth century.[18]

attempting combinations to fix prices. The growth of schools had far outrun the usual supply of bodies, and Old Donald died at a fortuitous moment in the price history of the body.[19]

One might suggest, rather sardonically, that the real crisis facing anatomists, especially those who lectured for a living, was not the supply of bodies, but their cost, which probably reached twenty guineas (a guinea was twenty-one shillings) at times during the 1820s. When prices went that high, lecturers might face ruin, and body snatchers might well overstep the bounds in which they had been operating. The best argument for this crisis comes not only from the sketchy records of prices that remain, but simply from the government's intervention in 1832, in the face of murders in Edinburgh in 1828, and London in 1831. From this perspective, we can see that Log, Hare, Burke, and M'Dougal were not peculiar figures, making a few pounds for themselves at the edge of an obscure and minor twist in the developing urban economies of university towns. They were thriving in the midst of a bizarre but also ordinary, and quite viciously free—and illicit—working out of supply and demand, resulting from customary habits of burial and religious beliefs, rather than from positive legal prohibitions against the sale or dissection of bodies. The body was problematic at law for it belonged to no one, presumably because no one in the past had had any interest in claiming property in such a thing.[20]

At the heart of the problem lay the local and national government officers who were generally in sympathy with the anatomists. Their sympathy no doubt stemmed from the history of body snatching, for it had been done first by medical students and doctors, with doctors starting to pay others to do the digging somewhere around 1800. After the discovery of paid labor—part and parcel of capitalism—the uneasy system of illicit digging and carting grew, subject to minor harassment and local riot, but generally condoned by those above.[21]

Burke and Hare as Entrepreneurs

This market, which affected Knox, was the context in which Burke and Hare planned to expand their business. As Burke put it in his *Courant* confession, "Hare and him had a plan made up, that Burke and a man were to go to Glasgow or Ireland, and try the same there, and to forward them to Hare." The editor of *The West Port Murders* also reported, presumably from a prison conversation, that Burke had said

that Hare and he intended taking a journey in the way of their business next spring, they were to proceed westward from Edinburgh, and after visiting the intermediate places, travel on to Glasgow, where they expected to find a rich harvest. They were to preceed thence to Belfast, by way of Greenock, which was also to be attempted on the route, and after doing what they could in the north of Ireland, to journey on to Dublin.

This extraordinary plan to cull the poor of Scotland and Ireland, adding a partner and home office, suggests that they knew a good deal about the market in bodies, and knew that Ireland was already supplying the Scottish market. Information about the Irish imports was being given to the Parliamentary Select Committee meeting in the same year, 1828. And Knox's doorman Paterson wrote about Edinburgh anatomists divvying up a shipment of Irish bodies in his slightly scandalous pamphlet published in 1829. What Burke and Hare knew about the market very probably came from Paterson, and he may have been one intended new partner, bringing with him expertise in the distribution of bodies in Edinburgh, as well as in importing them.[22]

What the editor of *The West Port Murders* said about their work is instructive, showing us a context that came to mind in 1829. They were, he said, "engaged in a species of profession which had indeed, like illicit distillation, or any contraband traffic, to be concealed from the authorities, but which, except for this annoying accompaniment, was pursued with as little compunction as any other profession would have been." It was work; it was systematic. So the anonymous editor situated it among a host of entrepreneurial crimes that had both plagued and shaped the early modern economy: shipwrecking, privateering and prize taking, poaching, smuggling, illicit distillation, and then body snatching, all marking contests to determine who could establish various rights to property.

Crime, Law, and the Shadow Economy

Thieves steal goods for their exchange value; social-political criminals poach, and join grain riots, for the use value of the object, like the loaf of bread stolen by Jean Valjean in *Les Miserables.* But most crime has not been social crime; and to study ordinary theft is chiefly to study who took what from whom, and to connect criminals to commodities in a changing economy. For the "habite and repute" thief in Edinburgh in 1828, theft was an entrepreneurial activity possible for those without capital, appealing to those who would be entrepreneurs. Hare kept pigs, and he and Log had a servant girl who fed them. As soon as her employers were arrested, she sold the pigs and disappeared, suggesting a pervasive awareness of value and opportunity that had little to do with simple destitution. But the categories used in courts disguise and homogenize the crimes and the goods, conflating Lucky Log with Betty McKinnon.[23]

Schumpeter's Entrepreneur

Joseph Schumpeter's fear of a "stationary economy" in *Capitalism, Socialism and Democracy* led him to place his faith in the entrepreneur, and his entrepreneur sounds just like Log, Burke, Hare, or Barbara Kerr. He wrote that "the function of entrepreneurs is to reform or revolutionize the pattern of production...by opening up a new source of supply of materials." And he added that "to undertake such new things is difficult and constitutes a distinct economic function." Schumpeter's focus on the entrepreneur as a role specific to capitalism gives us a category for our best thieves and resetters that is absent from Marx's work, not to mention from that of British Marxist historians writing about crime. And we can use Schumpeter's entrepreneurial function—"it consists in getting things done"—to draw the shadow economy and the larger economy together, to see economic life as a whole and to better judge the nature of the economic rationalism on which capitalism and its entrepreneurs fed.[24]

The Shadow Economy before 1828

The shadow economy and legitimate economic activity have overlapped for centuries. As the goods in circulation multiplied and were stored outside households in warehouses and at wharves, there was simply more to steal. In the 1820s, the Scottish merchant Patrick Colquhoun, lately moved to London, complained that thieves preyed on ships docked in London, and wrote extensively on the need for harbor police.[25] But complaints about harbor thieves were only one facet of a complex world. As an Atlantic and a world economy grew, the opportunities for theft, as well as the perceived necessity of fraud, either with customs officials, suppliers, or customers, also grew. Smuggling, false coining, piracy, slaving, prize taking, and shipwrecking had developed nicely in an early modern economy with a good many rough edges, where profits could be handsome, if not moral.

For Scotland in particular, smuggling developed under guise of patriotism after the Union with England in 1707. But illegal trade with the Americas and the West Indies, and a penchant for piracy against Hanse merchants had come even earlier.[26]

Commerce from the late Middle Ages through the nineteenth century was sometimes a battlefield where deceit and bribery figured boldly. Trade was both dogged by and carried forward by lawlessness. During the reign of Henry VI, in the fifteenth century, "the abbot of St Augustines's, Canterbury, aided by 'other evildoers,' boarded a French vessel off the Isle of Thanet, and appropriated ship and cargo."[27] This is a particularly striking example because the church was busy on the Continent with pressing those engaged in trade or worse, usury, to beware of sinning. The life of a Renaissance merchant adventurer could be fraught with sinfulness in the eyes of the church. Public debates on the evils of usury were held in the early 1500s, and it seems that by that time the need to bypass religious prohibitions had become pressing. And the dilemmas of usury would pale beside those of the trans-Atlantic slave trade. By the later 1500s, Elizabeth I was relying on income from the exploits of her slaver, John Hawkins, and her pirate, Francis Drake.[28]

To be brief, the growing productive capacities, themselves questionable at times, and needs of Europe filled markets and harbors, buoyed exploration, invited theft and fraud, and also invited innovation. Trade and manufacture were dogged by lawlessness at the same time that they were carried forward by men and women who broke with the law, custom, and morality of their contemporaries. If we consider our West Port felons in light of the three centuries before 1828, they fit into a story of crime that has shared a very blurry border with economic development. At times there must have been an uncomfortably thin line between those betrayals of old guild, estate, and corporate customs that would now be called the beginnings of capitalism, and crime.[29]

Burke, M'Dougal, Log, and Hare were the prodigies of the West Port in 1828; but their colleagues—the women who stole hams, pocket watches, wet laundry, blankets, Bibles, and the clothing off toddlers' backs—differed from them only in being less bold, less quick, less amoral, and less well-paid for their exploits. What was similar in the work of Maggie Robertson, a member of the ham-and-raisin-stealing gang, and Burke, Log, M'Dougal, and Hare? The bodies turned up in the rooms of an excellent and well-attended lecturer, the ham in a small grocery shop. Both dovetailed nicely with the existing economy, and there was a system in play far beyond necessity or depravity. These thieves and murderers were not attacking "the system," but were very much its creatures.

Watches, Time, and Work Discipline

If the bodies were extraordinary commodities in a furtive market, the hams and raisins were surely more ordinary. So were the linens, blankets, shirts, babies' shifts, trousers, and coats that were pawned or sold at Salt's, Divine's, Tonner's, the Equitable Loan Company, Sinclair's, and a public house in Leith Street. And with sufficient time, it would be possible to write the history of these simple things and the secondhand markets that offered cheap goods and quick loans to the respectable working classes and the anxious lower middle class. But the watch stolen by Barbara Kerr and her friends, and the watches almost stolen by Hannah Barton, and by Janet Morrison and her friends do have a history. The need for watches, like the need for uniform time, permeated the world with the industrial revolution. Not only the sale of labor, but the railroad timetable and the telegraph necessitated an exact reckoning of minutes and hours. But watches are small and finicky, and production was hard to mechanize. A good solid British watch with a gold case was worth about as much as a dead body in Knox's dissecting room, or around seven pounds for the gold alone. But by 1817, after the Napoleonic Wars were over, the British market was being flooded with cheap watches smuggled in from France and Switzerland. By the later nineteenth century, the competition would come from the United States, where mass production of decent watches at low prices flourished. Significantly, the first signs of mass production came in the 1820s.[30]

In other words, watches were still in fairly short supply in 1828, and British manufacture could not keep up with demand, especially for cheaper watches. Watches were subject not only to smuggling and theft, but to scams of various sorts, most commonly with watches of low quality or poor design being passed off as better pieces. Hannah Barton had made a living for a few years by stealing watches. And it was probably no surprise to the Edinburgh police that she was trolling the North Bridge for men waiting for coaches, since these men would have been at least somewhat likely to have watches, and money for the fare. And after M'Dougal was released from prison, and sent word to Burke that she needed money, he sent what money he had, and his "common old watch." Barbara Kerr lifted papers, notes, change, a watch, a silk handkerchief, and glasses from her gentleman. She immediately disposed of the watch by selling it to William Baslar in a Grassmarket bar, while her sister sold the chain and seal at Divine's. While separating the watch from its trimmings may have been a means of making it less identifiable, it also suggests that there were special networks for the reset of watches. For example, Margaret Veitch bought and sold stolen clothes, while her husband Thomas Low bought watches. There were systems at work among thieves, retailers, and consumers of all sorts, not just Burke, Hare, Paterson, and Knox.[31]

But it is well worth bearing in mind that while the Edinburgh police worked at catching the petty thieves as best they could, neither Dr. Knox nor Lord Advocate Rae had any interest in laying bare the scandal of the West Port. That was for Mrs. Gray to do, a poor woman about whom we know absolutely nothing, other than that she lodged with the murderers, and when offered money by M'Dougal, said "God forbid that my husband should be worth that for dead bodies." If the Grays were alarmed, the common people of Edinburgh were appalled, and information came to them, not from the lawyers or the indictments, but from William Burke, and the writers who dogged him and his old neighbors in the West Port for information. The ordinary and sometimes quite poor people who lived in the Grassmarket, the West Port, along the Cowgate and the old closes were possibly irritated, but not alarmed by the usual thieves like Barbara Kerr, Hannah Barton, or Davie Stark. When Elizabeth McKinnon stole shirts from Janet Lawson, Lawson told the "watch" and then caught up with her shirts and McKinnon at a pawnbroker's shop. But Burke was jeered on the gallows, and his three colleagues driven out of town by furious crowds not only because they were dangerous. They represented a protected system of murder and theft that had long abused the bodies of the poor and even the middling, and could not be matched in shamefulness by the thefts of blankets and beer, shirts and watches. After all, old blankets were bought by the poor, and perhaps by the lower middle classes; tea by many more people; and bodies by a very few, who would pay almost any price. The thousands of people who gathered to watch Burke hang knew the difference between petty theft, even of new goods, and an extension of economic law into a new aspect of human life. Perhaps a very few of the men who sat in judgment knew that a society may get the kind of crime it deserves, but it certainly gets the kind of crime it requires.[32]

Notes

Prologue

1. See NAS (National Archives of Scotland, previously Scottish Record Office) AD 14/28/61; these records (AD series) are precognitions, or depositions, taken by the Lord Advocate's Department in the course of investigating crimes, prior to indictment. All other archival references are to the NAS collections, and NAS will be omitted from following references.

2. Reset, as a crime, was the retailing of goods known to be stolen. Thieves seem to have sold to resetters, who then sold to final consumers or accepted retailers, and reset was a distinct specialty among criminals.

Introduction

1. Sir Walter Scott, *The Journal of Sir Walter Scott* (New York: Harper & Brothers, 1891), p. 543; see also Richard H. Hutton, *The Life of Sir Walter Scott Abridged from Lockhart's Life of Scott* (Philadelphia: John D. Morris & Company, n.d.), pp. 259–61. On George's procession, see John Prebble, *The King's Jaunt* (London: Collins, 1988). Scott was a monarchist, but he was a Hanoverian, not a Jacobite, and that difference was enormous, for it meant that Scott acknowledged the coming of a modern world. He merely wanted it to come on his terms, and with a place for the old hierarchy on the land, not on the terms of the urban middle classes.

2. See Eric J. Hobsbawm, *The Age of Revolution* (New York: New American Library, 1962); Harold Perkin, *The Origins of Modern English Society* (London: Routledge & Kegan Paul, 1969), p. 3; Karl Polanyi, *The Great Transformation: The Political and Economic Origins of Our Time* (New York: Rinehart & Company, 1944); and Rondo Cameron, *A Concise Economic History of the World* (New York: Oxford University Press, 1993).

3. Bruce Lenman, *An Economic History of Modern Scotland* (Hamden, Conn.: Archon Books, 1977), pp. 148–50; T. M. Devine, *The Scottish Nation* (New York: Viking, 1999), pp. 113, 141. On canal preservation and design, see Anthony Burton and Derek Pratt, *The Anatomy of Canals: The Early Years* (Stroud, Gloucestershire: Tempus Publishing, 2001); and Guthrie Hutton, *Scotland's Millennium Canals: The Survival and Revival of the Forth & Clyde and Union Canals* (Catrine, Ayrshire: Stenlake Publishing, 2002). The canals have become popular recreation

Notes to Introduction 143

sites recently across Europe; see Hamish Brown, *Exploring the Edinburgh to Glasgow Canals* (Edinburgh: The Stationery Office, 1997); Jean Stone, *Voices from the Waterways* (Gloucestershire: Sutton Publishing, 1997).

4. For a quick and easy introduction to this period, see Arthur Herman, *How the Scots Invented the Modern World* (New York: Crown Publishers, 2001). For debate over multiple Enlightenments, see Charles R. Sullivan, "Enacting the Scottish Enlightenment: Tobias Smollett's Expedition of Humphrey Clinker," *Journal of The Historical Society* 4:4 (2004): 415–46; and Gertrude Himmelfarb, *The Roads to Modernity: The British, French, and American Enlightenments* (New York: Knopf, 2004).

5. On that imperial world, the place to start is with P. J. Marshall, *The Oxford History of the British Empire*, vol. 2, *The Eighteenth Century* (Oxford: Oxford University Press, 1998); especially useful are the articles by P. J. Marshall, Bruce Lenman, and Jack P. Greene. For a more specific look at Scots in the Empire, see T. M. Devine, *The Tobacco Lords* (Edinburgh: Edinburgh University Press, 1975). On slavery and abolition, see C. Duncan Rice, *The Scots Abolitionists, 1833–1861* (Baton Rouge and London: Louisiana State University Press, 1981), and James Walvin, *England, Slaves and Freedom, 1776–1838* (Jackson and London: University Press of Mississippi, 1986). For India, 1766 is the year of Robert Clive's typically corrupt attempt at housecleaning among East India Company employees; while accusing other nabobs of accepting bribes, he collected more from Indian princes than any of his colleagues had dared to grab. He thereby touched off a split in the company, between the (Scottish) Johnstone party and his own. His anomalous position in Indian affairs probably contributed to his suicide not so many years later. See Lucy Stuart Sutherland, *The East India Company in Eighteenth-Century Politics* (Oxford: Clarendon Press, 1952); Abdul Majed Khan, *The Transition in Bengal, 1756–1775* (Cambridge: Cambridge University Press, 1969); on the Johnstones, especially John, see Bruce Lenman and Philip Lawson, "Robert Clive, the 'Black Jaghir,' and British Politics," *Historical Journal* 26 (December 1983): 801–29; and Arthur C. Murray, *The Five Sons of Bare Betty* (London: John Murray, 1936). Scots played a large role in the EIC's administration of Bengal, and they figure prominently in most work on the British in Bengal.

6. One authority on provision for the poor in Scotland is Rosalind Mitchison; see "The Poor Law," in T. M. Devine and Rosalind Mitchison, eds., *People and Society in Scotland*, vol. 1 (Edinburgh: John Donald Publishers, 1988), pp. 252–88; and T. C. Smout, ed., *The Search for Wealth and Stability: Essays in Economic and Social History Presented to M. W. Flinn* (London: Macmillan, 1979), containing essays by both Smout and Mitchison on attitudes governing the administration of aid to the poor. See also R. A. Cage, *The Scottish Poor Law, 1745–1845* (Edinburgh: Scottish Academic Press, 1981); and Christopher Smout, "The Culture of Migration: Scots as Europeans 1500–1800," *History Workshop Journal* 40 (Autumn 1995): 108–17. Mobility and migration were not unique to the nineteenth century, but population growth and the distances traveled had been increasing since perhaps the mid-eighteenth century, producing a Scots diaspora reaching across the Atlantic, and into India. More briefly, see Bruce Lenman, *Integration, Enlightenment, and Industrialization: Scotland, 1746–1832* (London: Edward Arnold, 1981), especially chapters 8 and 9, covering the years after 1815; and on the Irish, see Owen Dudley Edwards, *Burke & Hare* (Edinburgh: Polygon Books, 1984); and T. M. Devine, "Unrest and Stability in Rural Ireland and Scotland, 1760–1840,"

in Rosalind Mitchison and Peter Roebuck, eds., *Economy and Society in Scotland and Ireland 1500–1939* (Edinburgh: John Donald Publishers, 1988), pp. 126–39.

7. On the Union, see T. I. Rae, ed., *The Union of 1707: Its Impact on Scotland* (London: Blackie & Son, 1974); and W. C. Mackenzie, *Andrew Fletcher of Saltoun* (Edinburgh: Porpoise Press, 1935).

8. On Dundas, and the role of lawyers in post-Union Scotland, see Deborah A. Symonds, *Weep Not for Me: Women, Ballads, and Infanticide in Early Modern Scotland* (University Park: Pennsylvania State University Press, 1997), especially the notes to chapters 5 and 6 on law.

9. E. P. Thompson, *Whigs and Hunters: The Origin of the Black Act* (New York: Random House, 1975); Natalie Zemon Davis, *The Return of Martin Guerre* (Cambridge, Mass.: Harvard University Press, 1983); Christina Larner, *Enemies of God: The Witch-Hunt in Scotland* (Baltimore: Johns Hopkins University Press, 1981).

10. For G. R. Elton's still useful essay, "Crime and the Historian," see J. S. Cockburn, ed., *Crime in England, 1550–1800* (Princeton, N.J.: Princeton University Press, 1977), pp. 1–14; for the comments on it, see J. A. Sharpe, *Crime in Early Modern England, 1550–1750* (London and New York: Longman, 1984), p. 4–5.

11. The various examples of social criminals, based on my own definition of what the term ought to encompass, are drawn from Kenneth Logue, *Popular Disturbances in Scotland, 1780–1815* (Edinburgh: John Donald Publishers, 1979); Thompson, *Whigs and Hunters*; and Larner, *Enemies of God*; and Christopher A. Whatley, "The Union of 1707, Integration and the Scottish Burghs: The Case of the 1720 Food Riots," *Scottish Historical Review* 2:206 (October 1999): 192–218. The original use of the term seems to date to 1972. See E. J. Hobsbawm, "Distinctions between the Socio-Political and Other Forms of Crime," *Bulletin—Society for the Study of Labour History* 25 (Autumn 1972): 5–9; E. P. Thompson, "Eighteenth-Century Crime, Popular Movements and Social Control," *Bulletin—Society for the Study of Labour History* 25 (Autumn 1972): 9–11; Terry L. Chapman, "Crime in Eighteenth-Century England: E. P. Thompson and the Conflict Theory of Crime," *Criminal Justice History* 1 (1980): 139–55; David F. Greenberg, "Crime," in Thomas B. Bottomore, ed., *A Dictionary of Marxist Thought* (Oxford: Basil Blackwell, 1983), pp. 100–102. See especially Willem A. Bonger, *Criminality and Economic Conditions*, trans. Henry P. Horton (Boston, Mass.: Little, Brown & Co., 1916), as seminal, perhaps, for these Marxists; and John H. Langbein, "Albion's Fatal Flaws," *Past and Present* 98 (1983): 96–120, the most astute critic of this school; see also, somewhat more reflectively, if not on quite the same topic, Elizabeth Fox-Genovese, "The Many Faces of Moral Economy: A Contribution to a Debate," *Past and Present* 58 (1973): 161–68.

12. See Elton's still useful essay, "Crime and the Historian."

13. V. A. C. Gattrell, Bruce Lenman, and Geoffrey Parker, introduction to their edited volume, *Crime and the Law: The Social History of Crime in Western Europe since 1500* (London: Europa Publications, 1980), pp. 1–10, see especially p. 9.

14. For the reference to Engels, I am indebted to David Philips, *Crime and Authority in Victorian England: The Black Country, 1835–1860* (Totowa, N.J.: Rowman and Littlefield, 1977), p. 13; or see, directly, Friedrich Engels, *The Condition of the Working Class in England*, trans. and ed. by W. O. Henderson and W. H. Chaloner (Oxford: Basil Blackwell, 1958), p. 145.

Notes to Introduction

15. The classic recent books to define social crime are, in chronological order, Thompson, *Whigs and Hunters*; Douglas Hay et al., eds., *Albion's Fatal Tree: Crime and Society in Eighteenth-Century England* (Harmondsworth: Penguin, 1977); and John Brewer and John Styles, eds., *An Ungovernable People: The English and Their Law in the Seventeenth and Eighteenth Centuries* (New Brunswick, N.J.: Rutgers University Press, 1980); especially recommended in the latter is pp. 11–20, the introduction. It is also worth looking at Hobsbawm, "Distinctions between the Socio-Political," pp. 5–7; Thompson, "Eighteenth-Century Crime," pp. 9–11; and Chapman, "Crime in Eighteenth-Century England," pp. 139–55. Also see Langbein, "Albion's Fatal Flaws," for a critique of these various defenses of criminals.

16. For a succinct statement on Marx, see Allen W. Wood, "The Marxian Critique of Justice," *Philosophy & Public Affairs* 1 (Spring 1972): 244–82. On Sir George Mackenzie, the "Bluidy Mackenzie" to his enemies, see George W. T. Omond, *The Lord Advocates of Scotland from the Close of the Fifteenth Century to the Passing of the Reform Bill* (Edinburgh: David Douglas, 1883), pp. 200–225.

17. In the wake of social crime, it has become possible to talk about all criminals as if they were victims of a repressive state—one need only consider the tremendously influential work of Michel Foucault, in a book such as *Discipline and Punish: The Birth of the Prison* (New York: Vintage, 1979); or Jacques Donzelot, in *The Policing of Families* (New York: Pantheon, 1979), to see how the old Marxist concept of bourgeois self-interest, or the older notion of unjust statutes has been stretched to implicate not only a state's authority to define and punish crime, but authority itself, including the authority of mothers over children, in Donzelot. It is telling to compare these grand indictments of modern states with what appears repeatedly in books on crime in history, even those by Marxists: laws are fragile, indictments erratic, legal process and sentencing full of personally exercised power that flies in the face of what the statute intended.

18. The historian mentioned is J. A. Sharpe, "The History of Crime in Late Medieval and Early Modern England: A Review of the Field," *Social History* 7:2 (1982): 187–203; see esp. p. 198; see also Sharpe, *Crime in Early Modern England*, pp. 121–42, for a longer discussion of social crime, its usefulness, and its problems. On staying up all night, see William Roughead, *Burke and Hare*, Notable British Trials Series (Toronto: Canada Law Book Company, 1921), p. 2.

19. See J. M. Beattie, *Crime and the Courts in England, 1660–1800* (Princeton, N.J.: Princeton University Press, 1986), pp. 202–37; and John Jacob Tobias, *Crime and Industrial Society in the 19th Century* (New York: Schocken Books, 1967), pp. 150–53, among many.

20. See Barbara Hanawalt, *Crime and Conflict in English Communities, 1300–1348* (Cambridge, Mass.: Harvard University Press, 1979), pp. 115–18 on the medieval and Elizabethan figures; and Beattie, *Crime and the Courts in England*, pp. 239–40, and on women's lower conviction rates, pp. 437, 454. Beattie notes that more women were taken as offenders in urban Surrey than in rural Sussex. The figure of 20 percent for Scotland comes from the bound volumes of the *Records of the Lord Advocate's Department* for 1828, an index in which 532 men and 109 women were investigated. At least one woman occurs twice in the list, in separate investigations, and other men and women were sometimes taken as witnesses with immunity, so a figure based on actual indictments would be lower than 20 percent, but 20 percent probably more accurately reflects those who were criminally active.

21. Hanawalt, *Crime and Conflict*, pp. 115–25; J. M. Beattie, "The Criminality of Women in Eighteenth-Century England," *Journal of Social History* 8 (Summer 1975): 80–116. On witch hunts in Scotland, see Larner, *Enemies of God*; and on infanticide, Symonds, *Weep Not for Me*. There is an enormous literature on the witch hunts across Europe; for England see Alan Macfarlane, *Witchcraft in Tudor and Stuart England* (Prospect Heights, Ill.: Waveland Press, 1970).

22. See Macfarlane, *Witchcraft*; Hanawalt, *Crime and Conflict*, pp. 117–18; Beattie, "The Criminality of Women," pp. 80–116; Beattie, *Crime and the Courts in England*, pp. 239–40; Buchanan Sharp, *In Contempt of All Authority: Rural Artisans and Riot in the West of England, 1586–1660* (Berkeley: University of California Press, 1980), pp. 13, 19, 22, 23, 35, 36; and Keith Wrightson, *English Society, 1580–1680* (New Brunswick, N.J.: Rutgers University Press, 1982), pp. 202–4, 177–78. For Scotland, see Christina Larner, "Crimen Exceptum? The Crime of Witchcraft in Europe," in V. A. C. Gattrell, Bruce Lenman, and Geoffrey Parker, eds., *Crime and the Law: The Social History of Crime in Western Europe since 1500* (London: Europa Publications, 1980), pp. 49–75; Logue, *Popular Disturbances in Scotland*; and James D. Young, *Women and Popular Struggles* (Edinburgh: Mainstream, 1985).

23. On the rather new police establishment in Edinburgh, and the Bridewell or prison there is little in print; see older or English material: Elaine A. Reynolds, *Before the Bobbies: The Night Watch and the Police Reform in Metropolitan London* (Stanford, Calif.: Stanford University Press, 1998); anonymous, "Prisons," *Edinburgh Review* 36 (1822): 353–74; Henry Fielding, *An Enquiry into the Causes of the Late Increase of Robbers & with some Proposals for Remedying This Growing Evil* (London: A. Millar, 1751); Patrick Pringle, *Hue and Cry: The Story of Henry and John Fielding and Their Bow Street Runners* (New York: William Morrow & Co., n.d.); William Tait, *Magdalenism: An Inquiry into the Extent, Causes, and Consequences of Prostitution in Edinburgh* (Edinburgh: P. Richards, 1840); Patrick Colquhoun, *A Treatise on the Police of the Metropolis* (London: C. Dilly, 1797); see also Joy Cameron, *Prisons and Punishment in Scotland from the Middle Ages to the Present* (Edinburgh: Canongate, 1983); Linda Mahood, *The Magdalenes: Prostitution in the Nineteenth Century* (London: Routledge, 1990); Frances Finnegan, *Poverty and Prostitution: A Study of Victorian Prostitutes in York* (Cambridge: Cambridge University Press, 1979).

24. Given from common usage, without citation, in Jacques Barzun, ed., *Burke and Hare: The Resurrection Men* (Metuchen, N.J.: Scarecrow Press, 1974), p. xi.

25. Underworld, as a term, has fallen out of favor among scholars who associate it with nineteenth-century writing about the criminal classes, and especially unscholarly writing about denizens of the underworld, as if they lived in a geographically separate area. I use the term advisedly, then, to refer to public houses, streets, houses, and pawnshops that seem to have been frequented by thieves and other criminals, but that were also obviously part of the city.

26. Much has been written on the body snatchers. Bodies were first "lifted" by doctors and medical students. The dirty work was being hired out by the 1780s, as gangs took it on. At that point, competition had increased, and relatives were becoming wary, increasing the risks and making the work too dangerous for even the rowdiest students. For historical studies, see first Ruth Richardson's excellent *Death, Dissection and the Destitute* (London and New York: Routledge & Kegan Paul, 1987), which has a useful bibliography; and the now somewhat dated, but useful James Moores Ball, M.D., LL.D., *The Body Snatchers*, rpt. of 1928

Notes to Chapter 1

ed. (New York: Dorset Press, 1989); and these articles: Matthew H. Kauffman, "Another Look at Burke and Hare: The Last Day of Mary Patterson—A Medical Cover-Up?" *Proceedings of the Royal College of Physicians of Edinburgh* 27 (1997): 78–88; M. Durey, "Bodysnatchers and Benthamites," *London Journal* 2 (1976): 200–225; C. F. A. Marmoy, "The Auto Icon of Jeremy Bentham at University College," *Medical History* 11:2 (1958): 77–86; Ian Ross and Carol Urquhart Ross, "Bodysnatching in Nineteenth-Century Britain," *British Journal of Law and Society* 6:1 (1979): 108–18; R. E. Wright-St. Clair, "Murder for Anatomy," *NZ Medical Journal* 60 (1961): 64–69; Alan F. Guttmacher, M.D., "Bootlegging Bodies: A History of Body-Snatching," *Bulletin of the Society of Medical History of Chicago* 4:4 (January 1935): 353–402; H. P. Tait, M.D., "Some Edinburgh Medical Men at the Time of the Resurrectionists," *Edinburgh Medical Journal* 55 (1948): 115–123; A. T. H. Smith, LL.M., M.A., "Stealing the Body and its Parts," *Criminal Law Review* 10 (1976): 622–27; Hannibal Hamlin, "The Dissection Riot of 1824 and the Connecticut Anatomical Law," *Yale Journal of Biology and Medicine* 7:4 (1934–35): 275–89; Julia Bess Frank, "Body Snatching: A Grave Medical Problem," *The Yale Journal of Biology and Medicine* 49 (1976): 399–410. For a contemporary example, see Andrew Murr, "Bad News for the Body Trade," *Newsweek* (March 22, 2004): 42.

Chapter 1

1. *West Port Murders*, p. 331. This comes from Burke's January 3, 1829, confession; the best source of most of these documents, and the trial transcript of Burke and M'Dougal's trial can be found in Barzun, *Burke and Hare*. However, Barzun inexplicably did not include all three confessions, and the third, known as the *Courant* confession, which is most valuable, can be found easily only in *West Port Murders*, or in the *Edinburgh Evening Courant* (February 7, 1829) where it was originally published. For Burke's confessions in *West Port Murders*, see pp. 331–52. Other versions of the trial transcript exist, for example in *West Port Murders*, but the desirable and complete version is that taken down by John Macnee, emended by the lawyers and judges in the case, and published separately at the time; see *Trial of William Burke and Helen M'Dougal, Before the High Court of Justiciary, at Edinburgh, on Wednesday, December 24, 1828, for the Murder of Margery Campbell, or Docherty* (Edinburgh: Robert Buchanan, 1829), but Barzun's reprint is more accessible. For whatever it is worth, the transcript published in *West Port Murders* is about half as long as that in Macnee's *Trial*, probably because *West Port Murders* was rushed into print following Burke's hanging. For Burke's first two confessions reprinted in Barzun, *Burke and Hare*, see pp. 229–36.

2. On the death of the pensioner, see *West Port Murders*, pp. 331–33. This comes from Burke's confession of January 3, 1829; it is also reprinted in Barzun's *Burke and Hare*, pp. 231–36, but a complete series of all three confessions is in *West Port Murders*, pp. 331–52. The last, or *Courant* confession, from the *Evening Courant*, was made later, well after his trial. It is more reflective and perhaps more forthcoming than the first two, in which he chiefly sought to incriminate Hare, who had testified against him as king's evidence. On prying up the coffin lid, see *West Port Murders*, p. 331; on Log's pound, see *West Port Murders*, p. 350.

3. Camstone is white clay used to whiten hearths and doorsteps.

4. Lenman, *Economic History of Modern Scotland*, p. 119; Lenman gives four to six shillings a week as the possible wages of a handloom weaver in 1838, and we should note that this

was a depressed trade by then. *West Port Murders*, pp. 340–41; for the porter, see 333. Burke's three confessions are sometimes contradictory, in that he could not remember the order in which the victims were killed, and offered somewhat different details about each person in each. In general, the last version is the fullest account, but he does not repeat what he had said in the earlier ones, probably intentionally, since it would have little value to the men who besieged him for details.

5. *West Port Murders*, p. 341.

6. Barzun, *Burke and Hare*, p. 19; from an anonymous introduction to Macnee's trial transcript, *Trial*, attributed to C. K. Sharpe.

7. *West Port Murders*, pp. 124–32; statement of Janet Brown.

8. *West Port Murders*, pp. 124–32; statement of Janet Brown. A gill, when used for spirits, is one quarter of a mutchkin, which is equal to an imperial pint; see *The Concise Scots Dictionary* (Aberdeen: Aberdeen University Press, 1985), pp. 232, 431. I would assume it to be a good-sized glassful, but by no means as large as a pint glass.

9. *West Port Murders*, pp. 124–32; statement of Janet Brown. Ironically, Constantine's job as scavenger made him an employee of the Edinburgh police.

10. *West Port Murders*, p. 131.

11. *West Port Murders*, p. 335, for Burke's comment that he sent for Hare; I have assumed that that is where Elizabeth Burke went when she left the house, because no one else could have gone, unless her husband did not actually go to work that day. For "you sort," see *West Port Murders*, p. 131.

12. *West Port Murders*, pp. 335, 342. Burke's two confessions disagree on the body's temperature, and I have used the last confession as final, in which he cites four hours and a warm body; the earlier one had said five to six hours, and just cold.

13. *West Port Murders*, pp. 334–35, 342–43.

14. *West Port Murders*, pp. 335, 343–44.

15. *West Port Murders*, pp. 344–45; see also Hugh Douglas, *Burke and Hare: The True Story* (London: Robert Hale & Company, 1973); Douglas has reproduced some penny broadsides, and in chapter seventeen discusses the various popular plays on the murders, and Daft Jamie, see p. 161.

16. This approximation applies to liquor only, and comes from *Concise Scots Dictionary*, p. 431.

17. For quotes, see *West Port Murders*, p. 345. As for beds, see *West Port Murders*, p. 352; on the night of the last murder, Burke and Hare spent part of the time sleeping in the bed, with the corpse hidden nearby on the floor, and with their wives also on the floor. It seems possible that as the killings continued, the men were driven together by what they shared, as well as apart by what they did not wish to remember. The marriages and their partnerships seem often to have put them at cross-purposes.

18. *West Port Murders*, pp. 344–45, 347.

19. *West Port Murders*, pp. 344–45, 347.

20. *West Port Murders*, pp. 346–47.

21. See Macnee's *Trial*, pp. viii–ix, from the anonymously compiled preface attributed to C. K. Sharpe. The same text is available in Barzun, *Burke and Hare*, pp. 18–19.

Notes to Chapter 1   149

22. Barzun, *Burke and Hare*, p. 350; from a Christopher North piece, "The West-Port Murders," first published in "Noctes Ambrosianae" in *Blackwood's Magazine*, March 1829. Christopher North was the pseudonym of John Wilson: see Elsie Swann, *Christopher North* (Edinburgh: Oliver and Boyd, 1934).

23. *West Port Murders*, p. 78, declaration of Helen M'Dougal, November 3, 1828, unsigned; she cannot write.

24. *West Port Murders*, p. 347.

25. Barzun, *Burke and Hare*, provides the most easily accessible reprint of the transcript. Whether because the case was literally unprecedented, or Rae did not wish it to be accessible, no attempt was made to maintain an official record of the trial in the books of the High Court of Justiciary; all that is recorded there are the indictments, and the sentence. See note 1 above on the competing versions offered to the public commercially. For the list of witnesses, see Barzun, *Burke and Hare*, pp. 32–34.

26. Barzun, *Burke and Hare*, pp. 76–79, the testimony of Mary Stewart and Charles M'Lauchlan, or McLaughlan. Docherty was known as Margery M'Gonegal at Stewart's, and seems variously to have gone by the names Mary, Madgy, or Margery M'Gonegal, Duffie, Campbell, or Docherty. Her first husband had been Campbell, her second Duffie.

27. Barzun, *Burke and Hare*, pp. 79–80, the testimony of William Noble, the shop boy at Rymer's.

28. On the porridge, see Barzun, *Burke and Hare*, pp. 81–82, testimony of Ann Connoway; p. 108, James Gray; pp. 154–56, declarations of William Burke; pp. 158–59, declaration of Helen M'Dougal. The declarations, or statements made while in custody, before the trial, of both Burke and M'Dougal are generally unreliable, since they had to tell stories that did not incriminate themselves, but on the matter of eating breakfast, they seem acceptable. For those later complaints about Docherty by M'Dougal, see Barzun, *Burke and Hare*, p. 88, testimony of Mrs. Law, and note 42 below.

29. Barzun, *Burke and Hare*, pp. 101–2, testimony of Mrs. Gray; p. 108, testimony of Mr. Gray; p. 88, testimony of Mrs. Law.

30. Barzun, *Burke and Hare*, pp. 82–83, testimony of Ann Connoway; p. 102, testimony of Mrs. Gray.

31. Barzun, *Burke and Hare*, pp. 82–83, testimony of Ann Connoway on the party in Mrs. Connoway's house; p. 110, testimony of Mr. Gray, on Burke and the copper measure.

32. Barzun, *Burke and Hare*, p. 102.

33. *West Port Murders*, p. 337, Burke's confession of January 3, 1829.

34. *West Port Murders*, p. 337, Burke's confession of January 3, 1829; for the report of his conversation after the trial, see p. 109. For the opium rumor, see Barzun, *Burke and Hare*, pp. 15, 17.

35. Barzun, *Burke and Hare*, pp. 90–92, testimony of Hugh Alston; pp. 88–89, testimony of Janet Law; *West Port Murders*, p. 337, Burke's confession of January 3, 1829.

36. *West Port Murders*, p. 337, Burke's confession of January 3, 1829; Barzun, *Burke and Hare*, pp. 140–43.

37. *West Port Murders*, pp. 348–49, Burke's confession of January 3, 1829; Barzun, *Burke and Hare*, pp. 93–95, testimony of David Paterson; p. 93, testimony of Elizabeth Paterson.

We do not know when the body was stripped, but it was naked when discovered the next day, probably because resurrected bodies were always stripped of clothes to avoid prosecution for the theft of clothing; stealing a body was not chargeable, as bodies were not property at law.

38. Barzun, *Burke and Hare*, pp. 93–99, testimony of David Paterson; *West Port Murders*, pp. 337–38, Burke's confession of January 3.

39. Barzun, *Burke and Hare*, p. 100, testimony of John Brogan.

40. Barzun, *Burke and Hare*, pp. 85, 89, 95, 102, 121, from the testimony of Connoway, Law, David Paterson, Mrs. Gray, and Hare. Mrs. Brogan was variously identified as related to M'Dougal, and to Burke.

41. Barzun, *Burke and Hare*, pp. 85, 100, 103, the testimony of Mrs. Connoway, Mrs. Gray, and John Brogan. On wakes, and customs associated with death, see I. F. Grant, *Highland Folk Ways* (London, Boston, and Henley: Routledge & Kegan Paul, 1961), pp. 366–70 for Scotland; for the Irish, see Sean O'Suilleabhain, *Irish Wake Amusements* (Dublin and Cork: Mercier Press, 1979).

42. Barzun, *Burke and Hare*, pp. 89, 100, 103, testimony of Law, Mrs. Gray, and Brogan. For spaewife, fashous, and limmer, see *Concise Scots Dictionary*; a spaewife is a fortuneteller, perhaps by extension a witch or even con artist; fashous is troublesome; and a limmer is a scoundrel, and when used about a woman, also a whore.

43. Barzun, *Burke and Hare*, p. 348, Burke's confession of January 3, 1829.

44. Barzun, *Burke and Hare*, pp. 95, 101–7, testimony of Brogan, and Mrs. Gray.

45. Barzun, *Burke and Hare*, pp. 101–7, testimony of Mrs. Gray.

46. Barzun, *Burke and Hare*, p. 109, testimony of Mr. Gray.

47. Barzun, *Burke and Hare*, pp. 79–80, 86, 95–96, 111, testimony of William Noble, shop boy, Mrs. Connoway, David Paterson, and George M'Culloch; see also *West Port Murders*, p. 5, text of a report supposedly taken from "the officer who apprehended Burke." Paterson did not specify £8 or £10; those were the figures reported by Burke and Hare. Mrs. Connoway's account of their comings and goings, pp. 86–87, is useful, but also implicates her in the business, as she admits that Hare and M'Dougal were in and out of her house that evening, but insisted that neither said a word to her on these visits.

48. Barzun, *Burke and Hare*, pp. 86–87, 113–15, testimony of Mrs. Connoway and John Fisher; on John Finlay as Findlay, see AD 2/1, printed indictment of Burke.

49. Barzun, *Burke and Hare*, pp. 86–87, 113–15, testimony of Mrs. Connoway and John Fisher; on John Finlay as Findlay, see AD 2/1, printed indictment of Burke; on Log's jeering, see *West Port Murders*, p. 5, text of a report supposedly taken from "the officer who apprehended Burke."

Chapter 2

1. The aggregate figures for Scotland were taken from the *Records of the Lord Advocate's Department for 1828*, held by the National Archives of Scotland at West Register House, Edinburgh; the population figures, and other useful information can be found in A. J. Youngson, *The Making of Classical Edinburgh*, (Edinburgh: Edinburgh University Press, 1966), pp. 265–67; the NAS sources for the twenty-one women are listed in the bibliography at the

Notes to Chapter 2

end of this volume. For some comparison, see Beattie, *Crime and the Courts in England*, pp. 237–42; the percentage of women in his counts varies from 1.8 percent to 35.5 percent, broken down by region and type of crime, not chronologically.

2. See Youngson, *Making of Classical Edinburgh*, pp. 182–87, for information on the George IV Bridge, and chapters 3, 5, and 6 on other public building, particularly bridges, in Edinburgh.

3. Again, see Youngson, *Making of Classical Edinburgh*, pp. 182–87 on George IV Bridge, includes an excellent photograph of the bridge over the Cowgate in 1860.

4. For Margaret Veitch, see the Records of the Lord Advocate's Department, AD 14/28/30.

5. Keir Street was located conveniently off the West Port and Grassmarket, via the Vennel, while still near enough to Veitch's eastern neighborhood, which lay just the other side of George Heriot's School.

6. For Elizabeth Paterson, especially Archibald Grant's description of her, see the Records of the Lord Advocate's Department AD 14/28/17 and JC 26/522.

7. For Elizabeth Paterson, especially Archibald Grant's description of her, see the Records of the Lord Advocate's Department, AD 14/28/17; and the small papers of the High Court of Justiciary, JC 26/522.

8. For Margaret Stewart or Burrows, see the Records of the Lord Advocate's Department, AD 14/28/22; which are labeled David Stark. Stark, Mrs. Burrows, and her daughter Mary were all indicted. Older women may have found it easier to reset because they were dealing with similar women as dealers and brokers in pawnshops and secondhand clothing stores.

9. For Elizabeth or Betty McKinnon, or Mackinnon, see the Records of the Lord Advocate's Department, AD 14/28/50; and the small papers of the High Court of Justiciary, JC 26/522.

10. For the case of Elizabeth or Betty McKinnon, see the Records of the Lord Advocate's Department, AD 14/28/50; and the small papers of the High Court of Justiciary, JC 26/522.

11. For the quotation, see Janet Swanston's statement in the Records of the Lord Advocate's Department, AD 14/28/50.

12. For McKinnon's use of the word tipsy, see JC 26/522.

13. On the Edinburgh Bridewell, see Cameron, *Prisons and Punishment*, p. 47; a Bridewell was a jail, but one built with the reform of the criminal in mind, so rather more like a workhouse; the Edinburgh Bridewell was partly based on Jeremy Bentham's Panopticon, and was meant to turn minor criminals into working people.

14. For Jean McBeath, see the small papers of the High Court of Justiciary, JC 26/522.

15. The problem posed by alcohol consumption in the late eighteenth and early nineteenth centuries can quickly be reviewed in the works of the artist William Hogarth, i.e., *Beer Street* and *Gin Lane*, and in the rise of temperance societies in the early nineteenth century. Brewing gave way to distilling, a process enhanced by population growth, improved agriculture, and capital.

16. For the case of Hannah Hodgson or Barton, see the Records of the Lord Advo-

cate's Department, AD 14/28/19; and the small papers of the High Court of Justiciary, JC 26/523.

17. For the quotations, see AD 14/28/19.

18. For Burke and the prostitute with too much makeup, see *West Port Murders*, p. 180. The only other source of wealth that would have tempted a lone woman would have been the possessions of masters and mistresses, for those women who went into service. But that would have been hard for a poor city woman to do. The one case reported in 1828, that of Margaret Thomson or McKenzie, JC 26/522, was not in the Old Town.

19. For the case of Barbara Kerr et al., see the Records of the Lord Advocate's Department, AD 14/28/26; and the small papers of the High Court of Justiciary, JC 26/522. All subsequent references are to these documents.

20. For Paterson and Brown, see Brown's account of Paterson's murder, in *West Port Murders*, pp. 125–31; clearly they worked as a team, and Brown was no doubt helpful in keeping the memory of Paterson's disappearance alive, and harassing Constantine and Elizabeth Burke. For Kerr, see note 19 above.

21. For the case of Janet Morrison et al., see the Records of the Lord Advocate's Department, AD 14/28/79. All subsequent references are to these documents.

22. Most of this story comes from the statement of Marion, Marjory, May, or Mary Campbell, in AD 14/28/79. Whether she is to be believed in all points is doubtful, but she was the only one who was willing to talk in any coherent way, and some of her story is too odd to be fiction.

23. For Ellen Reece, and related stories, see John Jacob Tobias, *Crime and Industrial Society in the 19th Century* (New York: Schocken Books, 1967), pp. 93–96; Tobias records that Ellen Reece's account came from the Chadwick Papers, box 129, University College, London. On prostitution, see, for Scotland, Mahood, *The Magdalenes*; and for Northern England, the more direct [and not Foucaldian] Finnegan, *Poverty and Prostitution*.

24. The new Bridewell on Calton Hill was completed in 1795; see Youngson, *Making of Classical Edinburgh*, p. 122; and more importantly on that Bridewell, Cameron, *Prisons and Punishment*, pp. 47, 244, where Cameron points out that Calton Bridewell was the most like Bentham's Panopticon of any prison to be built. The word Bridewell is given by the *OED* as derived from St. Bride's Well, London, site of an early house of correction, or prison. On English gangs, see Beattie, *Crime and the Courts in England*, pp. 252–62; the English gangs appear to have been male, and unstable for a number of reasons, but this may not tell us anything about Scotland. For women among the grave-robbers, see the Records of the Lord Advocate's Department, AD 14/29/16, for Helen Begbie, from Melville Mill, Lasswade, who was taken with the gang that included an anatomist. The gang members in Walter Scott's *The Heart of Mid-Lothian* (1818) were Madge Wildfire and Mother Blood; see chapters 29 and 30 in any edition of the novel.

25. The Bible stealer was Mary Ann McDonald, AD 14/28/83.

26. This may well be the same Christian McKay who bought a watch from Barbara Kerr's sister; see AD 14/28/26; JC 26/522.

27. Elizabeth Fox-Genovese, paraphrasing remarks she had made on fashion, "each society gets the ―― it deserves," e-mail to author, January 9, 1996. And for a glimpse of how family and business fit together in the legal, public economy, see Leonore Davidoff

and Catherine Hall, *Family Fortunes: Men and Women of the English Middle Class, 1780–1850* (Chicago: University of Chicago Press, 1987).

28. On the frequency of petty theft as predominant form, see the important essay by J. A. Sharpe, "History of Crime," pp. 187–203; Sharpe, *Crime in Early Modern England*; and Beattie, *Crime and the Courts in England*.

29. On their dutiful, as well as suspicious, waiting (they may have suspected their husbands would hide the money from them) see *West Port Murders*, p. 5; testimony of Paterson pp. 45–46; testimony of M'Culloch pp. 51–52; see also the fuller accounts of the same testimony as given in Macnee, *Trial*, pp. 65–71, and pp. 82–87, respectively.

Chapter 3

1. For the classic British example of gibbet tales, see George Theodore Wilkinson, *The Newgate Calendar*, introduced by Christopher Hibbert (London: Sphere Books, 1991).

2. *West Port Murders*, pp. 10–11. See also the *Edinburgh Evening Courant* for the period of the discovery and trial, and much of 1829.

3. For the full list of faculty, see *West Port Murders*, p. 96; there were several assistants each for the lord advocate, and for both defense lawyers. One of the advocate deputes, later Sir Archibald Alison, published his autobiography in 1883.

4. On not letting anyone see them, see Burke's confession, *West Port Murders*, pp. 349–50; on verdicts and sentencing, see Barzun, *Burke and Hare*, the trial transcript, pp. 222–28; on the December 1 date, see Roughead, *Burke and Hare*, pp. 45–46, from Roughead's detailed but not always footnoted account.

5. On the figures in the trial, and the defending lawyers, see *West Port Murders*, p. 96; for Cockburn's statement on reversing positions, see *West Port Murders*, p. 89; and for Cockburn's cross-examination, see Barzun, *Burke and Hare*, pp. 124–38.

6. Roughead, *Burke and Hare*, pp. 40–45; quotation comes from p. 45. As to Hare and Log's declarations, Roughead implied (p. 43) that the government, after deciding to take Hare and Log as king's evidence, no doubt found their earlier tales, in what was inevitably a first round of lying, potentially embarrassing and apparently disposed of them. All the Burke and M'Dougal declarations can be found in *West Port Murders*, pp. 67–79. The three relevant petitions seem to have had an interesting life of their own; they were returned to the Scottish Record Office by one John A. Fairley, Esq. in 1929. They may have been valued souvenirs of the trial in the nineteenth century; they are now cataloged as EX GD 1/353/3, (November 3, Madgy McGonnegal, all four named); EX GD 1/353/4 (November 19, James Wilson [Daft Jamie], all four named); EX GD 1/353/5 (December 4, Mary Paterson, Burke and M'Dougal only named). The indictment, with handwritten marginalia of, probably, one of the prosecutors, survives, see AD 2/1. P.[eter] Hume Brown, *History of Scotland*, vol. 3, Cambridge Historical Series (Cambridge: Cambridge University Press, 1911), p. 403 on the phalanx of Tories; on the various newspaper debates on Rae, see *West Port Murders*, pp. 137–69, esp. p. 167 on the faults in Hare's testimony.

7. *West Port Murders*, p. 93.

8. *West Port Murders*, p. 98.

9. Roughead, *Burke and Hare*, pp. 46–47, on troops and police; for the news directly

Notes to Chapter 3

from the *Courant*, from which Roughead is quoting, see the *Edinburgh Evening Courant* for December 6 and 25, 1828. For newspaper sales, see *West Port Murders*, p. 107. For Lord Advocate Rae's closing address to the jury, see the trial transcript reprinted in Barzun, *Burke and Hare*, pp. 161–78, for quote see p. 162.

10. Barzun, *Burke and Hare*, p. 222.

11. On the legal questions, it is necessary to look at the trial transcript for those points when the court postponed hearing evidence to consider questions of procedure: based on the transcript reprinted by Barzun, published in 1829 as *Trial of William Burke and Helen M'Dougal*, see "Defences for Burke," "Defences for M'Dougal," "Speeches of the Counsel on the Relevancy of the Indictment," "Opinions of the Judges," Barzun, *Burke and Hare*, pp. 38–75; and then the "Objection and Debate on Hare Being Questioned as to His Concern in Other Murders," Barzun, *Burke and Hare*, pp. 124–34. I have given Barzun's pagination; those using an original copy of Macnee's *Trial* will find the pages given in its table of contents. On the sentence, see Barzun, *Burke and Hare*, p. 222. And for the tanning business, see William Roughead, "The Wolves of the West Port," in his *The Murderer's Companion* (New York: Readers Club, 1941), pp. 119–21. As for the skeleton, it still hangs today in Edinburgh in Surgeons' Hall, where it remains the property of the Edinburgh University Department of Anatomy; presumably some members of that institution oversaw the sale of Burke's skin.

12. Barzun, *Burke and Hare*, p. 28, from the anonymous preface to the trial credited to C. K. Sharpe.

13. Barzun, *Burke and Hare*, p. 210, Cockburn's statement to the jury, from the trial transcript. Lawyers in the case corrected the transcriptions of their remarks. We can only hope that the corrections were in favor of accuracy.

14. For the bodies taken from prisons, see Richardson, *Death, Dissection and the Destitute*, p. 106; for Rae's letter to Peel, see Wright-St. Clair, "Murder for Anatomy," pp. 64–69, especially pp. 65–66. This short article is of tremendous value in presenting Rae's letter; this is the only reference to it in the Burke and Hare literature.

15. For Roughead's comments, see Roughead, *Burke and Hare*, pp. 46, 48; for the printed indictment, see AD 2/1 Indictment against William Burke, etc (Murder); Knox and his associates are witnesses, pp. 44–48. One of those associates, Fergusson, rose to eminence as a surgeon. This copy has handwritten annotations for each witness in the margins. Very few records of the trial survive; there is no official record of the testimony at the trial, itself a remarkable event. All that survives in the court's journal are notes of points made by various lawyers, pertaining to procedure, and the verdict; witnesses are noted by name, with no attempt to give their testimony. This was not the usual procedure; usually Scots court records contain a fairly thorough record of what was said by all parties. No precognitions, the statements taken down by police or sheriff during the investigation, survive either. The only other documents still in the government's possession are the procurator-fiscal's petitions to the sheriff, dated November 3, November 19, and December 4, 1828, now kept as GD 1/353/3–5. These seem to have traveled into private hands, to be returned to the Record Office in 1929, see note 6 above.

16. For Cockburn see Henry Cockburn, *Memorials of His Time* (1856), p. 458; also quoted in Roughead, *Burke and Hare*, p. 87. See *West Port Murders*, and Macnee, *Trial*. This latter text,

Notes to Chapter 3

sometimes referred to as McNee's, was the one reprinted by Jacques Barzun, and which constitutes the nearest thing to an official transcript of the trial that we have. Readers of *West Port Murders* got only an eighty-seven-page transcript of the trials, while readers of Macnee's *Trial*, perhaps the more expensive report, got one hundred and ninety-nine pages from the trial, including the lawyers' arguments, which were greatly abridged in *The West Port Murders*.

17. See Cockburn's closing argument as given in Barzun, *Burke and Hare*, pp. 201–13; quotations come from pp. 202–3, and p. 206.

18. See Alexander Walker's *Trilogy*, as discussed in Robyn Cooper, "Alexander Walker's Trilogy on Woman," *Journal of the History of Sexuality* 2:3 (1992): 341–64. What I am referring to is known as "bourgeois womanhood." See my "Making of the Scots Bourgeoise," in *Weep Not for Me*, pp. 211–32, and the bibliography therein for some sense of the immense literature on this aspect of the industrial and democratic revolutions in Europe and the North American colonies.

19. For specifics of her release, unsubstantiated, see Roughead, *Burke and Hare*, pp. 60–61; for the rumor, and a vague account of her release, see *West Port Murders*, pp. 110–11, 354–55; for the money, see pp. 114–15. Roughead and *West Port Murders* give somewhat contradictory accounts of her scuffles in the West Port, testifying to the number of accounts and rumors about her at the time and forever after.

20. *West Port Murders*, pp. 221–46; see especially pp. 221–23; on his disease, see Roughead, *Burke and Hare*, p. 88; and *West Port Murders*, p. 115.

21. Roughead has his own account of the execution, but it is as usual thinly footnoted; see Roughead, *Burke and Hare*, pp. 59–65; see also *West Port Murders*, pp. 221–33.

22. For the population of Edinburgh, see *The First and Second Statistical Accounts of the City of Edinburgh, 1799 and 1845* (Edinburgh: West Port Books, 1998), pp. 5, 79. This account is taken from *West Port Murders*; see pp. 23–38. Parts of this section of *West Port Murders*, if not the entire work, appear to have been issued as pamphlets, as events occurred; see p. 235, and a reference to a portrait given in the third number. For comparative accounts in much the same tradition, see Wilkinson, *Newgate Calendar*; and the now classic collection of essays edited by Hay, *Albion's Fatal Tree*.

23. *West Port Murders*, p. 243.

24. *West Port Murders*, pp. 240–47; on the rank in life, see p. 244; on Boyle, see p. 245. For the phalanx, see Brown, *History of Scotland*, p. 403. Brown is useful on the early nineteenth century, using classic sources and a biographical technique that necessarily includes the lawyers of that time. For background on Lord Advocate Rae, and the politics of the times, see Omond, *Lord Advocates of Scotland*, pp. 256–98.

25. The prosecution of the weavers was led by Lord Advocate Alexander Maconochie, who would be Lord Meadowbank at the Burke and M'Dougal trial. Brown, *History of Scotland*, pp. 402–3; at times the lord advocate acted within the British parliamentary system as virtual home secretary for Scotland.

26. A maligned reformer, Stuart of Dunearn, and one of the *Sentinel*'s anonymous authors, who turned out to be the son of the noted eighteenth-century lawyer and author, James Boswell, shot at each other in the formally prescribed way. Boswell was killed, and

Stuart was tried for murder, but the jury acquitted him. The Tories might well have seen some writing on the wall at this point, but serious political reform still looked a long way off in 1822. Brown, *History of Scotland*, pp. 408–10; this was not the first great burst of growth to be shown by newspapers and journals—that had come in the 1790s, during the French Revolution; on older newspapers see Brown, *History of Scotland*, p. 334; and the much more useful comments on the late eighteenth-century press by Lenman, *Integration, Enlightenment, and Industrialization*, pp. 100–13.

27. See, in general, Brown, "The Victory of Reform," in *History of Scotland*, pp. 398–422, and Lenman, *Integration, Enlightenment, and Industrialization*, see especially pp. 101, 111, on newspapers.

28. *West Port Murders*, pp. 251–54. On Alexander Monro, third in a line of Monro lecturers, and a great failure, see John D. Comrie, *History of Scottish Medicine*, vol. 2 (London: For the Wellcome Historical Medical Museum by Balliere, Tindall & Cox, 1932), pp. 492–93. Monro's failure as anatomist and lecturer contributed greatly to Knox's success.

29. *West Port Murders*, pp. 255–58.

30. *West Port Murders*, pp. 355–59; there is also some mention of Log in Roughead, *Burke and Hare*, p. 61, but this is a bare paraphrase of *The West Port Murders* account.

31. Hare's defender in this complicated business referred to them as the "alleged mother" and "alleged sister," which he probably would not have tried if they had been at all known in the city. *West Port Murders*, pp. 272–305, "Proceedings against Hare"; these pages include Jeffrey's argument for the Wilsons, the lord advocate's statement, the information or petition given for Hare, and the opinions of the judges of the High Court of Justiciary who had to decide the matter; these are often abridgements. See also *West Port Murders*, pp. 137–69, covering the newspaper accounts of the debate over trying Hare; the case had the effect of forcing politically neutral papers to take sides.

32. *West Port Murders*, pp. 272–305, "Proceedings against Hare"; and pp. 137–69, "Discussions Relative to the Trial of Hare and the Socii Criminum." The most important statements in the former section were those of Jeffrey, for the Wilsons, and against the powers of the lord advocate; the lord advocate, for his own actions; and the detailed decisions of Lord Pitmilly, for the Wilsons; and the lord justice clerk, for Hare. All of these are abridged, and mixed with commentary, but useful, and containing a good deal of direct quotation.

33. On Hare's legal position, see *West Port Murders*, pp. 207–30, "Proceedings against Hare"; and George MacGregor, *The History of Burke and Hare and of the Resurrectionist Times* (Glasgow: Thomas D. Morrison, 1884), pp. 163–65, and for following on Rae, pp. 184–85. Rae made clear that he had, through the procurator-fiscal, told Hare "that if he would disclose the facts relative to the case of Docherty, and to such other crimes of a similar nature committed by Burke, of which he was cognisant, he should not be brought to trial on account of his accession to any of these crimes."

34. *West Port Murders*, pp. 291–92.

35. Brown, *History of Scotland*, see p. 403 on the phalanx. On the various newspaper debates on Rae, see *West Port Murders*, pp. 137–69, esp. p. 167 on the faults in Hare's testimony. Other papers and journals entered the debate, which was divided on Whig and Tory lines,

Notes to Chapter 4

but these three maintained a running argument at the time, and it is valuable to note the level of legal debate in which the public was interested.

36. *West Port Murders*, p. 312.

37. Roughead, *Burke and Hare*, pp. 73–74; see also *West Port Murders*, pp. 310–12.

38. *West Port Murders*, pp. 313–22; for Sandford, see p. 314; for the umbrella story, see p. 317; for the collar and the ostler, see pp. 318–19.

39. For the road to Carlisle, see *West Port Murders*, p. 324; for the rumors, see Roughead, *Burke and Hare*, p. 77.

40. The best quick life of Knox is in Roughead, *Burke and Hare*, pp. 78–92; Roughead cites most of the other important sources, and gives excerpts from newspaper reports; see also, as main documents on this largely invisible man, Henry Lonsdale, *A Sketch of the Life of Robert Knox, the Anatomist* (London: Macmillan, 1870); and Echo of Surgeons' Square (pseudonym for David Paterson), *A Letter to the Lord Advocate* (Edinburgh, 1829), reprinted in Barzun, *Burke and Hare*, pp. 242–76; and also reprinted in Barzun, *Burke and Hare*, pp. 346–57, the wonderful Christopher North satire, "West-Port Murders," that first appeared in the Noctes Ambrosianae of the Tory *Blackwood's Magazine* in March 1829. As Roughead noted, Lonsdale was a student of Knox, and his life of his mentor is something of a whitewash; see also Sir Robert Christison, *The Life of Robert Christison*, edited by his sons (Edinburgh and London: William Blackwood and Sons, 1885–86), for another view, pp. 309–11. Christison, a noted professor of law and medicine, was called by Rae to testify in the case. See also Knox's obituary, by Dr. Druit, "The Late Dr. Knox," *Medical Times & Gazette* 2 (December 27, 1862): 683–85.

41. His nemesis in the trial of Burke and M'Dougal, Dr. (later Sir) Robert Christison, who testified about the cause of Docherty's death for the prosecution, remarked in his memoirs that Knox ended his life as "lecturer, demonstrator, and showman, to a travelling party of Ojibbeway Indians." It may not have been true, but it was how Christison chose to remember him. For Christison's rather damning remarks on Knox, and his fate, see Christison, *Life of Robert Christison*, pp. 310–11. For other facts, see Roughead, *Burke and Hare*, pp. 78–92. There is also a good and newer, if brief account of Knox's troubles in Richardson, *Death, Dissection and the Destitute*, pp. 132–43, and 327, n. 103. For the letter, and the committee's report on Knox, see Lonsdale, *Life of Knox*, pp. 82–88.

42. Lonsdale, *Life of Knox*, pp. 72, 82–88 (letter to the press, and statement of the committee of inquiry), 92–93; Lonsdale claims that the bodies Burke and Hare offered him were no more than one-sixth of his total, from which I have calculated 96. Knox claimed to have over 400 students; see his letter to the press, reprinted in Lonsdale, *Life of Knox*, pp. 82–85. Roughead, *Burke and Hare*, put the figure at 504 students for the 1828–29 session; p. 80.

43. On Knox's entertaining lecture style, see Comrie, *Scottish Medicine*, pp. 501–2; and Lonsdale, *Life of Knox*, pp. 111–14, 138–42, 147–54.

Chapter 4

1. For the city's development, see Youngson, *Making of Classical Edinburgh*.

2. AD 2/1, p. 14. The italics are mine. This is the second page of the printed Indict-

ment Against William Burke, &, from the records of the Lord Advocate's Department. A sketch map was included, but is now lost from the records. Wester Portsburgh grew outside the southwest city gate, the West Port, and was not incorporated into Edinburgh until 1856; see E. F. Catford, *Edinburgh: The Story of a City* (London: Hutchinson & Co., 1975), front cover map.

3. These were not the unknowable warrens of Engels's Manchester; they were no more than a ten-minute walk from the High Court in Parliament Square, and the two closes that gave access to Burke and M'Dougal's house, Grindley's and Weaver's, had been there for some years. Closes are alleys, often no more than a few feet wide, and in hilly Edinburgh often include steps. The West Port originally referred to the western gate of the old city, but by 1828 appears on maps as the street running west from that site. The surrounding neighborhood was sometimes referred to as Wester Portsburgh, to differentiate it from the street itself. See, for example, the republication of the *1877 Ordnance Survey Map of Edinburgh Castle* (Edinburgh sheet 35) from Alan Godfrey, known as the Godfrey Edition; and Drew Easton, ed., *By the Three Great Roads: A History of Tollcross, Fountainbridge, and the West Port* (Aberdeen: Aberdeen University Press, 1988); and Steven Marcus, *Engels, Manchester, and the Working Class* (New York: Random House, 1974).

4. Accounts of the murders, the trial, and subsequent mobs included as much detail about Burke, Hare, M'Dougal, and Log as could be gleaned from voluble informants in their old neighborhood, and even stretched in *West Port Murders* to the results of phrenologists' studies of both men's heads; see p. 259. Madame Tussaud's son came from Paris to make a life mask of Hare, and a death mask of Burke. Out of these snatches of biography, odd speculations, and interviews, we know a good deal about the four murderers, and we can begin to build a picture of how the four worked together. A land was virtually a street address, as in Van Diemen's Land, and probably reflected the first owner of land or the building thereon, not all subsequent owners. As for Connoway's knowing the name of the land, she admitted as much when she testified that Docherty asked for a name, so she could return, and Connoway told her the name would do her no good, as that landlord owned three buildings in the area, all presumably known by the same name. For diagrams, see Macnee, *Trial*, p. 54; Barzun, *Burke and Hare*, p. 82; *West Port Murders*, facing p. 37. According to the map drawn for the trial, Burke and M'Dougal's house could be entered only by descending the common stair that opened from the nameless courtyard lying between Grindlay's Close and Weaver's Close, both of which alleys ran north from the West Port. Their neighbors' houses had doors near the stair, but Burke and M'Dougal, and friends, had to walk the length of the hall, turn right through another door, and then pass through what must have been a very dark inside hall before reaching their own door. See, among other descriptions, the diagram and text in MacGregor, *History of Burke and Hare*, pp. 84–85. For Tussaud's waxwork exhibit of Burke and Hare, see Marie-Helene Huet, *Monstrous Imagination* (Cambridge, Mass. and London, England: Harvard University Press, 1993); for the phrenologists, see *West Port Murders*, pp. 259–72. Burke's skull proved, to the great discredit of phrenologists, to be that of a good man, or woman, by some accounts. Roughead noted that Burke pretty much finished the phrenologists, since his head was so antithetical to their expectations.

Notes to Chapter 4

5. *West Port Murders*, pp. 16, 67; on cancer, pp. 115–16; living in Peebles, p. 173, and note on p. 173; pp. 170–85, 263, 351; on his children, see esp. p. 174; for the quote, see p. 177. See also MacGregor, *History of Burke and Hare*, pp. 233–34, for minister's letter. On the impact of improved transportation in small villages, George Douglas Brown's *The House with the Green Shutters* (Harmondsworth, Middlesex, England: Penguin Books, 1985), although a novel, is very useful.

6. *West Port Murders*, pp. 170–85; for Effie, see p. 343, from Burke's *Courant* confession.

7. *West Port Murders*, pp. 180–82, 208–9; for the books, see p. 178; for religious meetings, see p. 179; for children, see pp. 124, 202–3; for Cockburn, see his *Memorials*, p. 265.

8. Barzun, *Burke and Hare*, pp. 347–48; for the entire article, see pp. 346–57. For the reprinting of Wilson's article from *Blackwood's*, see Barzun, *Burke and Hare*, p. 349.

9. *West Port Murders*, pp. 112–13, for nightmares; p. 350, resurrectionists; p. 352, getting better victuals; and p. 188, spending fourteen pounds.

10. *West Port Murders*, p. 350.

11. *West Port Murders*, p. 113, attending Protestant churches; p. 102, instructing M'Dougal; pp. 112–13, 349, bad dreams; pp. 108–9, on Daft Jamie, and on reading "Scriptures;" p. 109 on praying for M'Dougal.

12. Leith, now a suburb of Edinburgh, was then a separate port on the Firth of Forth, just north of Edinburgh's New Town.

13. On M'Dougal, see *West Port Murders*, pp. 11, 101–2, 110, 353–54; and Barzun, *Burke and Hare*, pp. 23–24, 26–27, 158–61, 204–6.

14. On the books, see MacGregor, *History of Burke and Hare*, p. 49; as for the room being decent and well lit, see a later comment by John Wilson writing as Christopher North in Barzun, *Burke and Hare*, pp. 350–51.

15. See *West Port Murders*, p. 11; and Barzun, *Burke and Hare*, p. 26. The wording differs slightly in the two records.

16. For Sharpe's comment, see Barzun, *Burke and Hare*, p. 19; as for Burke looking uninviting, see p. 26; both are the preface attributed to C. K. Sharpe in Macnee, *Trial*. For M'Dougal's claim to be thirty-three, see *West Port Murders*, p. 75. On M'Dougal's age, see Barzun, *Burke and Hare*, p. 19, note; this was the addition of C. K. Sharpe, the supposed author of the preface to Macnee, *Trial*. For the original citation, see Macnee, *Trial*, preface, p. ix.

17. For M'Dougal, see *The West Port Murders*, pp. 11, 261–62 and various comments throughout, especially remarks made by Burke in his confessions and trial testimony, especially from Mrs. Law, Mrs. Connoway, and Mrs. Gray, who commonly saw her in her house.

18. For the words business and system, see for example Barzun, *Burke and Hare*, p. 225: "But really, when a system of such a nature is thus developed..." and see also Roughead, "Wolves of the West Port," pp. 117–76. Roughead adopts the tone and vocabulary of commentators of 1829 in using a business vocabulary to discuss Burke et al.

19. On Hare, see *West Port Murders*, pp. 306–12; and also Barzun, *Burke and Hare*, p. 24. For Hare's testimony at the trial, see Barzun, *Burke and Hare*, pp. 115–38.

20. For descriptions of Hare, see *West Port Murders*, pp. 103, 306–9, 325; and Barzun, *Burke and Hare*, pp. 28, 200, 210.

21. By Ireland's sketch of Hare, I mean the one published by him in *West Port Murders*, plate facing p. 272; Nimmo's appeared in Macnee, *Trial*, facing the title page; also in Barzun, *Burke and Hare*, p. 4. For Hare's comment on Burke, see *West Port Murders*, p. 308.

22. For the argument that both were hated because they were Irish, see Edwards, *Burke & Hare*.

23. *West Port Murders*, pp. 355, 358; some flicker of admiration for her toughness and "industry" is apparent here.

24. *West Port Murders*, pp. 355–59 for general description; p. 104 for short and stout; and see also Barzun, *Burke and Hare*, pp. 24–25 for her control and last word, and p. 112 for M'Culloch's comment, from his testimony.

25. *West Port Murders*, p. 352, for Burke on Log; for Log's decoying, see pp. 340–41, 344; for Janet Brown's account of Log attempting to strike her, see p. 130; on charging Burke one pound, see p. 350. Most of this comes from Burke's *Courant* confession, and he had reason to tell the worst about Log by then.

26. *West Port Murders*, p. 307.

27. *West Port Murders*, pp. 123, 107, 344; and on Docherty's box, see Barzun, *Burke and Hare*, p. 80, and p. 348 for John Wilson's [as Christopher North] description of Hare.

28. *West Port Murders*, pp. 352, 350; Barzun, *Burke and Hare* pp. 24–25, 139–46.

29. *Caledonian Mercury*, December 27, 1828; reprinted in Barzun, *Burke and Hare*, pp. 26–27.

30. *West Port Murders*, pp. 348–49.

31. *West Port Murders*, pp. 128, 341, 343, 348–49.

32. *West Port Murders*, pp. 344–45, 350, from the *Courant* confession.

33. *West Port Murders*, pp. 346–48.

34. *West Port Murders*, p. 104.

35. *West Port Murders*, p. 62; Barzun, *Burke and Hare*, p. 143.

36. *West Port Murders*, p. 352.

37. *West Port Murders*, pp. 4, 109, 217, 338, 344.

38. See the testimony of Mrs. Hare (not, we should note, Lucky Log) in Barzun, *Burke and Hare*, pp. 139–46; illustration of Mrs. Hare as an evil-looking mother is facing p. 139; see Cockburn's use of "natural," p. 204; compare with the "natural" phrase, in *West Port Murders*, p. 64.

39. Barzun, *Burke and Hare*, p. 210, from trial transcript.

40. The "she-devil" quote comes from the *Caledonian Mercury*, December 27, 1828; it was also cited in Barzun, *Burke and Hare*, p. 27. See Barzun, *Burke and Hare*, pp. 204–6 for Cockburn's arguments, and p. 204 on Log as a wife; for the condensed version of Cockburn's remarks also circulated, see *West Port Murders*, p. 90.

41. For Paterson's elaborate defense of himself, see Barzun, *Burke and Hare*, pp. 242–76; and for the story of Paterson offering Docherty around at a higher price than what was to be paid to Burke and Hare for her body, see Roughead, *Burke and Hare*, p. 88; Roughead calls Paterson Knox's janitor.

On Paterson as messenger, see Barzun, *Burke and Hare*, pp. 248–49 [letter]; and on M'Culloch carrying Daft Jamie, see pp. 268–69; for Burke's statement that only Paterson

Notes to Chapter 5

knew, see the additional statement he supplied to his official confession, *West Port Murders*, p. 340. On Scott's disgust, see Roughead, *Burke and Hare*, p. 89; this was given by Roughead as from *Journal of Sir Walter Scott*, 2:263. For Burke on their plans to expand the business, see his *Courant* confession, *West Port Murders*, p. 350.

42. On the cutting up of Daft Jamie, see David Paterson in Barzun, *Burke and Hare*, pp. 256–57 [letter]; see also AD 2/1, *Indictment against William Burke, etc.*, which contains a list of witnesses called by the lord advocate, anticipating a trial on the murders of Jamie, Paterson, and Docherty. Rae's search turned up a medical student, James Evans, who was noted in the margin of the document to have "dissected the right leg of a male subject" and who suspected that it was Jamie's leg. On Fergusson recognizing Mary Paterson, and the drawings, see Barzun, *Burke and Hare*, pp. 246–48; and on Burke's version, and quotes from him on Paterson, see *West Port Murders*, pp. 335, 341–42. On William Fergusson, destined for a notable career, see Roughead, *Burke and Hare*, p. 28; Sir William Fergusson was to be president of the Royal College of Surgeons of England, among other honors. On Liston's remarkable report, given only in paraphrase, see Richardson, *Death, Dissection and the Destitute*, p. 327 n. 103; for her discussion of fears of corpse violation, see pp. 95–97; and for speculation on Mary Shelley's awareness of the body trade, see pp. xiii, xvii.

43. *West Port Murders*, pp. 219, 332, 350, 351.

44. For the report on Knox, see Roughead, *Burke and Hare*, pp. 277–79; for what seems the fullest account of Christison's testimony, see Barzun, *Burke and Hare*, pp. 148–52; for his life, and his remark on Knox, see *Life of Sir Robert Christison*, p. 310.

45. For the protection, the police watching, and the argument over price, see Barzun, *Burke and Hare*, pp. 251–52.

46. Violence still abounded in 1828. Elizabeth McDonald in Leith hit her husband over the head with a large slate, JC 26/524; Catherine Liston appears to have stabbed a male attacker with her clam knife, AD 14/28/71. For the child murder in Inverness, see AD 14/28/276 and 277.

47. For the records, see JC 26/522; AD 14/50; JC 26/523; AD 14/17; AD 14/19; AD 14/22; AD 14/26; AD 14/30; AD 14/61; AD 14/79; AD 14/83; JC 26/524; AD 14/55.

Chapter 5

1. *West Port Murders*, p. 1.

2. To examine the full range of this author's dismay, see *West Port Murders*, pp. 1–2. Commentators, judges, and lawyers seem to have struggled to find the right words to convey their astonishment and horror.

3. For the invisible hand, see Adam Smith, *An Inquiry into the Nature and Causes of the Wealth of Nations* (New York: Modern Library, 1937), p. 423; and on the reputations of anatomists, Richardson, *Death, Dissection and the Destitute*, pp. 54–61, 161–74. Of course the anatomists had not looked quite so pure to many critics for several decades before 1828, but suspicions about body snatching, and lewd behavior with corpses were not fears of premeditated, market-driven murder.

4. For a recent discussion of the free market and bodies, see a book review by Jean

Notes to Chapter 5

Bethke Elshtain, "Everything for Sale," *Books & Culture* (May/June 1998): 8–11. On the timing of rapid change in Scotland, see Lenman, *Economic History of Modern Scotland*, pp. 101–3; Lenman places rapid although very regional growth between 1780 and 1840.

5. For Cobbett see Richardson, *Death, Dissection and the Destitute*, p. 100, quotation from *Cobbett's Weekly Political Register*, 1832.

6. On the Anatomy Act (2nd and 3rd William IV, Cap. 75) see Barzun, *Burke and Hare*, p. xi. On Jeremy Bentham, see Marmoy, "Auto Icon of Jeremy Bentham"; see also Durey, "Bodysnatchers and Benthamites." Bentham, the inventor of a prison scheme called the Panopticon, had a great interest in crime and the law, and Edinburgh's Bridewell was modeled on the Panopticon. See also recent work in jurisprudence by an admirer of Bentham's: Richard Posner, *The Problems of Jurisprudence* (Cambridge, Mass.: Harvard University Press, 1990).

7. London also had its skeleton, that of the "The Irish Giant" O'Brien, who was exhibited while living, and then displayed after his death in 1783 by the Scots-born anatomist John Hunter; see Richardson, *Death, Dissection and the Destitute*, pp. 57–58; see also George C. Peachey, *A Memoir of William & John Hunter* (Plymouth: William Brendon and Son, 1924).

8. Barzun, *Burke and Hare*, p. 227; see also Macnee, *Trial*, p. 199.

9. His suggestion was taken seriously, probably by Alexander Monro, the official university professor of anatomy who dissected Burke, and who had good reason to commemorate and rejoice in the notoriety of his freelance rival, Knox. On Alexander Monro, the third man of that name to hold the chair of anatomy at the University of Edinburgh, see Comrie, *History of Scottish Medicine*, pp. 492–502.

10. On systems, see Barzun, *Burke and Hare*, p. 28; or see Macnee, *Trial*, p. xviii; and 195–96 for Meadowbank; and *West Port Murders*, pp. 7, 9, 93–95, 247, 249, and Burke's comment on p. 349.

11. For Wilson's piece, "Characters of Burk [sic], Hare, and Dr. Knox," see Barzun, *Burke and Hare*, p. 346, where it is reprinted in full, pp. 346–57. On John Wilson writing as Christopher North, see Swann, *Christopher North*.

12. On heroic old criminals, see Tobias, *Crime and Industrial Society in the 19th Century*, pp. 122–24; and also Hanawalt, *Crime and Conflict*, pp. 7, 204–7, on the mythic Robin Hood. For Thomas Carlyle's phrase, see his essay "Chartism" in *Selected Writings* (Harmondsworth: Penguin, 1971), especially pp. 193–200. For Burke's memories of pennies clutched in dying fingers, see *West Port Murders*, p. 348.

13. For Fielding's comments, see Fielding, *Enquiry*, pp. 2–3; see also the discussion of change in Tobias, *Crime and Industrial Society in the 19th Century*, pp. 122–59; and Hanawalt, *Crime and Conflict*, pp. 7, 204–7 on gangs in the fourteenth century.

14. On shaming in England, see J. A. Sharpe, *Crime in Early Modern England*, pp. 47–48; the rough music of England has not been identified directly in Scotland, probably because of the kirk's local ability to sanction and fine through the kirk session, and because of the high rates of mobility of tenants among estates, suggesting that those who irritated each other were never together for long. Then again, the procession shaming Knox has been described as a skimmington by Richardson, *Death, Dissection and the Destitute*, p. 138. For a glimpse of the prostitute Paterson, enshrined as a glowing figure of a popular print, see the cover portrait on Edwards, *Hare and Burke*.

Notes to Chapter 5

15. The best evidence we have of the temporary suspension of social ties is in the habits of gallows crowds, who were generally on the side of the victim; see Adam Smith, *The Theory of Moral Sentiments*, ed. D. D. Raphael and A. L. McFie (Oxford: Clarendon Press, 1976), p. 88; and Peter Linebaugh, "The Tyburn Riot against the Surgeons," in Douglas Hay et al., eds., *Albion's Fatal Tree: Crime and Society in Eighteenth-Century England* (Middlesex: Penguin, 1975), pp. 65–117. On systematic individualism, see Elizabeth Fox-Genovese, ed., *The Autobiography of DuPont de Nemours* (Wilmington, Del.: Scholarly Resources, 1984), pp. 6–11. It may be that the great efforts made to reclaim criminals in the nineteenth century, especially women, were an unconscious outgrowth of the increasing difficulty of doing so, which a new criminal individualism suggests.

16. See Symonds, *Weep Not for Me*, pp. 211–31, and that portion of the bibliography on pp. 277–79, on women.

17. On the war between relatives and anatomists over bodies, with authorities often siding with the anatomists, see Richardson, *Death, Dissection and the Destitute*, pp. 52–99.

18. Richardson's *Death, Dissection and the Destitute* is the great source here, with Bransby B. Cooper, *The Life of Sir Astley Cooper, Bart.* (London: John W. Parker, 1843); James Blake Bailey, ed., *The Diary of a Resurrectionist 1811–1812* (London: Swan Sonnenschein Co., 1896), Hubert Cole, *Things for the Surgeon* (London: William Heinemann, 1964). Comrie, *History of Scottish Medicine*, John Knyveton, *The Diary of a Surgeon in the Year 1751–1752* (New York: D. Appleton-Century Co., 1937), and of course Burke's confessions. Rumors abounded, and perhaps none of the figures are exact, but the rough definition of the market probably is quite accurate.

19. For the information in this paragraph, and beyond, I am in debt to Richardson, *Death, Dissection and the Destitute*; see especially p. 102 on Lizars, and pp. 52–72, 100–103 for information most relevant to this work. See also T. Southwood Smith, "The Uses of the Dead to the Living," *Westminster Review* 1 (1824): 59–97, especially pp. 85–86 on the scarcity of bodies in Edinburgh, and the defection of students to Dublin and Paris; and Durey, "Bodysnatchers and Benthamites," pp. 200–225; especially pp. 200–203 on conditions before 1832.

20. The exceptions would be claims made to the body parts of saints by the church, and to historical figures such as pharaohs by their subjects and later by archeologists. The language of commodity is Richardson's; see her *Death, Dissection and the Destitute*, pp. 52–54, and on the London murders of 1831 by Bishop and Williams, see pp. 165, 193–97. Others have also used the language of business in discussing Burke, Hare, Log, and M'Dougal; see especially Jacques Barzun, who referred to their "story" as "one of the curiosities of capitalist enterprise;" see his *Burke and Hare*, p. v. See also the older commentator, Roughead, "Wolves of the West Port," pp. 117–76.

21. The choice of 1800 for the employment of gangs comes largely from the biographies of two notable anatomists, Sir Robert Christison and Sir Astley Cooper. Both were born before 1800, lived until roughly midcentury, and both remembered getting bodies themselves as students, and acknowledged the widespread use of gangs to do the same by the 1820s. See Christison, *Life of Sir Robert Christison*, pp. 170–80; and Cooper, *Life of Sir Astley Cooper*, pp. 339–408.

22. See *West Port Murders*, p. 350 for the *Courant* confession, and p. 204 for the reported

conversation; also Richardson, *Death, Dissection and the Destitute*, pp. 120, 136, 163, 173; and the Echo of Surgeons' Square, *A Letter to the Lord Advocate*. The latter is reprinted in Barzun, *Burke and Hare*, pp. 242–76.

23. Thompson, *Whigs and Hunters*; and his earlier "Eighteenth-Century Crime," pp. 9–11. Social crime, with its implicit sympathy for the situation of the criminal, accounts for a rather small percentage of the total crimes committed in eighteenth-century Britain, and other English social historians of crime have dealt with the "other" (and majority) of crimes as if they were rather dry and transhistorical stuff, related to moral flaws, population structure, war, and cyclic economic distress. This is the understandable result of records that allow one to study the judicial process and the decisions made. Legal records are very much about the law, and are meant to stand as proof of its proper administration, and this is easily where they take their readers. Despite the rather dry return of empirical studies, there have been cogent criticisms of Thompson from that school, as well as from those who do not study crime. On Thompson, social crime, and the British Marxists, see among others Gertrude Himmelfarb, *The Old Historians and the New* (Cambridge, Mass.: Belknap Press of Harvard University Press, 1987); Fox-Genovese, "Many Faces of Moral Economy," pp. 161–68; Langbein, "Albion's Fatal Flaws," pp. 96–120; Chapman, "Crime in Eighteenth-Century England," pp. 139–55; J. A. Sharpe, "History of Crime," pp. 187–203; Joanna Innes and John Styles, "The Crime Wave: Recent Writing on Crime and Criminal Justice in Eighteenth-Century England," *Journal of British Studies* 25:4 (1986): 380–435. Jean Valjean is the main character in Victor Hugo's *Les Miserables*. Hare's pig-feeder can be found in *West Port Murders*, p. 352.

24. Joseph A. Schumpeter, *Capitalism, Socialism and Democracy* (London: George Allen & Unwin, 1976), pp. 131, 125; and *The Theory of Economic Development: An Inquiry into Profits, Capital, Credit, Interest and the Business Cycle* (New York: Oxford University Press, 1961); and *Business Cycles: A Theoretical Historical and Statistical Analysis of the Capitalist Process, Abridged* (New York: McGraw Hill, 1964), both latter works deal in greater depth with the entrepreneur; and Richard N. Langlois, "Schumpeter and the Obsolescence of the Entrepreneur," paper presented at the History of Economics Society annual meeting, June 21, 1987, Boston. Electronic publication: http://www.ucc.uconn.edu/~LANGLOIS/SCHUMPET.HTML.

25. Henry Atton and Henry Hurst Holland, *The King's Customs. An Account of Maritime Revenue, Contraband Traffic, the Introduction of Free Trade, and the Abolition of the Navigation and Corn Laws, from 1801 to 1855*, vol. 2, Reprints of Economic Classics (New York: Augustus M. Kelley Publishers, 1967), p. 198. Also, Patrick Colquhoun, *A Treatise on the Commerce and Police of the River Thames*, rpt. from the London 1800 edition (Montclair, N.J.: Patterson Smith, 1969).

26. Colquhoun, *Treatise on the Commerce*; Michael Weisser, *Crime and Punishment in Early Modern Europe* (Atlantic Highlands, N.J.: Humanities Press, 1979); Donald A. Petrie, *The Prize Game: Lawful Looting on the High Seas in the Days of Fighting Sail* (Annapolis, Md.: Naval Institute Press, 1999). On Scots, see S. G. E. Lythe and J. Butt, *An Economic History of Scotland 1100–1939* (Glasgow & London: Blackie, 1975), pp. 56, 57, 63, 146; Lenman, *Economic History of Modern Scotland*, pp. 51, 61; and Henry Hamilton, *An Economic History of Scotland in the Eighteenth Century* (Oxford: Clarendon Press, 1963), p. 249 on illegal trade with North America. Along with piracy and shipwrecking came the use of the diving bell to recover cargo lost in

Notes to Chapter 5

shallow water; see Colin Martin, *Scotland's Historic Shipwrecks* (London: B. T. Batsford, 1998). Salvage rights differ from theft and ordinary piracy in being a legal form of theft, justified by cost and risk, and presumably, society's unwillingness to abandon what could be salvaged.

27. Whether this was piracy or some aspect of the internal conflict between York and Lancaster, Atton and Holland do not consider; see Atton and Holland, *King's Customs*, p. 43.

28. See Lisa Jardine, *Worldly Goods: A New History of the Renaissance* (London: Macmillan, 1996), pp. 321–30. The literature on slavery is immense; see briefly, David Brion Davis, *The Problem of Slavery in the Age of Revolution 1770–1823* (Ithaca and London: Cornell University Press, 1975); Orlando Patterson, *Freedom*, Volume I: *Freedom in the Making of Western Culture* (New York: Basic Books, 1991); Eugene D. Genovese, *A Consuming Fire: The Fall of the Confederacy in the Mind of the White Christian South* (Athens and London: University of Georgia Press, 1998). On Hawkins and Drake, see two recent books by Harry Kelsey, *Sir Francis Drake: The Queen's Pirate* (New Haven and London: Yale University Press, 2000); and *Sir John Hawkins: Queen Elizabeth's Slave Trader* (New Haven and London: Yale University Press, 2003).

29. Fraudulent imitation allowed northern Atlantic weavers and merchants to undermine Venetian woolen textiles' prominence in the Mediterranean by 1600. What was clever imitation to the English was a crime and a disaster to the Venetians. And when the Nordlingen woolen merchant Daniel Worner began to monopolize the town's textile sales, and convert master weavers into something very like employees in the late 1600s, those weavers took him to court. They won a small victory there in 1698, but lost the war to the next generation of Worners. For this information and more, I am indebted to the work of Charles R. Friedrichs and Richard Rapp on early modern European business and trade.

30. There are two classic sources for the history of the watch and time: David S. Landes, *Revolution in Time: Clocks and the Making of the Modern World* (Cambridge, Mass., and London, England: The Belknap Press of Harvard University Press, 1983), see pp. 274–96; and E. P. Thompson, "Time, Work-Discipline and Industrial Capitalism," *Past and Present* 38 (December 1967): 39–77.

31. For Hannah Barton, see AD 14/19; Burke and his watch see *West Port Murders*, p. 208; Barbara Kerr, see AD 14/26, and JC 26/522; for Margaret Veitch, see AD 14/30.

32. Barzun, *Burke and Hare*, pp. 101–7, testimony of Mrs. Gray. For Barbara Kerr, see AD 14/26, and JC 26/522; for Hannah Barton, see JC 226/523, AD 14/19; for Davie Stark, see the case of Margaret Stewart of Burrows (also old Mrs. Burrows), AD 14/22; for Elizabeth or Betty McKinnon, see JC 26/522, and AD 14/50.

Bibliography

Archival Sources, National Archive of Scotland

NAS AD 2/1, William Burke and Helen M'Dougal, December 24, 1828.
NAS JC 8/23, William Burke and Helen M'Dougal, December 24, 1828.
NAS JC 26/524, Elizabeth McDonald, August 19, 1828; Catherine Liston or Johnson, November 4, 1828.
NAS GD 1/353/3-5, William Burke, Helen M'Dougal, William Hare, Margaret Laird, November 3, November 19, December 4, 1828.
NAS JC 26/522, Elizabeth or Betty McKinnon.
NAS JC 26/522, Barbara Kerr, Margaret Thomson or McKenzie, Elizabeth Paterson.
NAS JC 26/523, Helen White or Williamson, Mary Ann McDonald, Hannah Hodgson or Barton.
NAS AD 14/28/17, Elizabeth Paterson.
NAS AD 1428/19, Hannah Hodgson or Barton.
NAS AD 14/28/22, Margaret Stewart or Burrows.
NAS AD 14/28/26, Barbara Kerr.
NAS AD 14/28/30, Margaret Veitch, Amos Low.
NAS AD 14/28/50, Elizabeth McKinnon.
NAS AD 14/28/55, Sarah Murray, or Mrs. Binnie.
NAS AD 14/28/61, Margaret Robertson.
NAS AD 14/28/79, Janet Morrison.
NAS AD 14/28/83, Mary Ann McDonald.
NAS AD 14/28/120, Mary Kirkland or McKenzie.

Primary Sources, Printed Books

Anon. *The Story of Daft Jamie, One of the Victims of Burke and Hare.* Edinburgh, 1829.
Anon. *West Port Murders.* Edinburgh: Thomas Ireland, Junior, 1829.
―――. *West Port Murders.* Edinburgh: Thomas Ireland, Junior, 1829; rpt., Edinburgh: West Port Books, 2001.
Barzun, Jacques, ed. *Burke and Hare: The Resurrection Men. A Collection of Contemporary Documents*

Bibliography

Including Broadsides, Occasional Verses, Illustrations, Polemics, and a Complete Transcript of the Testimony at the Trial. Metuchen, N.J.: Scarecrow Press, 1974.

Christison, Sir Robert. *The Life of Sir Robert Christison*, edited by his sons. Edinburgh and London: William Blackwood and Sons, 1885–86.

Cockburn, Henry. *Memorials of His Time*. 1856.

Colquhoun, Patrick. *A Treatise on the Police of the Metropolis*. London: C. Dilly, 1797.

———. *A Treatise on the Commerce and Police of the River Thames*. 1800. Reprint, Montclair, N.J.: Patterson Smith, 1969.

Cooper, Bransby B. *The Life of Sir Astley Cooper, Bart*. London: John W. Parker, 1843.

Echo of Surgeons' Square [David Paterson]. *A Letter to the Lord Advocate*. Edinburgh, 1829.

Fielding, Henry. *An Enquiry into the Causes of the Late Increase of Robbers & with Some Proposals for Remedying This Growing Evil*. London: A. Millar, 1751.

The First and Second Statistical Accounts of the City of Edinburgh, 1799 and 1845. Edinburgh: West Port Books, 1998.

Leighton, A. *Court of Cacus*. London, 1861.

Lizars, A. J. *A System of Anatomical Plates of the Human Body*. Edinburgh, 1822–26.

Lonsdale, Henry. *A Sketch of the Life of Robert Knox, the Anatomist*. London: Macmillan, 1870.

Macnee, John. *Trial of William Burke and Helen M'Dougal, Before the High Court of Justiciary, at Edinburgh, on Wednesday, December 24, 1828, for the Murder of Margery Campbell, or Docherty. Taken in Short Hand by Mr John Macnee, Writer*. Edinburgh: Robert Buchanan, 1829. Preface attributed to C. K. Sharpe; anonymous.

Medicus (pseud.). *An Exposure of the Present System of Obtaining Bodies for Dissection*. London, 1829.

Smith, Adam. *An Inquiry into the Nature and Causes of the Wealth of Nations*. New York: Modern Library, 1937.

———. *The Theory of Moral Sentiments*. Edited by D. D. Raphael and A. L. McFie. Oxford: Clarendon Press, 1976.

Stone, T. *Observations on the Phrenological Development of Burke, Hare, and Other Atrocious Murderers*. Edinburgh, 1829.

Tait, William. *Magdalenism: An Inquiry into the Extent, Causes, and Consequences of Prostitution in Edinburgh*. Edinburgh: P. Richards, 1840.

Primary Sources, Periodical

Blackwood's Edinburgh Magazine

Caledonian Mercury

Edinburgh Evening Courant, November 3, 1828; January 29, 1829; February 7, 1829.

Edinburgh Observer

Scotsman

Anon. "Prisons." *Edinburgh Review* 36 (1822): 353–74.

Druit, Dr. "The Late Dr. Knox." *Medical Times & Gazette* 2 (December 27, 1862): 683–85.

Gooch, B. "A Bill for Preventing the Unlawful Disinterment of Bodies." *Quarterly Review* 42 (1830).

Smith, Sydney. "Prisons," *Edinburgh Review* 36 (1822): 353–74.
Smith, T. Southwood. "The Uses of the Dead to the Living." Review of William Mackenzie, *An Appeal to the Public and to the Legislature, on the Necessity of affording Dead Bodies to the Schools of Anatomy, by Legislative Enactment*. *Westminster Review* 1 (1824): 59–97.

Secondary Sources, Books

Adams, Norman. *Scottish Bodysnatchers*. Musselburgh, Scotland: Goblinshead, 2002.
Atton, Henry, and Henry Hurst Holland. *The King's Customs: An Account of Maritime Revenue, Contraband Traffic, the Introduction of Free Trade, and the Abolition of the Navigation and Corn Laws, from 1801 to 1855*. Vol. 2. 1910. Reprint, New York: Augustus M. Kelley Publishers, 1967.
Bailey, James Blake, ed. *The Diary of a Resurrectionist 1811–1812*. London: Swan Sonnenschein Co., 1896.
Ball, James Moores, M.D., LL.D. *The Body Snatchers*. New York: Dorset Press, 1989. Reprint of the 1928 edition.
Beattie, J. M. *Crime and the Courts in England, 1660–1800*. Princeton, N.J.: Princeton University Press, 1986.
Bonger, Willem A. *Criminality and Economic Conditions*, trans. Henry P. Horton. Boston, Mass.: Little, Brown & Co., 1916.
Brewer, John, and John Styles, eds. *An Ungovernable People: The English and Their Law in the Seventeenth and Eighteenth Centuries*. New Brunswick, N.J.: Rutgers University Press, 1980.
Brown, George Douglas. *The House with the Green Shutters*. Harmondsworth, Middlesex, England: Penguin Books, 1985.
Brown, Hamish. *Exploring the Edinburgh to Glasgow Canals*. Edinburgh: Stationery Office, 1997.
Brown, P.[eter] Hume. *The History of Scotland*. Vol. 2–3. Cambridge: Cambridge University Press, 1905–11.
Burton, Anthony, and Derek Pratt. *The Anatomy of Canals: The Early Years*. Stroud, Gloucestershire: Tempus Publishing, 2001.
Burton, James Hill. *Narratives of Criminal Trials in Scotland*. 2 vols. London: Chapman and Hall, 1852.
Cage, R. A. *The Scottish Poor Law, 1745–1845*. Edinburgh: Scottish Academic Press, 1981.
Cameron, Joy. *Prisons and Punishment in Scotland from the Middle Ages to the Present*. Edinburgh: Canongate, 1983.
Cameron, Rondo. *A Concise Economic History of the World*. New York: Oxford University Press, 1993.
Carlyle, Thomas. *Selected Writings*. Edited by Alan Shelston. Harmondsworth, England: Penguin, 1971.
Catford, E. F. *Edinburgh: The Story of a City*. London: Hutchinson & Co., 1975.
Cockburn, J. S., ed. *Crime in England, 1550–1800*. Princeton, N.J.: Princeton University Press, 1977.
Cole, Hubert. *Things for the Surgeon*. London: William Heinemann, 1964.
Comrie, John D. *History of Scottish Medicine*. 2 vols. London: For the Wellcome Historical Medical Museum by Balliere, Tindall & Cox, 1932.

The Concise Scots Dictionary. Aberdeen: Aberdeen University Press, 1985.

Davidoff, Leonore, and Catherine Hall. *Family Fortunes: Men and Women of the English Middle Class, 1780–1850.* Chicago: University of Chicago Press, 1987.

Davis, David Brion. *The Problem of Slavery in the Age of Revolution 1770–1823.* Ithaca and London: Cornell University Press, 1975.

Davis, Natalie Zemon. *The Return of Martin Guerre.* Cambridge, Mass.: Harvard University Press, 1983.

Devine, T. M. *The Scottish Nation.* New York: Viking, 1999.

———. *The Tobacco Lords.* Edinburgh: Edinburgh University Press, 1975.

———. "Unrest and Stability in Rural Ireland and Scotland, 1760–1840." In Rosalind Mitchison and Peter Roebuck, eds., *Economy and Society in Scotland and Ireland, 1500–1939.* Edinburgh: John Donald Publishers, 1988.

Donzelot, Jacques. *The Policing of Families.* New York: Pantheon, 1979.

Douglas, Hugh. *Burke and Hare: The True Story.* London: Robert Hale & Company, 1973.

Easton, Drew, ed. *By the Three Great Roads: A History of Tollcross, Fountainbridge, and the West Port.* Aberdeen: Aberdeen University Press, 1988.

Edwards, Owen Dudley. *Burke & Hare.* Edinburgh: Polygon Books, 1984.

Elton, G. R. "Crime and the Historian." In J. S. Cockburn, ed., *Crime in England, 1550–1800.* Princeton, N.J.: Princeton University Press, 1977, pp. 1–14.

Emsley, Clive. *Crime and Society in England, 1750–1900.* London and New York: Longman, 1987.

Engels, Friedrich. *The Condition of the Working Class in England.* Edited and translated by W. O. Henderson and W. H. Chaloner. Oxford: Basil Blackwell, 1958.

Finnegan, Frances. *Poverty and Prostitution: A Study of Victorian Prostitutes in York.* Cambridge: Cambridge University Press, 1979.

Foucault, Michel. *Discipline and Punish: The Birth of the Prison.* New York: Vintage, 1979.

Fox-Genovese, Elizabeth, ed. *The Autobiography of DuPont de Nemours.* Wilmington, Del.: Scholarly Resources, 1984.

Gattrell, V. A. C., Bruce Lenman, and Geoffrey Parker, eds. *Crime and the Law: The Social History of Crime in Western Europe since 1500.* London: Europa Publications, 1980.

Genovese, Eugene D. *A Consuming Fire: The Fall of the Confederacy in the Mind of the White Christian South.* Athens and London: University of Georgia Press, 1998.

Grant, I. F. *Highland Folk Ways.* London, Boston, and Henley: Routledge & Kegan Paul, 1961.

Greenberg, David F. "Crime." In Thomas B. Bottomore, ed., *A Dictionary of Marxist Thought.* Oxford: Basil Blackwell, 1983.

Hamilton, Henry. *An Economic History of Scotland in the Eighteenth Century.* Oxford: Clarendon Press, 1963.

Hanawalt, Barbara. *Crime and Conflict in English Communities, 1300–1348.* Cambridge, Mass.: Harvard University Press, 1979.

Hay, Douglas, et al., eds. *Albion's Fatal Tree: Crime and Society in Eighteenth-Century England.* Harmondsworth: Penguin, 1977.

Herman, Arthur. *How the Scots Invented the Modern World.* New York: Crown Publishers, 2001.

Himmelfarb, Gertrude. *The Old Historians and the New.* Cambridge, Mass.: Belknap Press of Harvard University Press, 1987.

———. *The Roads to Modernity: The British, French, and American Enlightenments.* New York: Knopf, 2004.
Hobsbawm, Eric J. *The Age of Revolution.* New York: New American Library, 1962.
Huet, Marie-Helene. *Monstrous Imagination.* Cambridge, Mass. and London, England: Harvard University Press, 1993.
Hutton, Guthrie. *Scotland's Millennium Canals: The Survival and Revival of the Forth & Clyde and Union Canals.* Catrine, Ayrshire: Stenlake Publishing, 2002.
Hutton, Richard H. *The Life of Sir Walter Scott Abridged from Lockhart's Life of Scott.* Philadelphia: John D. Morris & Company, n.d.
Jardine, Lisa. *Worldly Goods: A New History of the Renaissance.* London: Macmillan, 1996.
Kelsey, Harry. *Sir Francis Drake: The Queen's Pirate.* New Haven and London: Yale University Press, 2000.
———. *Sir John Hawkins: Queen Elizabeth's Slave Trader.* New Haven and London: Yale University Press, 2003.
Khan, Abdul Majed. *The Transition in Bengal, 1756–1775.* Cambridge: Cambridge University Press, 1969.
Knyveton, John. *The Diary of a Surgeon in the Year 1751–1752.* New York: D. Appleton-Century Company, 1937.
Landes, David S. *Revolution in Time: Clocks and the Making of the Modern World.* Cambridge, Mass., and London, England: The Belknap Press of Harvard University Press, 1983.
Larner, Christina. "Crimen Exceptum? The Crime of Witchcraft in Europe." In V. A. C. Gattrell, Bruce Lenman, and Geoffrey Parker, eds., *Crime and the Law: The Social History of Crime in Western Europe since 1500.* London: Europa Publications, 1980.
———. *Enemies of God: The Witch-Hunt in Scotland.* Baltimore: Johns Hopkins University Press, 1981.
Lenman, Bruce. *An Economic History of Modern Scotland.* Hamden, Conn.: Archon Books, 1977.
———. *Integration, Enlightenment, and Industrialization: Scotland, 1746–1832.* London: Edward Arnold, 1981.
Linebaugh, Peter. "The Tyburn Riot against the Surgeons." In Douglas Hay et al., eds., *Albion's Fatal Tree: Crime and Society in Eighteenth-Century England.* Middlesex: Penguin, 1975.
Logue, Kenneth. *Popular Disturbances in Scotland, 1780–1815.* Edinburgh: John Donald Publishers, 1979.
Lythe, S. G. E., and J. Butt. *An Economic History of Scotland, 1100–1939.* Glasgow & London: Blackie, 1975.
Macfarlane, Alan. *Witchcraft in Tudor and Stuart England.* Prospect Heights, Ill.: Waveland Press, 1970.
MacGregor, George. *The History of Burke and Hare and of the Resurrectionist Times.* Glasgow: Thomas D. Morrison, 1884.
Mackenzie, W. C. *Andrew Fletcher of Saltoun.* Edinburgh: Porpoise Press, 1935.
Mahood, Linda. *The Magdalenes: Prostitution in the Nineteenth Century.* London: Routledge, 1990.
Marcus, Steven. *Engels, Manchester, and the Working Class.* New York: Random House, 1974.
Marshall, P. J. *The Oxford History of the British Empire.* Vol. 2, *The Eighteenth Century.* Oxford: Oxford University Press, 1998.

Martin, Colin. *Scotland's Historic Shipwrecks.* London: B. T. Batsford, 1998.
Mitchison, Rosalind. "The Poor Law." In T. M. Devine and Rosalind Mitchison, eds., *People and Society in Scotland.* Vol. 1. Edinburgh: John Donald Publishers, 1988.
Murray, Arthur C. *The Five Sons of Bare Betty.* London: John Murray, 1936.
Omond, George W. T. *The Lord Advocates of Scotland from the Close of the Fifteenth Century to the Passing of the Reform Bill.* Edinburgh: David Douglas, 1883.
O'Suilleabhain, Sean. *Irish Wake Amusements.* Dublin and Cork: Mercier Press, 1979.
Patterson, Orlando. *Freedom.* Vol. 1, *Freedom in the Making of Western Culture.* New York: Basic Books, 1991.
Peachey, George C. *A Memoir of William & John Hunter.* Plymouth: William Brendon and Son, 1924.
Perkin, Harold. *The Origins of Modern English Society.* London: Routledge & Kegan Paul, 1969.
Petrie, Donald A. *The Prize Game: Lawful Looting on the High Seas in the Days of Fighting Sail.* Annapolis, Md.: Naval Institute Press, 1999.
Philips, David. *Crime and Authority in Victorian England: The Black Country, 1835–1860.* Totowa, N.J.: Rowman and Littlefield, 1977.
Polanyi, Karl. *The Great Transformation: The Political and Economic Origins of Our Time.* New York: Rinehart & Company, 1944.
Pollock, Otto. *The Criminality of Women.* Westport, Conn.: Greenwood Publishing Group, 1978.
Posner, Richard. *The Problems of Jurisprudence.* Cambridge, Mass.: Harvard University Press, 1990.
Prebble, John. *The King's Jaunt.* London: Collins, 1988.
Pringle, Patrick. *Hue and Cry: The Story of Henry and John Fielding and Their Bow Street Runners.* New York: William Morrow & Co., n.d.
Rae, T. I., ed. *The Union of 1707: Its Impact on Scotland.* London: Blackie & Son, 1974.
Reynolds, Elaine A. *Before the Bobbies: The Night Watch and the Police Reform in Metropolitan London.* Stanford: Stanford University Press, 1998.
Rice, C. Duncan. *The Scots Abolitionists 1833–1861.* Baton Rouge and London: Louisiana State University Press, 1981.
Richardson, Ruth. *Death, Dissection and the Destitute.* London and New York: Routledge & Kegan Paul, 1987.
Roughead, William, ed. *Burke and Hare.* Notable British Trials Series. Toronto: Canada Law Book Company, 1921.
———. *The Murderer's Companion.* New York: The Readers Club, 1941.
Schumpeter, Joseph A. *Business Cycles: A Theoretical Historical and Statistical Analysis of the Capitalist Process.* Abridged. New York: McGraw Hill, 1964.
———. *Capitalism, Socialism and Democracy.* London: George Allen & Unwin, 1976.
———. *The Theory of Economic Development: An Inquiry into Profits, Capital, Credit, Interest and the Business Cycle.* New York: Oxford University Press, 1961.
Scott, Sir Walter. *The Journal of Sir Walter Scott.* New York: Harper & Brothers, 1891.
Sharp, Buchanan. *In Contempt of All Authority: Rural Artisans and Riot in the West of England, 1586–1660.* Berkeley: University of California Press, 1980.

Sharpe, J. A. *Crime in Early Modern England, 1550–1750.* New York: Longman, 1984.
Smout, T. C., ed. *The Search for Wealth and Stability: Essays in Economic and Social History, Presented to M. W. Flinn.* London: Macmillan, 1979.
Stone, Jean. *Voices from the Waterways.* Gloucestershire: Sutton Publishing, 1997.
Sutherland, Lucy Stuart. *The East India Company in Eighteenth-Century Politics.* Oxford: Clarendon Press, 1952.
Swann, Elsie, *Christopher North.* Edinburgh: Oliver and Boyd, 1934.
Symonds, Deborah A. *Weep Not for Me: Women, Ballads, and Infanticide in Early Modern Scotland.* University Park: Pennsylvania State University Press, 1997.
Thompson, E. P. *Whigs and Hunters: The Origin of the Black Act.* New York: Random House, 1975.
Tobias, John Jacob. *Crime and Industrial Society in the 19th Century.* New York: Schocken Books, 1967.
Walvin, James. *England, Slaves and Freedom, 1776–1838.* Jackson and London: University Press of Mississippi, 1986.
Weisser, Michael. *Crime and Punishment in Early Modern Europe.* Atlantic Highlands, N.J.: Humanities Press, 1979.
Wilkinson, George Theodore. *The Newgate Calendar.* Introduction by Christopher Hibbert. London: Sphere Books, 1991.
Wrightson, Keith. *English Society, 1580–1680.* New Brunswick, N.J.: Rutgers University Press, 1982.
Young, James D. *Women and Popular Struggles.* Edinburgh: Mainstream, 1985.
Youngson, A, J. *The Making of Classical Edinburgh.* Edinburgh: Edinburgh University Press, 1966.

Secondary Sources, Periodical

Beattie, J. M. "The Criminality of Women in Eighteenth-Century England." *Journal of Social History* 8 (Summer 1975): 80–116.
Bruford, A., and M. MacDonald. "Burkers and Resurrectionists." *Tocher Journal* 5 (1972).
Chapman, Terry L. "Crime in Eighteenth-Century England: E. P. Thompson and the Conflict Theory of Crime." *Criminal Justice History* 1 (1980): 139–55.
Charlesworth, Andrew. "An Agenda for Historical Studies of Rural Protest in Britain, 1750–1850." *Rural History* 2:2 (1991): 231–40.
Clark, Henry C. "Women and Humanity in Scottish Enlightenment Social Thought: The Case of Adam Smith." *Historical Reflections/Réflexions Historiques* 19:3 (1993): 335–61.
Cohen, Patricia Cline. "Unregulated Youth: Masculinity and Murder in the 1830s City." *Radical History Review* 52 (1992): 33–52.
Cooper, Robyn. "Alexander Walker's Trilogy on Woman." *Journal of the History of Sexuality* 2:3 (1992): 341–64.
Durey, M. "Bodysnatchers and Benthamites." *London Journal* 2 (1976): 200–225.
Elshtain, Jean Bethke. "Everything for Sale." *Books & Culture* (May/June 1998): 8–11.
Fox-Genovese, Elizabeth. "The Many Faces of Moral Economy: A Contribution to a Debate." *Past and Present* 58 (1973): 161–68.

Frank, Julia Bess. "Body Snatching: A Grave Medical Problem." *Yale Journal of Biology and Medicine* 49 (1976): 399–410.
Garland, David. "Criminological Knowledge and Its Relation to Power: Foucault's Genealogy and Criminology Today." *British Journal of Criminology* 37:4 (1997): 403–22.
Guttmacher, Alan F. "Bootlegging Bodies: A History of Body-Snatching." *Bulletin of the Society of Medical History of Chicago* 4:4 (January 1935): 353–402.
Hamlin, Hannibal. "The Dissection Riot of 1824 and the Connecticut Anatomical Law." *Yale Journal of Biology and Medicine* 7:4 (1934–35): 275–89.
Henderson, Anthony R. "Prostitution and the City." *Journal of Urban History* 23:2 (1997): 231–39.
Hobsbawm, E. J. "Distinctions between the Socio-Political and Other Forms of Crime." *Bulletin—Society for the Study of Labour History* 25 (Autumn 1972): 5–7.
Innes, Joanna, and John Styles. "The Crime Wave: Recent Writing on Crime and Criminal Justice in Eighteenth-Century England." *Journal of British Studies* 25: 4 (1980): 380–435.
Jewson, N. D. "Medical Knowledge and the Patronage System in 18th Century England." *Sociology* 8 (1974): 369–85.
Kauffman, Matthew H. "Another Look at Burke and Hare: The Last Day of Mary Patterson—A Medical Cover-Up?" *Proceedings of the Royal College of Physicians of Edinburgh* 27 (1997): 78–88.
King, Peter. "Decision-Makers and Decision-Making in the English Criminal Law." *Historical Journal* 27:1 (1984): 25–58.
Klein, Dorie. "The Etiology of Female Crime: A Review of the Literature." *Issues in Criminology* 8:2 (1973): 3–30.
Langbein, John H. "Albion's Fatal Flaws." *Past and Present* 98 (1983): 96–120.
Langlois, Richard N. "Schumpeter and the Obsolescence of the Entrepreneur." Paper presented at the History of Economics Society annual meeting, Boston, Mass., June 21, 1987. www.ucc.uconn.edu/~langlois/schumpet.html.
Lenman, Bruce, and Philip Lawson. "Robert Clive, the 'Black Jaghir,' and British Politics." *Historical Journal* 26 (December 1983): 801–29.
Marmoy, C. F. A. "The Auto Icon of Jeremy Bentham at University College." *Medical History* 11:2 (1958).
Mui, Lorna H. and Hoh-Cheung. "Smuggling and the British Tea Trade before 1784." *American Historical Review* 74 (1968): 44–73.
Murr, Andrew. "Bad News for the Body Trade." *Newsweek* (March 22, 2004): 42.
North, Christopher [John Wilson]. "The West-Port Murders." *Blackwood's Magazine* (March 1829).
Ross, Ian, and Carol Urquhart Ross. "Bodysnatching in Nineteenth-Century Britain." *British Journal of Law and Society* 6:1 (1979): 108–18.
Sharpe, J. A. "The History of Crime in Late Medieval and Early Modern England: A Review of the Field." *Social History* 7:2 (1982): 187–203.
Sindall, Rob. "Middle-Class Crime in Nineteenth-Century England." *Criminal Justice History* 4 (1983): 23–40.
Smith, A. T. H. "Stealing the Body and its Parts." *Criminal Law Review* 10 (1976): 622–27.

Smout, Christopher. "The Culture of Migration: Scots as Europeans 1500–1800." *History Workshop Journal* 40 (Autumn 1995): 108–17.

Sullivan, Charles R. "Enacting the Scottish Enlightenment: Tobias Smollett's Expedition of Humphrey Clinker." *Journal of The Historical Society* 4:4 (2004): 415–46.

Tait, H. P. "Some Edinburgh Medical Men." *Edinburgh Medical Journal* 55 (1948): 116–23.

Thompson, E. P. "Eighteenth-Century Crime, Popular Movements and Social Control." *Bulletin—Society for the Study of Labour History* 25 (Autumn 1972): 9–11.

———. "The Moral Economy of the English Crowd in the Eighteenth Century." *Past and Present* 50 (February 1971): 76–136.

———. "Time, Work-Discipline and Industrial Capitalism." *Past and Present* 38 (December 1967): 39–77.

Tur, R. H. S. "What is Jurisprudence?" *Philosophical Quarterly* 28:111 (April 1978): 259–332.

Weiner, Carol Z. "Sex Roles and Crime in Late Elizabethan Hertfordshire." *Journal of Social History* 8 (Summer 1975): 38–60.

Whatley, Christopher A. "The Union of 1707, Integration and the Scottish Burghs: The Case of the 1720 Food Riots." *Scottish Historical Review* 2:206 (October 1999): 192–218.

Wood, Allen W. "The Marxian Critique of Justice." *Philosophy & Public Affairs* 1 (Spring 1972); 244–282.

Wright-St. Clair, R. E. "Murder for Anatomy." *NZ Medical Journal* 60 (1961): 64–69.

Index

Adams, David, xi, xii
advocate depute, 75, 101, 153n. 3
  Alison, Archibald, 75, 153n. 3
  Dundas, Robert, 75
  Wood, Alexander, 75, 101
Allan, Elizabeth, xi, xiii
Alston, Hugh, 35, 40, 67, 149n. 15
anatomy, 17, 18, 82, 83, 110, 120–23, 126–28, 133, 142n. 3, 147n. 26, 154n. 21, 162n. 6, 168, 174
  Anatomy Act of 1832, Lord Warburton's, 128
Anderson, Bell, 65, 66, 68
Armagh, 108
assythment (blood money), 95

Barclay, John, 98
Barton, Hannah, 60, 102, 139–41, 165n. 31
Baslar, William, 62–64, 123, 124, 140
Beacon, The, 90
Begbie, Helen, graverobber, 69, 152n. 24
Bentham, Jeremy, 128, 133, 147n. 26, 151n. 13, 152n. 24, 162n. 6, 173
  Benthamite, 128, 147n. 26, 162n. 6, 163n. 18, 172
Bertram the Cowfeeder, xi
Bibles, 70, 138, 152n. 25
Big Hamilton's Close, 64, 124
Black, Dr. Alexander, police surgeon, 50, 122
Blackfriar's Wynd, xi, xiii, 124
Blackwood's Edinburgh Magazine, 90, 103, 129, 149n. 22, 157n. 40, 159n. 17, 167, 173
body, human, 23, 24, 27, 31, 32, 35, 42, 44–47, 49, 51, 78, 81, 82, 91, 92, 105, 112, 121, 128, 129, 135, 139, 150n. 37, 165n. 17,
  as commodity, 18, 29, 34, 50, 69, 98, 111, 113, 120, 122, 123, 125, 127, 133, 134, 136, 146n. 26, 147n. 26, 148n. 12, 160n. 41, 161n. 42, 162n. 6, 168, 172, 173
Boyle, David, Right Honorable, 75, 89, 128, 129, 155n. 24
Bridewell, 58, 59, 60, 62, 65, 68, 69, 146n. 23, 151n. 13, 152n. 24, 162n. 6
Bristo Port, 55
Brogan, John, 32, 43, 46, 68, 115, 116, 150n. 39
Brooks, Ann, 62
Brown, Janet, 26, 28, 67, 95, 114, 148nn. 7–9, 160n. 25
Brown, John, 55
Bruce, Hugh, advocate, 75
Bruce, James, 3
Burke, Constantine, 25–28, 86, 95, 114, 148n. 9, 152n. 20
Burke, Elizabeth, wife of Constantine, 26, 28, 148n. 21, 152n. 20
Burke, William, xiii, 1, 17, 22, 23, 80, 83, 101, 102, 106, 127, 140, 147n. 1, 148n. 21, 149n. 28, 154n. 11, 158n. 2, 161n. 42, 166, 167
Burrows, old Mrs., 57, 69, 72, 102, 124, 151, 165, 166

Caledonian Mercury, 79, 81, 94, 107, 113, 119, 129, 160n. 28, 167

175

Index

Calton Hill, 58, 97, 152n. 24
Calton Jail, 85, 86
Campbell, Marion, or May, 65–67, 152n. 22
Campbell, Michael, 35
Campbells of Argyll, 51
Candlemaker Row, 62, 64
Canongate, North Back of, 52, 58
Catholic Emancipation, 4
Catholics, 4, 22, 102, 105, 108
  Irish, 4, 22, 34, 35, 46, 58, 102, 104, 105, 108, 110, 114, 135, 136, 143n. 6, 150n. 41, 160n. 21, 162n. 7, 170
Christison, Dr. Robert, 122, 157nn. 40–41, 161n. 44, 163n. 21, 167
clearances, highland, 3
Clerk, John, 90
Cockburn, Henry, 6, 75–77, 80, 81, 83, 84, 89, 90, 94, 103, 104, 109, 117, 119, 153n. 5, 154nn. 13, 16, 155n. 17, 159n. 7, 160nn. 38, 40, 167
Colquhoun, Patrick, 137, 146n. 23, 164nn. 25, 26, 167
Connoway, Mrs. Ann, and Mr. John, 36–38, 40, 43, 44, 46, 49, 50, 84, 118, 149nn. 28, 30, 31, 150nn. 40, 41, 47–49, 158n. 4
Corn Laws, 3, 164n. 25, 168
courts, 5, 15, 16, 21, 137, 145nn. 19–20, 146n. 22, 151n. 1, 152n. 24, 153n. 28, 168
  baron, 15
  Church, 15
  High Court of Justiciary, 6, 15, 17, 74, 93, 95, 147n. 1, 149n. 25, 151nn. 7, 9–10, 14, 152nn. 16, 19, 156n. 31, 158n. 3, 167
  police, 15
Cowgate, xi, xvi, 25, 45, 52, 54, 55, 57, 59, 64, 65, 73, 87, 124, 140, 151n. 3
Cowgate Port, 25, 45
Crawford's Close, 58
crime, ix, x, xi, xiii, 7–16, 52, 53, 60, 64, 71, 72, 74, 76–81, 83, 84, 94, 112, 119, 126, 128–32, 136–38, 141
  arson, 8, 14
  bestiality, 15
  deforcement, 15
  false coining, 15, 137
  homicide, 14
  incest, 15
  infanticide, or child murder, 7, 14–16, 77, 132, 144n. 8
  kidnapping, 14, 120
  notorious adultery, 15
  rape, 8, 12, 15
  riot, 1, 2, 7, 8, 10, 15, 74, 85, 92, 135, 136, 144n. 11, 146n. 22, 147n. 26, 163n. 15
  social crime, 8–12, 15, 53, 136, 144n. 11, 145nn. 15, 17–18, 164n. 23
  theft, xiii, 8, 9, 13, 15, 52, 67, 71, 102, 124, 125, 130, 136–38, 140, 141, 150n. 37, 153n. 28, 165n. 26
  witchcraft, 7, 14–16, 131, 144n. 9, 146nn. 21–22, 150n. 42, 170, 173
criminal underworld, xiii, 13, 74
  underworld, xiii, 13, 18, 53, 54, 72, 74, 127, 146n. 25

Davie Street, 55
Davis, Natalie Zemon, 7, 144n. 9, 169
Docherty, Mary, aka Madge Campbell, M'Gonegal, or Duffie, 17, 34–42, 44, 47, 48, 50, 59, 67, 70, 74, 78, 80, 81, 84, 94, 103, 112–16, 118, 120, 122, 147n. 1, 149nn. 26, 28, 156n. 33, 157n. 41, 158n. 4, 160nn. 27, 41, 161n. 42, 167
Donald the Pensioner, 23, 24, 111, 134
Donaldson, Robert, 65, 66, 68
Doyle, Jane, 67
Duff, Betty, 66
Dumfries, 112
Dundas, family, 6, 75, 144n. 8
  Robert, advocate depute, 75

East India Company, 3, 143n. 5, 171
East Meal Market Stair, 64
East Smith's Close, 64
Edinburgh Advertiser, 95
Edinburgh Evening Courant, 78, 86, 147n. 1, 153n. 2, 154n. 9, 167
Edinburgh Observer, 95, 167
Edinburgh Police Establishment, 16, 53, 56, 61, 140, 148n. 9
Edinburgh Review, 90, 93, 146n. 23, 167, 172

Index

Effie the cinder gatherer, 30, 103, 115, 159n. 6
Elton, G. R., 8, 144nn. 10, 12, 172
Engels, Friedrich, 7, 10–12, 144n. 14, 158n. 3, 169, 170
Enlightenment, ix, 2, 3, 5–7, 11, 18, 21, 126, 129, 143nn. 4, 6, 172, 174
entrepreneur, 4, 18, 28, 119, 127, 135–37, 164n. 24, 173
Equitable Loan Company, 55, 124, 139
Erskine, Henry, 6

Factory, Tureen Street power loom, 110
Fergusson, Mr. William, 120, 121, 123, 154n. 15, 161n. 42
Finlay or Findlay, John, officer, 50, 150n. 48
Fisher, John, police officer, 50, 150n. 48
Forth & Clyde Canal, 2, 142n. 3, 169
French Revolution, 6, 89, 90, 156n. 26

gangs, xiii, 16–18, 62, 65, 71, 72, 77, 95, 102, 107, 110, 112, 120, 130, 132, 139, 146n. 26, 152n. 24, 162n. 13, 163n. 21
Gayfield Square, 56
George IV, Bridge, 53–55, 64, 151nn. 2, 3
George IV, King, 1, 3
Gibb, Betty, 65, 66
Glasgow, 2, 4, 5, 22, 35, 57, 86, 92, 93, 102, 110, 130, 135, 143n. 3, 156n. 33, 164n. 26, 168
Glasgow Chronicle, 93
Grassmarket, ix, xvi, 21, 22, 25, 52, 55, 62–65, 73, 85, 90, 100, 101, 102, 124, 140, 151n. 5
grave robbers. *See* resurrectionists
Gray, Mr. and Mrs., 33, 35, 36, 38, 43, 44, 46–52, 74, 84, 95, 140, 149nn. 28–31, 150nn. 40–42, 44–46, 165n. 32

Haldane, old Mrs., 33, 116
Haldane, Peggy, 34, 116
Hallow-fair, 22
Halloween, 17, 34, 37, 41, 116, 118
harbor police, 137
Hardwell Close, 60
Hare, Mrs. *See* Log, Lucky
Hare, William or Willie, xiii, 17, 18–20, 22–34, 36–44, 46, 48–52, 56, 67, 72, 74–86, 88, 90, 92–98, 101–3, 105, 106, 108–120, 123, 124, 126, 127, 131–140, 143
Harper, Mrs., public house, 62
Hastie's Close, 57, 124
High Court of Justiciary, 6, 15, 17, 74, 93, 147n. 1, 149n. 25, 151nn. 7, 9, 10, 14, 152nn. 16, 19, 156n. 31, 158n. 3, 167
High Street, xiii, 21, 52, 54, 60, 73, 85, 87, 88
Hobsbawm, E. J., 2, 142n. 2, 144n. 11, 145n. 15, 169, 173
Hostler, Mrs., washerwoman, 34
household, 16, 18, 23, 24, 28, 32, 34, 38, 55–58, 62, 64, 67–71, 84, 101, 103, 105, 107, 111–17, 119, 124, 137
Hume, Baron David, 83
Hyndford's Close, 60

indentured servants, 4
Inverness, 66, 161n. 46
Ireland, 37, 92, 110, 133, 143n. 6, 172
Irish. *See* Catholics, Irish

Jacobites, 5, 6, 142n. 1
Jeffrey, Francis, 6, 76, 77, 89, 90, 93, 94, 156n. 31
Jones, Thomas Wharton, 49, 82, 122
Joseph the miller, 29
judges, 11, 49, 74, 75, 94, 118, 129, 147n. 1, 154n. 11, 156n. 31, 161n. 2
  lord justice clerk, 48, 49, 75, 81, 89, 128, 156n. 32
  Lord Meadowbank, Alexander Maconochie, 75, 79, 81, 118, 129, 155n. 25, 162n. 10
  Lord Pitmilly 75, 156n. 32

Keir Street, 55, 124, 151n. 5
Kerr, Barbara, 62–65, 67, 120, 124, 137, 139–41, 152nn. 19–20, 26, 165nn. 31–32, 166
king's evidence, 48, 52, 76, 78, 81, 94, 109, 112, 132, 147n. 2, 153n. 6
  immunity of Hare, 17, 77, 93, 94, 145n. 20
  socii criminum, 94, 156n. 32

King's Park, 60
Knox, Dr. Robert, 15, 17, 19, 23–25, 28–30, 35, 42–44, 47, 49–51, 69, 70, 72, 76, 77, 79, 82–84, 86, 88, 89, 90, 97–99, 105–10, 114, 115, 119–24, 127, 135, 136, 139, 140, 154n. 15, 156n. 28, 157nn. 40–43, 160n. 41, 161n. 44, 162nn. 9, 11, 14, 167

lantern, dark, xi, xii
Larner, Christina, 7, 144nn. 9, 11, 170, 173
Law, Mrs., 36, 43, 46
Lawnmarket, 57, 87, 124
Lawrie, Mrs., lodging-house keeper, 26, 27, 95
Lawson, Janet, 58, 59, 141
Leith, port of, 53, 56, 106, 124, 161n. 46
　Street, 55, 139, 159n. 12
　Wynd, 124
Libberton's Wynd, 57, 85–87, 124
Liquor, 38, 62, 148n. 16
　alcohol, 39, 44, 60, 151n. 15
　dram, 22, 26, 29, 30, 43, 47, 59, 62, 112
　drunk, xiii, 24, 27, 29, 30, 33, 37–39, 42, 46, 51, 53, 62, 84, 107, 109, 115, 130
　rum and bitters, 26
　small beer, 60, 141, 151n. 15
　sober, 27, 61, 66, 86, 103
　spirits, 29, 43, 148n. 8
　tipsy, 59, 60, 151n. 12
　whiskey, 24, 26, 27, 34, 36–39, 41, 44, 46, 47, 105, 107, 111, 118, 121, 125
　wine, 87
Liston, Catherine, 161n. 46, 166
Liston, Robert, 121–23, 161n. 42
Little Anderson's Close, 53, 65
Lizars, A. J., 133, 163n. 18, 167
lock-up-house, 39, 86, 87
Log, Lucky, xiii, 17, 18, 22–25, 27, 28, 30, 31, 33, 36–38, 40–44, 48–53, 56, 62, 68, 72, 74, 76, 78, 83, 92, 93, 95, 103, 108, 110–19, 124, 131–33, 136, 137, 153n. 6, 156n. 30, 158n. 4, 160nn. 25, 40
　Laird, Margaret, 22, 110, 166
Log's Lodgings, 22, 28, 30, 33, 38, 43, 58, 64, 73, 103, 109, 111, 114, 124
Lonsdale, Henry, 98, 157nn. 40–43, 167
Lord Advocate, 6, 13, 52, 76, 82, 89, 90, 93–95, 120, 122, 140, 142n. 1

Rae, William, 6, 75–79, 81–84, 89, 90, 92, 94, 95, 98, 118, 140, 144n. 7, 149n. 25, 153n. 6, 154nn. 9, 14, 155n. 24, 156nn. 33, 35, 157n. 40, 161n. 42
Lord Advocate's Department, 13, 52, 142n. 1
Low, Thomas, 140

McBeath, Jean, 59–61, 71, 151n. 14
M'Culloch, George, 43, 49, 50, 111, 119, 150n. 47, 153n. 29, 160n. 24
McDonald, Elizabeth, 161n. 46, 166
McDonald, John, 64
McDonald, Mary Ann, 152n. 25, 166
M'Dougal, Ann, 115
M'Dougal, Helen or Nelly, xiii, 17–20, 22, 23 25–44, 46–53, 56, 67, 68, 70, 72–80, 82, 86, 90, 96, 98, 101–3, 105–8, 110, 111, 113–19, 122, 126, 127, 129, 131–34, 138, 139, 140, 147n. 1, 166, 167
Macintosh, William, drover, 65, 66, 68
McKay, Christian, shopkeeper, xi, xii, 64, 71, 123, 124, 152n. 26
McKinnon, Elizabeth or Betty, 54, 58–62, 71, 137, 141, 151nn. 9–10, 12, 165n. 32, 166
McLaughlan, Charles, 35, 149n. 26
Maclean, James, 106, 111
Macnee, John, 25, 147n. 1, 155n. 16, 167
M'Neil, Duncan, advocate, 75
Maddiston, 106
Market, 83, 120, 124, 127, 133, 135, 136, 139, 161n. 4, 163n. 19
Marx, Karl, 2, 10, 11, 127, 137, 145n. 16, 167, 174
Marxists, English, 8, 9, 137, 164n. 23
Metternich, 2
migration, 4, 130, 173
　Irish migrants, 4, 104, 110, 114
Miller, Alexander, 82
Milne, David, advocate, 75
mob, 88, 90, 91, 96, 97
Moncrieff, Sir James W., advocate, 75–77, 89, 90
Monro, Alexander (Tertius), 82, 91, 98, 156n. 28, 162n. 9
Montagu, Mary Wortley, 3
Morningside, 55

Index

Morrison, Janet, 62, 65, 66–68, 71, 72, 124, 139
Muiravonside, 106
Musselburgh, 56

Napier, Mark, advocate, 75
natural. *See* women, nature of
Newhaven, 53
Newington, 49, 72, 97
Niddry Street, 59
North Bridge, 53, 58, 61, 62, 92, 102, 140
Nudgent, Thomas, 60

Old Town, ix, xi–xiii, 1, 4, 18, 21, 25, 27, 35, 52–55, 57, 59, 61, 63, 65, 67, 69, 71–73, 92, 101, 102, 114, 123, 125, 152n. 18
opium, 39, 149n. 34

Panopticon, 7, 151n. 13, 152n. 24, 162n. 6
Parliamentary Select Committee, on anatomy, 122, 134, 136
partnership, 32, 43, 68–71, 84, 112–17, 119, 148n. 17
Paterson, David, museum keeper, 42, 68, 82, 95, 120, 122, 123, 149n. 17, 150nn. 38, 40, 47, 157n. 40, 167
Paterson, Elizabeth (sister of David), 42, 43
Paterson, Elizabeth, thief, 56, 57, 151nn. 6–7, 166
Paterson, James, 56
Paterson, Mary, 17, 26–29, 78, 121, 153n. 6, 161n. 42
Paterson, William, tailor, 65, 66, 68
Patton, George, advocate, 75
pawnshops, xiii, 19, 22, 52–55, 58, 59, 123, 139, 141, 146n. 25, 151n. 8
Peel, Sir Robert, Home Secretary, 82, 154n. 14
Perkin, Harold, 2, 142n. 2, 170
pickpocket, 8, 60
piracy, 125, 137, 138, 164n. 26, 165nn. 26–27
Pleasance, the, 35, 52, 60
police. *See* Edinburgh Police Establishment; harbor police
Poor Law, new, 4, 168, 173
Portobello, 61, 97
Princes Street, 56

Privy Council, Scotland, 6
prostitute, 22, 28, 60–62, 64, 65, 67, 68, 84, 95, 102, 120, 121, 127, 131, 146n. 23, 152n. 18, 162n. 14, 169

Quarterly Review, 90, 167
Queensferry, 59

Reece, Ellen, 67, 152n. 23
Reform Acts, English and Scottish, 1, 3, 6, 89, 145n. 26, 170
Reid, Alexander, xii, xiii, 70, 71
reset, resetters of stolen goods, 57, 71, 123, 140, 142n. 2, 151n. 8
Robertson, Margaret or Maggie, xi–xiii, 4, 19, 69–72, 102, 120, 139, 166
Robertson, Patrick, advocate, 75
Roughead, William, ix, 12, 78, 82, 171
Royal Exchange, 2, 21, 54
Rymer, Mr., xii
  cellar of, xii, 71
  grocer, 19, 30, 35, 36, 43, 49, 105, 112, 149n. 27

St. Ann's Yards, 60
Salt's, dealer, 54, 58, 59, 124, 139
Sandford, Mr., advocate, 96, 157n. 38
scaffold, 86, 88, 106
scavenger, 26, 103, 148n. 9
Schumpeter, Joseph, 137, 164n. 24, 171, 173
Scotland, as nation, ix, x, 3–6, 15, 95, 138
Scotsman, The, 90, 167
Scott, Archibald, Procurator-Fiscal, 78
Scott, Sir Walter, 1, 3, 12, 69, 90, 120, 142n. 1, 152n. 24, 161n. 41, 170, 171
Scott's Land, 58
sedition, 90
Selkirk, 55
Sentinel, The, 90, 155n. 26
shadow economy, xiii, 13, 16, 18, 100, 101, 124, 126, 127, 129, 131, 133, 135–37, 139, 141
Sharpe, C. K., 25, 107, 148nn. 6, 21, 154n. 12, 159nn. 16–17, 167
she-devils, 113, 119, 160n. 40
shot (victim), 116, 118
Simon's Square, 60
Simpson, Abigail, pensioner, 24, 111
Sinclair's pawnshop, 124, 139

Sinclair, Robert, grocer, 58
slavery, 3, 143n. 5, 165n. 28, 169
Smith, Adam, 2, 3, 126, 161n. 3, 163n. 15, 172
Smith, T. Southwood, 133, 163n. 18, 167
smuggling, 125, 136–38, 140, 173
social crime. *See* crime, social
socii criminum. *See* king's evidence
South Bridge, 53, 54, 58, 59, 124
Stark, David or Davie, 57, 141, 151n. 8, 165n. 32
Stewart, Margaret. *See* Old Mrs. Burrows
Stewart, Mary, 35, 149
Stuart, Serjeant John, 61
Surgeons' Square, 88, 97, 157n. 40, 167
Swanston, Janet, grocer, 26–28, 58, 59, 151n. 11
system, of murder or reset, 55, 67, 72, 80, 83, 101, 108, 116, 123, 126, 127, 129, 130, 132, 133, 135, 136, 139–41, 159n. 18, 162n. 10, 167

Tait, George, Sheriff-Substitute, 94
Taylor, Janet, 62, 64, 65
tea, xi, 4, 19, 26, 70, 71, 107, 124, 141, 173
tea chests, boxes, 19, 24, 49, 113
Telford, James, 3
thief, 12, 17, 55, 56, 58, 59, 61, 71, 72, 129, 131, 136
Thompson, E. P., 7, 144nn. 9, 11, 145n. 15, 164n. 23, 165n. 30, 171, 172, 174
Thomson, John, brushmaker, 61, 62
Thomson, Margaret, 152n. 18, 166
Tonner, Mrs., 57, 87, 124, 139
Tory, 6, 77, 83, 89, 90, 156n. 15, 157n. 40
Tranent, 71

Union Canal, 2, 23, 101, 102, 106, 110, 111, 142n. 3, 169
usury, 138

Veitch, Margaret, 55–57, 62, 124, 140, 151nn. 4–5, 165n. 31, 166

Wakley, Thomas, 122
watches, xiii, 18, 38, 52, 55, 60, 62–67, 71, 123, 124, 138, 139–41
West Bow, 63–65
West Port, xiii, 19–22, 25–42, 45, 47, 52, 55, 64, 79, 80, 83, 84, 89, 100, 101, 110, 120, 127, 129, 138, 140
Wester Portsburgh, 20, 21, 101, 158n. 3
West Port Murders, The, 75, 79, 83, 86, 89, 109, 111, 112, 126, 129, 135, 136
Whig, 6, 7, 75–78, 83, 84, 89, 90, 93, 103, 104, 144nn. 9, 11, 145n. 15, 156n. 15, 164n. 23, 171
Whiskey Row, xi, xii
Wilson, James, or Daft Jamie, 17, 30, 68, 76, 78, 84, 88, 93, 94, 112, 115, 122, 131, 148n. 15, 153n. 6, 159n. 11, 160n. 41, 161n. 42, 166
Wilson, John (Christopher North), 103, 129, 149n. 22, 159n. 14, 160n. 27, 162n. 11, 173
witch hunts, 14, 16, 146n. 21
women, as criminals, 13–16, 18
 femininity, 107, 119
 maternal, 118, 119, 132
 nature of, 83, 84, 118, 119, 160n. 38
 womanhood, 117, 119, 132, 133, 155n. 18
Wood, Alexander, 75, 101
Wood, James, xi–xiii
World economy, 3, 4, 137

Notorious Murders, Black Lanterns, & Moveable Goods: The Transformation of Edinburgh's Underworld in the Early Nineteenth Century was designed and typeset in Centaur by Kachergis Book Design of Pittsboro, North Carolina. It was printed on 60-pound Joy White and bound by Thomson-Shore of Dexter, Michigan.